MW00563658

Plains Histories

John R. Wunder, Series Editor

Also in Plains Histories

food
control
and
resistance

Rationing of Indigenous Peoples in the United States and South Australia

Tamara Levi

Foreword by Walter R. Echo-Hawk

Texas Tech University Press

This book is typeset in Minion Pro. The paper used in this book meets the minimum requirements of ANSI/NISO Z39.48-1992 (R1997). ∞

Designed by Kasey McBeath

Library of Congress Cataloging-in-Publication Data
Names: Levi, Tamara J. | Echo-Hawk, Walter R.
Title: Food, control, and resistance : rationing of indigenous peoples in the United States and South Australia / Tamara Levi ; plainsword by Walter R. Echo-Hawk.
Description: Lubbock, Texas : Texas Tech University Press, 2016. | Includes bibliographical references and index.
Identifiers: LCCN 2015044925 (print) | LCCN 2015046739 (ebook) | ISBN 9780896729636 (hardcover : alkaline paper) | ISBN 9780896729643 (paperback : alkaline paper) | ISBN 9780896729650 (E-book)
Subjects: LCSH: Indians of North America—West (U.S.)—Government relations—History. | Aboriginal Australians—Australia—South Australia—Government relations—History. | Pawnee Indians—Food—Nebraska—History. | Osage Indians—Food—Indian Territory—History. | Aboriginal Australians—Food—Australia—Murray River Region (N.S.W.-S.A.)—History. | Narrinyeri (Australian people)—Food—Australia—Raukkan (S.A.)—History. | Rationing—Political aspects—West (U.S.)—History. | Rationing—Political aspects—Australia—South Australia—History. | Government, Resistance to—West (U.S.)—History. | Government, Resistance to—Australia—South Australia—History.
Classification: LCC E78.W5 L47 2016 (print) | LCC E78.W5 (ebook) | DDC 323.1197—dc23
LC record available at http://lccn.loc.gov/2015044925

16 17 18 19 20 21 22 23 24 / 9 8 7 6 5 4 3 2 1

Texas Tech University Press
Box 41037 | Lubbock, Texas 79409-1037 USA
800.832.4042 | ttup@ttu.edu | www.ttupress.org

For Jason

Contents

Illustrations

Plainsword

In age after age, traditional food has defined indigenous life and culture. Tribal people subsisted first by hunting, fishing, gathering, and planting, and then by processing nutritious healthy food so obtained from the bosom of Mother Earth. Then and now, traditional subsistence economies have shaped indigenous cultural identities and ways of life. Food is at the forefront of tribal conversation among healthy Salmon People, Whaling Tribes, Buffalo Nations, Plant Gatherers, Corn People, and Acorn Eaters. Indigenous social orders revolve around subsistence activity, and spiritual ties to food are common in tribal habitats. However, that bond is long-forgotten by an industrialized world that eats genetically engineered food from supermarkets. For urbanites, animal factories and corporate farms are the natural order of things, not habitat in the natural world.

During the Age of Colonialism, control over food was used in Settler States to bring indigenous peoples to their knees. Rations were doled out, or withheld, to accomplish the aims of the colonist state. The politics of starvation guided assimilation of tribal people into the body politic, as some Settler States used coercion, not consent, to build the political order. Though colonialism has been repudiated by the international order, its legacy is still seen and felt today in many nations. Tribal people are struggling in the post-colonial world to (1) preserve their remaining indigenous habitats, (2) assert sovereignty over food, and (3) establish human rights to hunt, fish, and gather in indigenous territories and use natural resources to maintain traditional economies and spiritual ties to the natural world. That struggle is best understood against the backdrop of colonialism, and its imprints are still seen in modern Settler States.

Food, Control, and Resistance: Rationing and Indigenous Peoples in the United States and South Australia is a comparative study of the use of food in the colonization process. It examines how the control of food was used and manipulated in the United States and Australia to assert dominion over the indigenous peoples during the colonization process. *Colonialism* was a worldwide phenomenon since 1492, when the nations of Europe embarked to colonize the world. European-style colonialism is defined as "the involuntary exploitation of or annexation of lands and resources previously belonging to another people, often of a different race or ethnicity, or the involuntary expansion of political hegemony over them, often displacing, partially or completely, their prior political organization."[1] During the Colonial Era (circa 1492–1960), most of the world was colonized by European powers. The non-European populations of those lands are variously called "indigenous," "tribal," or "aboriginal" peoples—they are the inhabitants of lands colonized by Europeans who resided there before the colonists arrived. For them, colonialism was a harsh, life-altering experience because it invariably meant invasion of their country, warfare, disease, appropriation of their land and natural resources, destruction of indigenous habitats and ways of life, and sometimes genocide, ecocide, and ethnocide. The colonists' goal was to occupy the land, no matter what the cost.

The impacts of colonization can be viewed through the lens of large-scale social trauma.[2] We tend to glorify the history of colonization in the United States and Australia as the "winning of the west," but there is no escaping the "dark side" of dispossession: it took a terrible toll on the natives in terms of population and land loss, destruction of tribal habitat and culture, and the loss of political integrity. Acute human suffering of this nature and magnitude has several names. Social scientists describe suffering seen in traumatized communities of the kind caused by catastrophic historical events as post-traumatic stress disorder (PTSD), historical trauma, or historical unresolved grief. The systematic destruction of ecosystems by settler states becomes genocidal when aimed at harming indigenous peoples or destroying their food base. One example is the near extermination of buffalo in the United States to bring the Plains tribes to their knees. Genocide experts call it "ecocide."[3] The replacement of indigenous food bases with rations set the stage for the politics of starvation, which involved the use of food to advance government policies aimed at stamping out indigenous culture and forcibly assimilating tribal people into Settler State societies. That process is called "cultural ethnocide" when intentional acts by the state contribute to the disappearance of a culture, even though its bearers are not physically destroyed.[4]

As shown in this book, control over food was a potent tool used in the United States and Australia as part of the colonial enterprise. It was used to wrest land from indigenous peoples, assert dominance over them, and to implement national policies with profound impacts on the targeted subjects. Four case studies examine that program. Chapter One describes the backdrop of colonialism and details the role of rations in the colonization process. Chapters Two and Three discuss rations as policy tools of the United States and Australia. Chapter Four is a Pawnee Nation case study in the United States; Chapter Five studies rationing for the Osage Nation. Chapters Six and Seven investigate the Moorundie Ration Depot and the Point McLeay Mission, respectively. Chapter Eight gives conclusions reached by the author following her riveting comparative study of these practices.

Today the United States and Australia are modern nations subject to many major influences, but the concept of the Settler State fairly describes their basic systems for addressing domestic indigenous issues. The Settler State model is a familiar byproduct of colonialism: it arises in former colonies where European settlers stayed after independence was achieved, but did not merge with the indigenous population. Instead they retained the language, religion, and culture of their distant homeland and kept intact the pre-existing colonial structure for dealing with Aborigines. Even after the colonization process ran its course, the embedded system lingers—its imprint in Settler State institutions and legal systems continues to cloud indigenous life and affairs.

The comparative study presented in this book is apt. The nations compared—the United States and Australia—have similar histories. Both are former British colonies. Both inherited the Settler State legacy. Both have indigenous peoples. Both used predominantly colonial legal, economic, social, and political systems for addressing indigenous affairs, so the historical treatment of indigenous peoples is similar. Notions of race and racism infused their public mindset, social policies, and legal regimes. The Law of Colonialism remains implanted in their domestic law. Both nations face similar indigenous challenges in the twenty-first century. The paramount question confronting their legal systems is this: to what extent shall native peoples be secure in their political, property, cultural, and human rights as indigenous people? The paramount political challenge is, then, to strike a more just balance in determining the rights, relationships, and responsibilities among indigenous and non-indigenous peoples. In both nations, the challenge is to discard the legacy of colonialism and replace it with a more just framework.

It is timely to critically examine the colonization process. At the dawn of this century, the United Nations approved the UN Declaration on the Rights of Indigenous Peoples (UNDRIP) in 2007. The US and Australia, themselves historically Settler States, initially voted against the UNDRIP; ultimately both endorsed it in 2009 and 2010. The US and Australia were among the last of one hundred fifty nations to endorse the UNDRIP, and now they are slow in implementing its provisions.

Nevertheless, the UNDRIP ushers the post-colonial world into a Human Rights Era for indigenous peoples. In forty-six articles, the UNDRIP sets forth minimum human rights standards for protecting the survival, dignity, and well-being of indigenous peoples. It creates a comprehensive framework for defining indigenous political, self-government, property, cultural, religious, land, natural resource, environmental, educational, social, and economic rights. It requires member nations to take "effective measures" to protect such rights. It does not create "new" or "special" rights for native peoples. Rather, it compiles human rights drawn from the larger corpus of modern international human rights law to tell nations how to apply that body of law to indigenous peoples, so that these peoples can enjoy the same human rights that the rest of humanity takes for granted. The remedial purpose is clear: to correct the lingering ill-effects of colonialism.

It is unsettling that contrary to popular myth and Western political theory, *Food, Control, and Resistance* shows that the two nations under discussion were not founded on consensus, but rather coercion, where indigenous peoples are concerned. It is noteworthy that many UNDRIP standards pertain to food.[5] As modern nations embrace indigenous human rights, vulnerable native peoples will henceforth be protected from coercive food manipulation at the hands of the state. In the Human Rights Era, free and democratic nations should rest on the consent of the governed and have respect for the human rights of all sectors of a society, including indigenous peoples. Free nations need not be founded on the politics of starvation, nor maintained by coercion.

Walter R. Echo-Hawk, author of *In the Courts of the Conqueror:
The 10 Worst Indian Cases Ever Decided*

Acknowledgments

Many people are owed thanks for their assistance in the process of creating this book. First and foremost, many thanks go to Dr. John Wunder for his guidance and assistance while I attended the University of Nebraska and afterward. Thanks to the staff of the numerous archives and state libraries in the United States and Australia that I visited on this journey. Thank you to my friends and colleagues at Jacksonville State University. Most importantly, thank you to my family for your love and support.

food
control
and
resistance

Chapter 1

Food in Colonial and Indigenous Societies

In March 1872 Jemmy Ducks and Young Buffaloe, two young Aboriginal men from the Lower Murray Lakes Region between Mannum and Milang in South Australia,[1] were suspected of committing a crime, and warrants were issued for their arrest. The police had trouble locating the two young men because other Aborigines were keeping watch and supplying them with food from their ration distributions. The police believed that they would

> never leave their own country, no matter what crime they may have committed; as their acquaintance with the locality, and the support and assistance which they receive from their own countrymen, make it the most pleasant, and at the same time the safest place for them, the other natives will never give any reliable information about them.[2]

In order to discourage Aborigines from assisting the fugitives, officials ceased the distribution of rations to the entire Native population of the area. They did not think withholding food from specific individuals would have any effect because of the cultural traditions of sharing food with those who do not have any. Despite the fact that the ill and the elderly had no means of supporting themselves, the distribution of rations was halted.[3]

The next year was a difficult year for Pawnees in Nebraska. The bison hunts in 1873 failed because of continuous attacks made on Pawnees by Lakotas. While the majority of the tribe went on a hunt, Pawnee lodges were burned and food caches raided. Small groups of hunters were attacked as they spread out to encircle bison herds. Even when a hunt was successful, Pawnees had to leave the carcasses, unable to clean and dress the animals without fear of Lakota attacks. Since Pawnee crop harvests were barely enough to keep the tribe temporarily alive, the people needed government rations to survive.[4] In the midst of this crisis, the United States government chose to urge acculturation by encouraging Pawnees to send their children to the Pawnee Manual Labor School. When in the summer of 1873 the Pawnee school was quite empty, the US government informed the Pawnee chiefs that unless they sent their children to the school, the tribe would not receive the desperately needed flour rations. The government even sent soldiers to each band to ensure that the children were sent.[5]

Relations among indigenous peoples and colonial societies and governments are fraught with misunderstandings, competition for land and resources, and political and military power imbalances. Whether an intruding group is focused primarily on resource extraction or transplanting permanent settlement, colonialism has vast implications for both indigenous peoples and colonizers. Settler colonization in particular, in all its various manifestations, created lasting legacies. Davia Stasiulis and Nira Yuval-Davis define settler societies as "societies in which Europeans have settled, where their descendants have remained politically dominant over indigenous peoples, and where a heterogeneous society has developed in class, ethnic and racial terms."[6] Settler societies, particularly the governments, created a variety of methodologies to assert dominance over and acculturation of indigenous populations. These methods influenced land use, gender roles and relations, culture, language, and subsistence patterns to name but a few. The subsequent cultural imperialism resulted in a simultaneous mix of acculturation (i.e., adoption of Christianity and English) and exclusion (from political, social, and legal power) of indigenous peoples.[7] The continuing struggle of indigenous peoples around the world for recognition and rights is a lasting legacy of settler colonialism.

Comparisons of different settler societies can open avenues for exploration not apparent when studying a single national history alone.[8] While different settler societies have unique motivations, cultures, and developments, they all have similar roots. Stasiulis and Yuval-Davis argue that "colonial settlers . . . kept Europe as their myth of origin and as a signifier of superiority even when formal political ties and/or dependency on European colonial powers had been abandoned."[9] A comparison of colonial practices in the United States and Australia can be especially informative. Both nations have their roots in the settler colonialism of the British Empire. As such, not only is there a common basis in terms of law and legal tradition, but also a similar starting point for defining indigenous relations—particularly with South Australia, the first free colony in Australia. Margaret Jacobs identified several similarities between the Australian colonial experience and the expansion of the United States across the West. Both nations developed similar, romanticized, notions of the "frontier"—a place where heroic European and Euro-American explorers and settlers struggled against wilderness and ultimately persevered. Settlers, and governments, of both nations tended to view the indigenous population as that of a people (or peoples) inevitably, sometimes tragically, in decline—the "vanishing Indian." Australia and the United States both developed an ideology of racial superiority and the inevitable dominance of that superior culture, a manifest destiny.[10]

British experience in eastern North America informed later policy in Australia just as colonial experiences influenced the policies and practices of the United States. From this common base, however, the United States and Australia diverge. Imperial competition influenced the very basis of indigenous relations in the two countries. The United States, faced with competition from France, Spain, and Britain for trade and alliances with Native nations, recognized a certain, although fleeting, amount of sovereignty. Australia, on the other hand, with little outside competition for dominance, granted Aborigines virtually no rights to territory.[11] The United States developed a Native policy designed, at least in part, to facilitate the continued expansion of Anglo-American settlement, including the confinement of Native peoples to reservations. In South Australia, indigenous policy developed to facilitate the creation of an aboriginal labor force, initially relying far less on the idea of confinement, and was more directly influenced by the growing humanitarian movement in Britain. The indigenous populations of North America and Australia differed markedly, from population size to political and cultural structures, but strategies to deal with the pressures of forced acculturation were remarkably similar. The study of different environments, time periods, and indigenous populations in the United States and South Australia highlights questions in comparison that individual studies overlook. It allows an examination of governmental thoughts and intentions that transcend political systems and national borders, contributing to the discussion of how settler colonialism shaped—and continues to influence—the resulting societies. The study will also highlight the agency of the populations targeted by indigenous policies, contradicting the popular view of indigenous peoples as helpless victims of colonial aggressors. Indigenous peoples were active participants, making choices, albeit often from an increasingly desperate list of options, to best ensure their own survival.

Comparative studies including the United States and Australia are increasingly popular, encompassing environmental history, colonialism, indigenous studies, and more. Stuart Banner made a comparison of colonial land policies in the Anglo-American Pacific Rim in *Possessing the Pacific*. Margaret Jacobs's *White Mother to a Dark Race* is a study of indigenous child removal in the United States and Australia. Another important aspect of colonial indigenous relations involved the control of food. Food studies, particularly focusing on what foods and food ways can reveal about peoples and cultures, has also grown in recent years. The combination of a study of settler colonialism and how these governments manipulated access to food is an important facet of colonial-indigenous relations. The control of food also allowed these settler societies to maintain an image of humanitarianism, assisting their indigenous populations rather than killing them. As part of what John Wunder termed "New Colonialism"—the move from a focus on the acquisition of land to a focus on acculturation or assimilation of indigenous peoples—control of food by government agents influenced many aspects of indigenous life with the aim of continuing to open new lands for colonial use.[12] Several works have addressed this issue in Australia, including Robert Foster's "Feasts of the Full Moon" and *White Flour, White Power* by Tim Rowse.[13] However, few works on United States indigenous policy address the use of food in more than passing, and there has been little comparison of the use of food by colonial governments as a tool of assimilation.

I argue that the distribution of food rations as indigenous policy by the United States and South Australia had similar foundations. Both governments desired greater access to lands occupied by indigenous peoples; however, straightforward exile or extermination did not fit with prevailing national ideologies encompassing humanitarian thought and Christian duty. As a means to achieving their goals, the governments developed indigenous policies in which the control of food played a crucial role.

Food is an important element in life. It is necessary for survival. However, the meanings surrounding food go beyond simple nutrition and subsistence. Food plays a central role in the social and cultural life of a people. Carole Counihan argues that cultural food ways impart knowledge about social and political structures, gender roles, family, community relations, and much more.[14] The control of food, therefore, is an effective method to influence or alter the behavior of a people. Beyond the coercive tactic of withholding food, with its incumbent threat of hunger or starvation, the type of foods, methods of distribution, and control over preparation and consumption can all be used not only to influence behavior but also to erode traditional cultural practices and knowledge.

Because of the significance of food, colonial governments both provided and manipulated it, in the form of rations, as part of their acculturation practices directed at indigenous peoples, such as experienced by the Murray Lakes Aborigines and the Pawnees. Acculturation and civilization goals for indigenous peoples asserted by colonial governments inevitably involved force, coercion, control, punishment, withdrawal, the breaking of promises and written agreements, and death; and food often emerges as an integral assimilative tool. Peter Scholliers observes that new "food regimes" imposed on a people maintain some features of the old.[15] This implies that the manipulation of identity through food is not total, that the target of the new food regime is able to maintain some elements of the old system. This could include food ways, ceremonial and ritual uses and their significance, and cultural and social mores and values. In this way, diet and identity cannot simply be given or dictated but are "interpreted, adapted or rejected according to one's needs, means and intentions."[16]

This process was used on the indigenous Ainu communities of northern Japan. The interaction between Ainus and Japanese began approximately in the tenth century with Japanese expansion onto the northern island of Hokkaido. This early contact was sporadic, and it was not until the Tokugawa shogunate, 1600–1868, and the Meiji government, 1868–1912, that an official native policy was created to deal with the Ainus. During the Tokugawa period Ainus were not considered to be fully Japanese. As direct control over Hokkaido grew more important as a counter to Russian expansion, assimilation of Ainus became a focus of government policy, and control of food was recognized as a powerful tool for that purpose.[17] Included in the Instructions to Officials in Charge of the Management of Ezo, issued in 1799, was this directive:

> Teach the [Ainus], in due time, how to raise crops and live on cereals and to become used to our way of life. Even before you teach them to cultivate the land try to change their diet from meat to grain by telling them that cereals are much better than meat. Then when the time comes to teach them how to raise crops their progress will be much better.[18]

Despite these assimilation attempts of the colonial Japanese, partially through the manipulation and distribution of food, Ainus were not completely assimilated. Ainus maintained certain elements of their culture.

Food occupies a seminal position in the indigenous creation of power. Within the Omaha nation, candidates for the Honhewachi, a society of honorary chieftainship, a position of influence and honor, were required to pass bowls of sacred food to members of the society and provide a feast for chiefs and guests at the initiation ceremony.[19] Often the process of a man moving into a position of power or chieftainship involved not only acts of bravery but also acts of charity, such as providing food for those in the tribe who did not have any.

Food also functions as a vehicle for the transfer of knowledge. In addition to knowledge of traditional food sources and their uses, information on food preparation and ritual significance is passed on from one generation to the next. This knowledge facilitates the continuation of both group and individual identities. Writing in *Consuming Passions*, Peter Farb and George Armelagos found that "perhaps the most common explanation for the variety of eating customs is enculturation—that through the learning experience members of the younger generation come to accept the traditional ways of their society."[20] An example can be seen in the patterns of land use of Yanyuwas in Northern Territory, Australia. Here the ways in which food is collected allow for sustainability. Yanyuwa rules of food consumption ensure that nothing is wasted and that places where hunting is prohibited are set aside to allow for breeding areas.[21] These food rules and practices teach children important cultural ideas while maintaining practices that allow for continued group sustainability in a tribe's territory.

In many indigenous cultures gender roles are partially defined by food gathering, preparation, and eating. Food and gender can be linked in several different ways. Foods tasks are often divided according to gender. In addition, the distribution of foodstuffs and even what foods are prohibited can be based on gender.[22] In indigenous hunting-gathering societies or societies with hunting and small-scale agriculture, women often gather or cultivate most of the vegetable foods, providing the basic and most consistent part of the diet. Men are responsible primarily for the hunting or fishing, a food supply not as reliable as vegetation. As the importance of gathering foodstuffs lessens with the introduction of new products and processes from dominating colonial cultures, the position and status of women within indigenous societies begins to change—and in many cases is diminished.[23] In addition to no longer being the primary provider of food, the knowledge that women possess of the environment, plant foods, and methods of preparing those foods becomes less important. With the introduction of wheat flour in Australia, for example, the time-consuming process of creating a type of flour from wattle seed was abandoned. Eventually Aboriginal knowledge of how to collect and process wattle seed was no longer considered important and in many areas was lost completely. When flour was withheld, Aborigines then had no access to this vital food staple.

Food ways also strengthen kinship ties and help maintain social cohesion within the group. In many cultures the practice of sharing food through lines of kinship not only ensures that all members of the group have access to adequate food but also strengthens family ties and helps maintain the political and social power structures. Within Omaha culture it is customary to return borrowed cooking pots with some food still in them as a measure of thanks and as a way to help provide food. The !Kung in southern Africa are among the many cultures in which food sharing is particularly important, creating a system of mutual obligation that acts as a social safety net.[24] Colonial authorities often used food to try to break up a group's social cohesion, as the South Australian police did when attempting to capture Jemmy Ducks and Young Buffaloe.

Food also links indigenous peoples directly to their homelands. The knowledge necessary to find plant foods and to process some plants in such a way as to make them palatable and nontoxic, as well as the knowledge of migratory and behavioral patterns of animals, are important pieces of environmental and geographical knowledge. As children are taken along on hunts or accompany foraging parties, they begin to learn these life lessons. In addition, at the same time they are being introduced to their tribal territory, they travel to areas of cultural and religious significance and learn to recognize important weather patterns. Food is one way in which people connect to the land, and for many cultures land is of seminal cultural importance.

Since it can affect so many aspects of the life of a people, from physical survival to cultural survival, food became an integral part of native policy for many colonial governments. When the types of foods eaten and food ways were recognized as being distinctive, changing diets and eating practices became an early step in attempts to force indigenous populations into new societies. Culture changes such as this also provided the stimuli for altering land usage patterns, molding them to fit the dispossession ideals of the encroaching society.

The recognition of the power of food and patterns of forced acculturation occurred throughout the world, including in the United States and Australia, where colonial acculturation and civilization practices included the manipulation of food ways. The usefulness of food in encouraging or coercing behavior and culture change are alluded to by South Australia Protector of Aborigines Edward John Eyre, who pointed out that the more dependent on European resources Aborigines became, the more an "almost unlimited influence might be acquired over the native population."[25] While these food policies had profound effects on the indigenous populations, they alone could not completely change the cultures of Native peoples. If this is the case, then why did so many governments use food as an integral part of indigenous policies? One possible reason is the number of cultural traits that the control of food could influence.

Food control is especially effective in colonial attempts to affect indigenous behavior and culture because of food's role in the creation of identity. Social psychologists define identity as a person's own definition in terms of group membership. Identity "allows one to situate oneself and the Other, to give a sense to existence, and to order the world."[26] Identity functions through different mediums: the individual, a peer group, a contrasting group, or remote groups that produce ideology. Peter Scholliers argues that food is an essential element in the formation and expression of identity—that the expression "you are what you eat" goes beyond ideas of nutrition.[27] Part of the way people define their own group, as well as those of other peoples, is through food. "People eating similar food," adds Scholliers, "are trustworthy, good, familiar, and safe; but people eating unusual food give rise to feelings of distrust, suspicion and even disgust."[28] This also extends to the preparation of familiar foods and the percentage of a particular food source, such as a steer, that is utilized. Food, therefore, is a fundamental component of indigenous culture. It is important in religion, ceremonies, celebrations, cultural knowledge and transmission, as well as physical survival.

Food is an essential element in many ceremonies and rituals, with some foods being more valued for their symbolic roles than their nutritional value.[29] Martha Royce Blaine, in *Pawnee Passage*, suggests that for the Pawnees the act of eating itself was deserving of respect.[30] Many American Indian ceremonies involve a ritual feast as an integral component, such as those of the Shell Society of the Omahas.[31] For the Hidatsas and Mandans, the performance of the Corn Dance Feast of the Women is necessary for thanking the Old Woman Who Never Dies, who sends them plant seeds. Elderly women hang dried meat as a sacrifice and then dance. The dancing women are fed meat, and they give blessed kernels of corn to be mixed with the tribe's planting seeds.[32] Today food still plays an important role in indigenous community gatherings, such as graduation celebrations, hand games, and memorials.

Food taboos also influence culture, ceremony, and religion. Food choices often rely on an "implicit and preliminary definition of what is edible and what is inedible that differs from culture to culture and from one era to another."[33] In many indigenous cultures certain foods are forbidden because they represent the people themselves, their totem, or are considered to be ancestors. Other foods are taboo because they are reserved for the gods or spirits alone. Breaking food taboos is a serious action that can have grave cultural and intercultural consequences. For example, in the Sepoy Rebellion in colonial India, the breaking of important food taboos helped spark a rebellion of native soldiers of the East India Company against British forces in 1857. The sepoys learned that the grease on the cartridge casings they used was made from cows and pigs. Since the soldiers had to bite the ends of the cartridges off to load their guns, this was taboo for both Muslim and Hindu sepoys.[34] Hence, food taboos can cause intercultural division and conflict, especially as those taboos are broken.

Food and food ways are an integral part of the way peoples define themselves as a group, as well as the way they define others. They influence gender roles, division of time, and patterns of movement. The ways in which a group views food influences their social and political structures and their cultural mores. Since food ways are an influential part of indigenous culture, the control and manipulation of food sources can be a powerful tool in colonization.

To alter native culture and identity, many colonial governments developed various methods using the control of food through the distribution of rations to indigenous peoples. Rations were used to effect many different outcomes, based on the specific desires of the issuing body and the receivers of the goods. Each brought their own cultural understandings, beliefs, and expectations to the table. Environment, economics, and culture also influenced the processes and results of ration systems, for both the issuers and the receivers.

Given its importance, how has rationing been defined? Tim Rowse, in *White Flour, White Power*, defines rationing as "the non-Aboriginal practice—whether based on custom or on policy—of providing food, clothing and other goods (such as blankets and tobacco) to Indigenous people."[35] It is important to note, however, that the practice of providing food and goods is much more complex than a simple distribution of objects. As Rowse has observed, rationing was a point of direct interaction between the different cultures. A government issuing the rations had specific ideas in mind in terms of the meaning of the distribution, what the goods were to be used for, and what the desired result of the exchange would be. The peoples receiving the rations had their own cultural understandings of the distribution and how those goods fit into their world, altering the end result of the colonial perception of the interaction.[36] So, while each side participated in the distribution and receipt of rations, they did not necessarily come together with the same expectations or even similar understandings of the process in which they were involved. Despite these possible misunderstandings of each other's intentions, the process had definite, albeit complex, consequences for both the people receiving the goods and the governments distributing them.

One significant effect of the control of rations by colonial governments was on the sovereignty of indigenous peoples. By distributing food at specific locations, a government could attempt to encourage nomadic indigenous peoples to become more sedentary, and this in turn allowed the government to control more easily the areas in which the peoples lived. Influencing the location of indigenous communities had several potential goals. In some instances the indigenous peoples were encouraged to congregate in areas away from expanding white settlement. This had a dual goal of clearing land for expansion and reducing the potential for conflict between native peoples and settlers. Missionaries also believed it would be easier to Christianize and "civilize" indigenous peoples in concentrated settlements away from the potentially corruptive influence of frontier settlers.

The ability of the government to withhold food also affected sovereignty. To capture Jemmy Ducks and Young Buffaloe, the South Australian police stopped the distribution of flour because they felt the only way to succeed was to restrict Aboriginal sovereignty. The police knew the Aboriginal community would protect the fugitives, either to ensure they were punished according to tribal customs or because they had not broken any tribal laws and did not deserve punishment.[37] However, these attempts did not always succeed in completely disrupting indigenous sovereignty. Indigenous peoples often continued to assert levels of sovereignty long after mobility and land had been lost.

Robert Foster argues, "Rations became an alternative economic resource, exploited in the context of traditional seasonal movements, as well as providing the basis for new patterns of movement."[38] In some cases the distribution of food at specific locations was incorporated into the movement patterns of the people, continuing traditional seasonal patterns while including the new source of subsistence. Gathering Native groups in one location at a certain time of year allowed governments more easily to negotiate land cessions and open trade with Native peoples, as well as to disseminate information.

Initially rations were incorporated as supplements to regular diets, serving as novel foodstuffs and as an additional economic source. As traditional foods became scarce, such as with the depletion of the bison in the American West and the kangaroo in some areas of Australia, or as access to food-gathering areas was restricted, people began depending more and more on rations as a primary source of food. Removing opportunities for indigenous peoples to procure food using traditional methods through both restrictions on movement and extinction of game had negative effects on sovereignty. As dependence on the introduced goods became stronger, the colonial government could exert increased influence on indigenous political structures and where and when indigenous peoples moved, reducing political options and the freedom of movement those peoples had enjoyed.

The control of food provides an easy tool through which to influence the internal structure of a group by controlling where and through whom food can be obtained. In many instances, encroaching governments chose "chiefs" or "kings," persons they wanted to deal with, either because they did not recognize the existing power structure or they determined that an existing leader was not partial to government desires. Part of the process of instilling power in the chosen people was for them to be responsible for distributing the rations to the rest of the group. Another method of influencing internal group dynamics and behavior was the withholding or threat of withholding supplies. Colonial governments used food as a coercive element by threatening the withdrawal of rations for behavior outside government-approved bounds and as punishment for the group or individuals. In this way, government sought to encourage actions that fit into its overall indigenous policy and visions for civilized society.

Governments and humanitarians have often used rationing as integral policies of assimilation programs. Food determines in part a group's identity and who is not a member of the group.[39] It can also provide a potential area of common ground on which natives and settlers can interact. Therefore, many coercive acculturation practices forced changes from traditional foods and eating practices to those of the dominant assimilating culture. Part of the reasoning of the colonials lay in the idea that if indigenous peoples ate what the encroaching culture did and in the manner that the encroaching culture did, they would then begin to act like that culture and might eventually be absorbed into it. The use of indigenous foodstuffs and eating practices became taboo to the assimilating culture and therefore had to end. Threatening to withhold a tribe's rations to ensure school attendance was another effective tool for assimilation. Not only was the United States government able to coerce Pawnee parents into sending their children to school, it also placed those children in a controlled environment away from their traditional society, a position the government believed was ideal for encouraging the children to give up their tribal culture.

Sovereign indigenous land use was attacked through rationing as well.

If an indigenous group could be convinced or coerced into eating the same types of foods as the larger culture, then the way they used the land could also be changed to conform to colonial government ideas of what was proper. This then freed areas previously used predominantly for hunting and gathering for settlement, farming, mining, or industry.

Rations were also distributed to groups who had already been dispossessed of their lands. The humanitarian and governmental response to dispossession and potential starvation was often to attempt to ease the remaining years of a people who was expected to gradually die out. In this way the humanitarian groups attempted to fulfill their Christian duty by ensuring humane treatment for those who had suffered from the worst of settler colonization.[40]

The introduction of new foodstuffs and the change from a diet of native plants and animals to one of processed foods, combined with changes in movement patterns and subsistence activities, caused numerous nutritional and health changes. Most Native diets were composed of a wide variety of plant and animal sources that, when combined with preparation methods, provided for complete nutritional needs. Processed foods, such as white flour and sugar, replaced native counterparts and reduced the amount of time and energy needed to produce food. However, the new foods, while containing higher concentrations of calories, were also void of much of the nutritional value of native plants.[41] As rations increasingly became the main source of subsistence, the decrease in nutrition and exertion led to health deficiencies and diseases such as diabetes, which had not existed in many Native societies prior to contact. These problems, combined with alcohol, poverty, and depression, continue to affect indigenous populations today. In many countries, including the United States and Australia, the native population is at a much higher risk of morbidity and mortality than national averages.

Humanitarians led much of the thought on rationing policies in the nineteenth century. Philanthropic groups, influenced heavily by evangelicalism and Britain's eighteenth-century antislavery campaign, believed the solution to the poverty and strife suffered by indigenous peoples was individual moral reform. Humanitarians were convinced of their own racial and cultural superiority and believed it their duty to offer the benefits of their definition of civilization to those who had suffered from the expansion of settler society.[42]

Key to these beliefs was humanitarians' understanding of what constituted civilization. Many white American and Australian reformers associated the idea of civilization with establishing social order. This included
assumptions about the superiority of settled patterns of living, European
and Euro-American understandings of gender roles, and the superiority and benefits of Christianity.[43] Humanitarians saw the goals of freeing,
protecting, and civilizing the colonized as part of their evangelical and
nationalistic duty.[44]

Governments, especially in the nineteenth century, saw the humanitarian impulse for "protection" as beneficial. Creating a common ground
with indigenous groups and encouraging the adoption of "civilization"
had the potential to reduce expenses.[45] As Julie Evans has argued, humanitarian ideals "could appear to redress an obvious injustice while also supporting the primary interests of the settler population to maximize access
to the land."[46] Humanitarian policies were not always easily applied, however. Governments often had to balance humanitarian ideals with the demands of settlers who cared little for the plight of their indigenous neighbors.[47] This dichotomy resulted in increased complexity of policy and a
discord between stated policy and actual implementation.

A consistent fear of governments and humanitarians was the "pauperization" of the recipients as a result of rationing policies. They worried that
if indigenous peoples received rations and other goods, for what was perceived as free by many, over an extended period of time, it would encourage laziness and inhibit the adoption of European civilization. Humanitarians and governments valued individualism and considered any form
of welfare as a threat to any progress made in instilling the value of work.

This fear of creating a permanent dependent class of peoples battled
against the idea that the Christian governments of the United States and
South Australia had a moral and ethical obligation to compensate indigenous peoples for their loss of territory and means of subsistence.[48] Eyre
questioned, "What recompense can he make them for the injury he has
done, by dispossessing them of their lands, by occupying their waters and
by depriving them of their supply of food?"[49] He and many humanitarians
believed that the distribution of rations was the only practical means of
compensation.[50]

Many ration recipients themselves considered the distributions as partial payments for lands and resources lost. Systems of reciprocity demand-

ed that people with abundant means, who had caused the dispossession of another group, should provide some form of compensation. Many also considered that the food and goods distributed served as payment for lands ceded, particularly in the United States where rations and annuities were included in treaty stipulations.

The loss of cultural knowledge that accompanied the distribution of rations helped break down cultural patterns of power by lessening the importance of elders and their knowledge of traditional survival skills, thus reinforcing the growing dependence on European goods for subsistence. This dependency became an important element in cross-cultural relations, and it continues to be an element in scholarly debates and indigenous political movements around the world.

Dependency is a complicated issue with as many different interpretations as there are scholars. No empirical measure of dependency exists because there is no single system of dependency. Dependency theory, initially developed by scholars writing on African and Latin American political economies and international relations, was first defined as "the process by which peripheral regions are incorporated into the global capitalist system and the political, economic, and social distortions that result."[51] Historian Richard White, writing on the Choctaw, Pawnee, and Navajo nations, defines dependency theory as more of a framework for historical inquiry and as the "conditioning of one economy by another."[52] Dependency is also a common term in Australian Aboriginal history. Richard Baker, in *Land Is Life*, distinguished between dependence as an interdependence in social, cultural, and religious areas based on trust and reciprocity, and dependence created through the contact process and an increasing reliance on European goods.[53]

The growing dependency of indigenous groups on an encroaching culture and the use of dependency theory as a framework for analysis does not mean that these groups were isolated prior to colonization. Many, if not most, indigenous cultures were part of local, regional, and long-distance trade routes through which goods, ideas, and disease traveled. The difference was power. Many of these contacts were made either on an equal footing or with a lesser power difference. As contact grew between indigenous peoples and the colonizing cultures and traditional resources and land became scarcer, dependency increased.

Indigenous peoples, however, were not without choices or agency in how they chose to deal with these increasing changes. Richard White has identified three ways in which indigenous groups chose to deal with the imposed changes. One method was to try to maintain culture, religion, and subsistence patterns with as little change as possible. The other extreme involved the purposeful embrace of modernization, deliberately replacing traditional methods with introduced ones. The less extreme of both these strategies was slow, incremental change—introducing new elements into existing forms, such as replacing stone tools and weapons with metal or meal from native plants with wheat flour.[54]

The governments of the United States and Australia, as well as many other nation-states from the nineteenth through the twentieth centuries, used rations to attempt to control indigenous movement, encourage European-style habits, decrease indigenous independence, and increase dependence on European goods. Food became an effective tool in governmental attempts to assimilate indigenous peoples. However, indigenous peoples took rations for their own reasons, with their own interpretations of the process, and incorporated them into their cultural systems, oftentimes frustrating the assimilation plans of the governments.

Thus, the policies and processes involved in issuing rations to indigenous peoples provide a window into the complex contact histories of these societies. An examination of the policies can reveal not only political and economic goals of the colonial governments but the humanitarian ideals of the issuing society. The ways in which indigenous peoples used the rations and the differing understandings they attached to the system can also expose some of their complex reactions to encroaching societies and the agency that native groups maintained over their own cultures. A comparative study of past ration policies and their ramifications on both colonial and indigenous cultures also provides a context for understanding current situations, including indigenous sovereignty concerns, political economies, and health issues.

The process of colonization and attempted cultural change of indigenous peoples occurred throughout the world. A comparative study of the ration systems in the United States and Australia, two nations that dealt with indigenous peoples through different policies with the similar goal of assimilation, discovers similarities and differences between the two colonial nations and raises questions of a nature not explored in noncomparative studies. Although Native Americans and Australian Aborigines were very different from each other culturally and the governments of the United States and Australia approached relations with them differently, the indigenous peoples used similar methods to resist assimilation efforts and maintain their cultural identities.

This book will compare the rations systems of the United States and Australia in the mid- and late nineteenth century. Fundamental differences exist between the United States and South Australia in terms of indigenous policy. The United States relied on treaty making through 1871, and treaty terms continued to be important in determining ration distributions and annuity payments after that date. South Australia did not rely on treaties, making its ration policies less consistent and more decentralized. Despite the differences in governmental policies and focus, and the differences in cultures, the two settler societies had similar foundations and often faced similar problems. By this period both governments had established approaches, although by no means static, to indigenous relations and acculturation. Viewpoints held by settlers and government agents toward expansion and indigenous peoples were comparable. In addition, many of the results of rationing in the American Great Plains and South Australia were similar. Through the examination of four case studies of indigenous peoples located on the Pawnee and Osage reservations in Nebraska and Oklahoma and the Moorundie and Point McLeay ration sites in South Australia, the complex policies and goals of each government's ration system, as well as the impact that rations had on indigenous peoples, will be analyzed.

The four case studies were chosen for several reasons. The time frame and context within frontier expansion is roughly similar. The surviving ration records in both the United States and South Australia are most complete for these four locations. The four also cover a range of approaches, power relations, and indigenous reactions. Pawnees and Osages had similar experiences with removal from their homelands, but each reacted to the ration system in very different ways, according to cultural patterns and values and the specific circumstances they found themselves in. Pawnees faced long periods of crisis and starvation while Osages were in a position to argue for the end of rationing and the receipt of money instead. The South Australian case studies include two of the types of sites used to distribute rations. Moorundie was a government-established ration depot that attempted to draw in many different peoples from the surrounding area, resulting in many different culture groups residing in the same area, the largest being from the Meru language family.[55] Point McLeay, or Raukkan, was a mission established by the South Australia Aborigines' Friends' Association that focused on converting and supporting primarily Ngarrindjeris from the Lower Murray Lakes region. Although run by missionaries, much of the rations and financial support for Point McLeay came from the South Australian government.

This study will also look at how the introduction of European foods supplanted native foods and subsistence knowledge and how new foods affected the health of indigenous populations. It will examine the manipulation by indigenous peoples of the rations system for their own benefit— including selling rations for cash and giving rations to relations who were not eligible to receive rations themselves—and the adaptation of ration supplies into a uniquely indigenous food and social system, rather than the outright adoption of European food habits. Through the examination of these case studies, a more thorough understanding of colonial-indigenous interaction in the nineteenth century, as well as insight into some of the sources of current indigenous rights and health issues such as high rates of Type II diabetes, can be attained.

Finally, this study will consider the response of the populations receiving the rations. Each society interpreted rationing within its own cultural context and understanding of its relationship with the government. Native American treaties established rations as part of the payment granted a nation for ceded lands, and the people viewed them in that way—a right already established. Aboriginal Australians also viewed food rations as a type of payment for resources lost because of colonial expansion. When the system, goods, and governmental responses failed to fit their cultural understandings, Pawnees, Osages, Moorundie Aborigines, and Ngarrindjeris resisted, further complicating the outcomes of rationing policies.

While the quiet disappearance or complete assimilation of indigenous populations was not achieved, governmental use of food as a tool of coercion profoundly affected native societies in the United States and South Australia. Language, religion, and lifestyle were all impacted. However, instead of eventually relieving the governments of responsibility for indigenous inhabitants, the policies increased dependence in the nineteenth and early twentieth centuries. Viewed through the experiences of the communities on the Pawnee and Osage reservations and at Moorundie and Point

McLeay, the story becomes more than a list of changing policies and lists of goods; it is given a human face.

By April 1872 the withholding of rations to the Lower Murray Lakes Aborigines had begun to have the desired effect. Some living in the area between Mannum and Milang became willing to assist the police in catching Jemmy Ducks and Young Buffaloe. Both were captured, even though a settler who feared being charged with supplying Aborigines with alcohol had further aided Young Buffaloe. Through the act of withholding the flour distributions until the capture of the fugitives, the South Australian police and officials in the Aborigines Office believed they had established a precedent—that in the future, when they needed to influence the behavior of Aborigines, they would simply threaten to withhold rations to achieve their desired outcome.[56]

Similarly, with the failed summer hunt and meager crops, Pawnees were forced to send their children to the Pawnee Manual Labor School, despite their strong feeling against such an action. Food was difficult to obtain and starvation was a very real possibility for the people. By sending their children to the school, Pawnee parents guaranteed that their children received daily meals, while at the same time ensuring that the tribe's rations would continue to be distributed. The United States government was able to influence the behavior of Pawnees through the manipulation of their rations, especially at a time when the tribe had little other means of subsistence. Despite the distrust of Pawnee parents regarding the school, they allowed their children to go because of the tribe's overwhelming need for food.[57]

The governments of both South Australia and the United States were able to manipulate food to ensure a desired outcome. Whether it was cooperation in apprehending wanted indigenous peoples like Jemmy Ducks and Young Buffaloe or coercing parents to allow their children to attend school, as with Pawnees in 1873, the effectiveness of governmental power over food is apparent. Without taking those measures, it is unlikely that the South Australian and United States governments would have achieved the same results as easily as they did.

Chapter 2
Rations and United States Policy

The distribution of goods, including food, has been a part of indigenous policies in North America since the beginning of Euro-American colonization. With the exception of Russian contact in Alaska, where the *promyshlenniki* operated (surprise attacks on Native villages, obtaining hostages in order to coerce men into providing furs and pelts), most European nations preferred to develop working (although inequitable) relationships with Native nations. Both the British and French used gifts to gain peace with and the allegiance of Native American nations. The Dutch made food gifts to form trade alliances in the northeast. Spanish missionaries, as part of their conversion efforts in the southwest and California, encouraged the adoption of European foods and eating habits, using Native labor on mission farms and implementing regimented daily meal schedules.[1]

The United States continued the practice of giving presents to chiefs in order to compete with the British in Canada and the Spanish in the North American west and southeast. The government first offered goods, including food, as part of Native American policy with the 1791 Treaty of Holston with the Cherokees. In partial payment for land cessions, Cherokees were granted "certain valuable goods, to be immediately delivered to the undersigned Chiefs and Warriors, for the use of their nation."[2] The United States, not fully appreciating the scope of Native cultural diversity and aiming for expediency, adopted a single body of policy through which to deal with Native American nations. The result of attempting to apply a single formula to relations with vastly different tribes was a policy that rarely worked as intended and was fraught with problems and exceptions.

This "one size fits all" approach was also applied to rations. United States ration policy developed over time with adjustments made as primary concerns in Washington, DC, shifted from treaty making to confinement on reservations to "civilization." A general knowledge of ration policy and its changes is necessary to better understand the issues and the impact that rations had on Pawnees and Osages in the mid- to late nineteenth century.

The practice of distributing presents, food, supplies, and money took the form of annuities. Annuity payments were based on the value of lands ceded by Native nations as determined by the US government. Included in negotiated treaties and official agreements, specified annual payments were made to tribal members for periods ranging from twenty years to perpetuity. Unfortunately, the annuity system had significant problems built into it. Since most payments were made in food and goods, tribes lost a good deal of the value of their payments to distributors, middlemen, and transporters. Inferior goods and high transportation costs over long distances were only the beginning of the problems the annuity system caused.[3] Those problems extended beyond the actual distribution of annuities into the twentieth century when payments and the undervaluation of tribal lands by US government agents became the focus of numerous cases heard by the Indian Claims Commission and the US Court of Claims.

Tribes were granted annuity credit and goods in exchange for ceded lands. Despite the desires of many tribes, the government rarely paid the full annuity in cash, paying instead in farm equipment, rations, or other goods.[4] Most government officials and humanitarians did not believe that American Indians were capable of handling cash in a way they saw as correct or beneficial. They argued that the cash only ended up in the pockets of unscrupulous traders and increased problems with Native drunkenness. Fulfilling treaty obligations in this way, the government was able to save more money than would be possible by distributing cash, despite the ongoing protests by numerous tribes for such payments. This method also allowed the government to use the tribes' own moneys to pay for the goods that were being used to encourage their assimilation, such as in the 1825 Osage treaty, where the funds were used to supply farming equipment, hire agency farmers, and provide timber-frame houses for the four principal chiefs.[5]

The reasoning behind the use of annuity goods varied from a true humanitarian, though paternalistic, desire to help to assertions of control and expediency. Throughout the nineteenth century many humanitarians believed that the United States had a moral obligation to purchase Indian lands with cash or goods, that because the American nation was removing Natives' means of subsistence it was obligated to support those affected until they could be taught a new way of life or they faded from existence. While there may have been some genuine concern when discussing the distribution of rations, much of the discussion centered on the continuance of peace and good relations, which would make further settlement of the continent easier. The government argued that it was cheaper to feed and "civilize" the tribes rather than fight an ongoing war as settlement spread across the continent.

Many officials, such as the governor of Michigan Territory, Lewis Cass, thought that the easiest and most cost-effective way to maintain peace between American Indians and settlers was to provide goods to supplement their subsistence efforts. Cass believed that many of the raids and conflicts that occurred in Michigan Territory were the result of a loss of tribal lands and thus hunting territory. This concern, however, was directed more to the safety of white settlers rather than the continued existence of tribal nations in their homelands.[6]

Later in the nineteenth century, most federal officials viewed annuity payments as a means to influence or control tribal behavior, using distribution points and threats of withholding goods as tools of coercion. Others saw annuity goods as important in the process of "civilizing" the indigenous peoples and of inducing the adoption of white culture, including work and food habits. These "humanitarians" viewed Native culture as a destructive force and believed the only way to save American Indians from extinction was for them to be assimilated completely into Euro-American society. Either way, the procurement and distribution of annuity goods became a constant source of debate and tension among all parties.

As the relationship between the federal government and Native nations evolved in the nineteenth century into a process of treaty negotiations, the distribution of food rations took on increasing importance. Rations were usually provided for the large groups gathered to participate in the negotiations, and in 1834 Congress authorized the president to grant rations to Native Americans visiting military posts and relocating at Indian agencies.[7] Through this practice the government hoped to encourage a specific behavior, the eventual settlement of Native Americans at potential reservations and the opening of western lands to white settlement. To expedite the process, to avoid entire tribes assembling at any one time, and to undermine existing tribal political structures, early distributions were given to the chiefs or Indian men chosen by whites for leadership so that they could make distribution among tribal members. Congress, however, passed legislation in 1847 that stopped this practice, stipulating the direct per capita payment of annuities rather than distribution through "chiefs."[8] Congress believed that this policy ensured the equitable distribution of the rations and goods and prevented chiefs from arranging distributions based on cultural and social mores that needed to be altered.

In the 1850s Commissioner of Indian Affairs Luke Lea saw problems with this system. He wanted a return to a policy of distribution through chiefs, believing this would allow the federal government to enhance the influence of those individuals it recognized as chiefs and alter tribal political culture, regardless of the desire of the particular Indian nation. Lea also feared that a continued bypassing of the chief's power to distribute goods according to cultural norms would only result in disorder.[9] Others believed that the only way to ensure that each individual received an equal share of the tribe's annuity goods was to maintain the policy of per capita distributions.

These differences of opinion concerning annuities reflected differing views on the status of Indian nations. On the one hand, if the tribes were "domestic dependent nations"[10] with individual governments, then the leaders of these governments—the chiefs—should be granted a certain amount of deference, such as allowing them to distribute the goods, foods, and money from annuities. However, if the eventual goal of federal Indian policy was the "civilization" of and eventual absorption of Native Americans into the larger American population, the continuation of tribal power, represented by the chief, should be avoided. Some believed that the per capita distribution of goods would encourage individualism and, therefore, the desire for private property.

As more and more land was lost and traditional methods of subsistence began to decline, tribes became more dependent on the distribution of rations and annuity goods. This process was actively encouraged by the federal government and aided by the expansion of settlement and the buffalo hunters who substantially decreased the range and size of the bison herds on the Great Plains. In 1848 Commissioner of Indian Affairs William Medill wrote,

> [A]s the game decreases and becomes scarce, the adults will grad-
> ually be compelled to resort to agriculture and other kinds of labor
> to obtain subsistence, in which aid may be afforded and facilities
> furnished them out of the means obtained by the sale of their for-
> mer possessions.[11]

Commissioner Francis A. Walker expressed a similar sentiment nearly a quarter century later in 1872:

> Can any principle of national morality be clearer than that, when
> the expansion and development of a civilized race involve the rap-
> id destruction of the only means of subsistence possessed by the
> members of a less fortunate race, the higher is bound as of simple
> right to provide for the lower some substitute for the means of
> subsistence which it has destroyed? That substitute is, of course,
> best realized, not by systematic gratuities of food and clothing
> continued beyond a present emergency, but by directing these
> people to new pursuits which shall be consistent with the prog-
> ress of civilization upon the continent; helping them over the first
> rough places on "the white man's road," and, meanwhile, supplying
> such subsistence as is absolutely necessary during the period of
> initiation and experiment.[12]

Regardless of the form and method of the distribution of federal rations, or indeed the legal and humanitarian arguments for rationing, the
policy faced nearly constant problems. By 1875 the standard issue, established during the previous decade when many Plains tribes were still able
to subsist at least partially on the hunt, was inadequate to feed people for
whom it was their only support.[13] The 1877 ration plan provided for an
average distribution of three pounds (gross) of beef, one-half pound each
of flour and corn, an ounce and a half of pork or bacon, a little more than
an ounce of sugar and rice, approximately half an ounce of coffee and
beans, and very small amounts of salt, tobacco, soap, and leavening per
person per week. Not all reservations received all components of the standard issue. Cornmeal often replaced the corn or rice, and tobacco was distributed irregularly. When either the beef or flour supply was insufficient,

the rationed amount of the other was generally increased (if additional amounts were available).[14] This practice meant that tribes could have little except beef or flour to subsist on for extended periods of time, especially when there were supply or transportation problems.

Table 2-1. Standard Weekly Ration Issued on
Indian Reservations in 1877 (per 100 rations)

Goods	Amount	Goods	Amount
Beef	300 lb. gross	Pork or Bacon	10 lb.
Flour	50 lb.	Salt	1 lb.
Corn	50 lb.	Tobacco	0.5 lb.
Sugar	8 lb.	Soap	1 lb.
Beans	3 lb.	Leavening	0.5 lb.
Coffee	4 lb.	Rice	5 lb.

Source: John Q. Smith, Procedural Issuances of the Bureau of Indian Affairs: Orders and Circulars, 1854–1860, RG75 (M1121), 1876, National Archives.

The rations were distributed to each head of a household, as defined by the US government. This restrictive definition attempted to negate traditional patterns of family and community responsibility. Treaties and agency laws stipulated that rations could not be shared beyond the nuclear family, excluding grandparents, aunts, uncles, and other extended family members. Distributing the food in this way also created difficulties in the continuation of tribal gatherings and obligations to help provide for the widowed, elderly, ill, and orphaned. However, despite rules prohibiting the sharing of rations, the practice of communal distributions continued in various forms on most reservations well into the twentieth century.

Rations were issued weekly, but agents were also responsible for guaranteeing that the supplies lasted the entire year. Often, the ration supplies were short, rancid, or missing altogether, resulting in less than adequate food supplies. Letters and reports from many Indian agents included warnings of insufficient food for distribution and starving and destitute people. On January 3, 1877, Cyrus Beede, Osage agent, reported conditions on the Osage reservation: "Cold weather, ground covered with snow, no flour, and between three and four thousand hungry Indians wanting bread is deplorable."[15] In many cases the amount of supplies delivered to the agencies were not enough to form full rations for an extended period of time. This can be seen in the reports of William Burgess, Pawnee agent, in the spring of 1874, when for several months small portions and partial rations were all that were issued.[16] There are also multiple reports of rancid flour, spoiled cornmeal and tobacco, and cattle so skinny hardly any meat could be obtained from slaughter.

Issues with the quality, quantity, and types of rations and other goods were major problems for the government, military, and tribes from the early nineteenth century. During the 1830s and 1840s the United States government signed treaties with many eastern tribes, providing for their removal to the area west of the Mississippi River. Most of these treaties promised the granting of transportation and provisions for the journey. There were numerous instances where these promises were not kept. Sometimes not enough food and blankets were sent; other times unscrupulous contractors and distributors overcharged for substandard goods en route. The most well-known instance of this is the Cherokee Trail of Tears. Cherokees traveled west in several groups, some of which were under military command while others went under the control of contractors. The contractors received $65 per person from the federal government to pay for the necessary food, medicines, and goods for the journey. In many cases the contractors, together with the distributors along the trail, provided inadequate food at exorbitant prices.[17]

Severe difficulties emerged again during the winter of 1874–1875 when many tribes recently confined to southern Plains reservations faced starvation, and agents were forced to give permission for hunts off the reservations. The situation was further exacerbated by the warfare that occurred on the plains during this period. While hunters were driven by hunger to leave their reservations to procure food, they had to range far to find herds and risked being attacked by the US Army and enemy tribes. These desperate conditions continued into 1877 with droughts, crop failures, and insect invasions.[18]

Distance was another significant problem. Many villages were far from the agency buildings; with very limited transportation and weekly distributions, much of the people's time was spent traveling to and from distributions. Conditions such as these proved to be a point of protest from tribes. In an 1878 Osage council meeting, Wah-ti-anka described the state of the rations being distributed:

> We have rations bought by the Commissioner for us. I know they are cheap for to look at them shows that; he must have found them some place where they were thrown away and got them for nothing. I think my people are brave to eat them. These rations are a damage to us. We live a long way from the Agency and it takes two days to come and get them, our homes are poor and we have a great many, for they are poor. If we could come only once a moon it would be better.[19]

Problems with rations and supplies became a constant for the Bureau of Indian Affairs and for the people being issued the goods. In many instances the flour or bacon issued was rancid, which in turn caused further health problems. The 1928 Meriam Report, which resulted from an investigation into the problems of the federal administration of Indian affairs, found that the "most important single item affecting health is probably the food supply."[20] Despite attempts by the US government to inspect the supplies, problems persisted in part due to the remoteness of camps within the reservations and the distance from government warehouses.[21] In an 1892 report of the Commissioner of Indian Affairs, the problems of distance and quality were noted in relation to the beef ration:

> The practice long obtained, grounded on the necessity of economizing to the upmost [sic] degree, of purchasing beef on the hoof and receiving in the fall a sufficient supply to last through the winter. No adequate provision, however, was made for sheltering the cattle or for properly feeding them, so that, as a natural result, when they were issued they had deteriorated in weight and very materially in quality.[22]

At other times excessive transportation costs were charged or scales were rigged, all to the benefit of contractors.

The desire of reformers and federal government officials was that once confined to reservations, Native Americans would quickly develop agricultural skills and become self-supporting farmers. A temporary system of distributing rations would support them only during this process. Humanitarians wanted the issuing of rations and the distribution of annuity goods to be as brief as possible to avoid the "pauperization" of the Indians.[23] They feared that if Native Americans received for too long food and goods perceived as free it would inhibit their embrace of white civilization.[24] Humanitarians believed that in order to develop a strong sense of individualism, private property, and a work ethic, all of which they viewed as essential American qualities, the recipients should be required to work for their rations, and only for the period it took for them to become successful farmers or ranchers.

However, the change from hunter to agriculturalist did not occur as quickly as non-Indians had hoped. In 1885 the Board of Indian Commissioners found that "by rations dealt out whether needed or not, we have interfered to suspend the efficient teaching by which God leads men to love and honor labor."[25] Many reservations were located in areas where traditional agriculture was difficult, if not impossible. A tragic and disastrous example occurred at Bosque Redondo in arid southeast New Mexico. Here in 1864–1865, the US military forced the relocation of 8,000 Navajos to a reservation along with several thousand Mescalero Apaches. The land could not support the large number of people settled there, even with irrigation, nor could it support the herds of goats and sheep. A. B. Norton, superintendent of the reservation, reported that "The soil is cold, and the alkali in the water destroys it. . . .The Indians now dig up the muskite [mesquite] root for wood, and carry it . . . for 12 miles."[26] The poor quality and low quantity of rations meant that the Navajos and Mescaleros at Bosque Redondo suffered from starvation, malnutrition, and illness. By 1868 the reservation was considered such a failure that the Navajos were allowed to return to a reservation in their homeland.[27] Problems such as those at Bosque Redondo were compounded by the distribution of insufficient and inadequate equipment and tools and the government's belief that the assimilation process would be a simple one of providing examples in the form of agency and reservation school farmers for the Indians to emulate. This meant that in many instances the issue of rations had to continue indefinitely.

Despite the call by many Indian policy reformers to change the ration and annuity system, the US government could not simply withdraw the aid. In addition to rations becoming the main source of subsistence for large numbers of people, in many cases the distribution of goods was a part of treaty stipulations. The annuities, rations, and goods distributed were often subtracted from the amounts the US government paid Indian tribes for ceded land. Some treaties provided annuities for a set number of years while others stipulated perpetual annuity disbursements. By the late nineteenth century the cry of humanitarians and American citizens who believed the disbursements were an additional and nonessential government expenditure became enough to force the government to alter its policies. Therefore, in 1874, in an effort to quiet the criticism and further encourage the development of a work ethic, an act was passed requiring all capable males, ages eighteen to forty-five, to perform labor on the reservation in return for rations and supplies.[28]

The last third of the nineteenth century witnessed the US federal government using rations extensively to coerce cultural change among Native peoples. An act passed on March 3, 1875, reinforced the previous work requirements and added that rations given in payment of labor could not be sold or exchanged and could only be shared with dependents and their nuclear family.[29] A circular sent out in 1883 provided further instructions on the matter:

> [Y]ou will not be allowed to issue sugar, tea, coffee, or tobacco to your Indians unless in payment of labor performed by them for themselves or the agency, except to the sick or very old and infirm, in which case a certificate from the physician, or two disinterested white persons, as to such disability.[30]

This not only altered the flow of supplies on the reservations, but it disrupted cultural patterns of kinship responsibility.[31] This change in procedure caused other problems as well. Many Indians believed they had already paid for the rations and supplies with the lands they had ceded to the United States. They were entitled to those goods through their treaties, and they should not have to pay for them again in the form of labor. It constituted a form of indentured servitude or slavery and often represented violations of existing treaties.

It is evident that some agencies had problems implementing the rations-for-labor policy. In 1882 the Bureau of Indian Affairs issued a circular stating that "the former rulings, of this Office, that all able bodied male Indians shall labor for their support, will be observed, and your employees should be such as will best assist them in their efforts."[32] Unfortunately, work was often difficult to arrange. The remoteness of many reservations, along with laws restricting travel beyond reservation borders, limited the opportunities for labor. Even around the agencies, work was often hard to find. Although the federal government ordered agents not to hire whites if tribal members could be used, jobs were often limited to fencing, assisting agency farmers, and other minor tasks. The work was tedious and sometimes demeaning, further exacerbating the tensions on the reservations and relations with the US government.

Another policy change aimed at increasing the "civilizing" influence of rations was made in 1889–1890. On November 1, 1889, the Bureau of Indian Affairs sent a circular to agents addressing the methods used in the distribution of beef rations. The predominant method of issue was for Native peoples to slaughter the cattle themselves and then distribute the meat and hides. The families of the men who did the slaughtering generally received a larger portion of the meat or the hides and offal in payment for their services. On several reservations, such as the Lakotas in South Dakota and Kiowas and Comanches in Oklahoma, cattle were killed using methods similar to those used on buffalo hunts, thus maintaining hunting skills and preserving some cultural aspects associated with the hunt.[33] This practice was viewed as barbaric by many government agents and humanitarians and resulted in the issuing of new instructions to agents in July 1890 concerning the beef ration:

> The killing is to be done in a pen, in as private a manner as possible, and by a man who understands the duty, and who uses the most speedy and painless method practicable; and during the killing children and women are specially prohibited from being present. . . .
>
> The consumption of the blood and intestines by the Indians is strictly prohibited. This savage and filthy practice which prevails at many agencies must be abolished, as it serves to nourish brutal instincts, and is, as I am well informed, a fruitful source of disease. . . .
>
> The beef will be delivered to men, and not to women, unless in cases of special exigency.
>
> In short, I intend that this branch of the work, which at many agencies has been so conducted as to be a scandal on the service and a stimulus to the brutal instincts of the Indians, shall become

an object lesson to them of the difference in this respect between the civilized man and the savage.[34]

In addition to turning the beef issue into a lesson on those parts of the animal considered edible by a "civilized" society and the proper method of preparation, the policy change effectively tried to end the last vestiges of the hunting culture of many tribes.

The goal of completely ending ration distributions was never far from the minds of the US Congress or the nation's humanitarians. In 1892, in an attempt to reduce—and ultimately phase out—ration distributions while not violating treaty stipulations, Congress passed an act that, in part, addressed this concern. In section eight of an Indian Appropriations Act, the Secretary of the Interior was granted the authority to distribute the value of goods and rations owed in cash. Once an individual or tribe was deemed "civilized enough"—capable of responsibly purchasing their own food and other necessities—they could petition to receive their distribution in cash.[35] This was to be an indication that the goals of "civilization" and the ration policy had come to a successful close.

As the nineteenth century drew to a close, public outcry over the ration system continued to grow. Reformers believed that many tribes were on the verge of adopting "civilization" through federal efforts to teach them farming and the system of Indian schools. One of the final steps in this process would be the ending of ration distributions. For their part, many tribes continued fighting to receive their annuities in cash rather than in rations and goods. They believed that they could purchase better-quality supplies themselves rather than using what the US government's representatives had been able to procure. The process of ending rationing and annuity payments was hastened by the signing and implementation of the 1887 Dawes Severalty Act, a federal law prohibiting communal ownership of land and forcing the adoption by individual tribal members of private property. While the distribution of rations ended in the early twentieth century (with the exception of Indian schools), the Bureau of Indian Affairs continued the practice of distributing foodstuffs, now called commodity goods, on many reservations. As with the ration goods of the nineteenth century, most commodity foods come from government surplus and are not designed to be the sole means of subsistence, nor are they particularly nutritious. Commodity foods are high in sugar, fat, and sodium and contribute to continuing health problems, particularly high rates of diabetes.

Many American Indian nations were granted rations and annuity goods through their treaties with the United States. However, they did not view the rations in the same way that government officials did. When rations were given to chiefs to distribute to the tribe, they did so according to their cultural and social values, not by distributing the same amount to each family, as the government had in mind. The federal government desired the tribal members to become self-supporting farmers and viewed rations as a temporary situation. As a result, many agents wanted to require men to work in exchange for rations. Many Native Americans, on the other hand, viewed the annuity goods as direct compensation for lands ceded through treaty negotiations, not as a reward for labor. Additionally, when individuals received rations intended for themselves or their nuclear family only, they often shared the food with extended family and friends, canceling government attempts to control behavior by only giving rations to certain persons.

Rationing on the reservations did not always strictly conform to the policies developed in Washington. Each agent and reservation faced its own problems with supplies and conditions. Individual agents took different approaches and had different concerns. Local conditions influenced the level of dependency on the government. Each Native nation tried to incorporate rations into its cultural and social framework. The story presented by the official records and policies shows only one aspect of Native rationing. An examination of the rationing process and its impact on individual reservations is needed to create a more complete picture. Therefore, with an understanding of the development of ration policy and the problems therein, it remains to explore the effects of federal ration policies in detail with case studies of rationing on the Pawnee and Osage reservations, as well as examining the ways Native peoples used the system and goods within their own cultural and social frameworks.

Chapter 3

Rations and South Australian Policy

South Australian colonial history differs from the history of the American West in many ways. Differences in environment, population, and cultures create different issues and responses. Each place and people has a distinct history. However, despite these differences, the common foundation of settler colonialism can be seen in similar attitudes and comparable themes in settler expansion and indigenous interactions. Ration policies in South Australia, indeed the entire Aboriginal policy system, were very different from those that were in use in the nineteenth-century United States. Historian Anne Pattel-Gray states that Britain's policies in Australia were "in sharp contrast to British policy in New Zealand, Papua New Guinea, Canada, and the US colonies."[1] The very premise upon which the colonial-Aboriginal relationship was built—a tradition of natural law[2]—created an official relationship devoid of treaties. Since Native Americans and Maoris had more stratified societies and could offer more prolonged resistance, settlers had less of an advantage. Aborigines, with the exception of Tasmania, did not often engage in organized warfare, limiting the effectiveness of their resistance. The competition between Britain, France, and Spain for control of North America also created differences in experience from Australia. While Native Americans received weaponry and metal utensils from competing nations, Aborigines rarely received such goods.

The differences in time during which initial colonization took place also helped create distinctive colonial-indigenous experiences in the United States and Australia. While sustained early contact with indigenous peoples in North America took place in the early seventeenth century, the British did not colonize Australia until the end of the eighteenth century, in the middle of the Industrial Revolution. This gave the British a greater weapons advantage over Aborigines than American settlers had had over Native Americans. The massive population movements facilitated in Australia by the Industrial Revolution also helped increase the drive to acquire more land and more raw materials at a faster pace than in previous colonial enterprises.[3] Despite drastic differences in outlook and policy implementation, and the cultural differences between the numerous Native American and Australian Aboriginal nations, many similarities between the two regions exist in their goals of assimilation, as well as with indigenous resistance, adaptation, and perseverance. Stemming from their origins as settler societies, the similarities and differences will reveal more than a study of either location in isolation.

Unlike the early settlers in North America, and later the United States, who acknowledged in Native cultures at least vaguely familiar forms of organization (leadership, social and political systems, organized forms of warfare), the explorers, settlers, and prison transportees in Australia did not recognize Aboriginal forms of political and social organization. Since the Europeans did not acknowledge any existing Aboriginal leadership, they created it. Unlike US government attempts to designate chiefs who would be friendly to their desires, where the goal was reshaping tribal power structures, similar suggestions in Australia were motivated more by desires to "civilize." In an 1891 *Queenslander* (Brisbane) story, A. D. Douglas suggested that a king and sub-kings should be designated within Aboriginal tribes, who would be held responsible for the behavior of their community. The kings would receive additional rations of tobacco and flour but would loose their rations if those charged with crimes were not turned in.[4] Although this suggestion was not widely implemented, designating particular Aborigines as "king" was practiced in some locations, but little to no power accrued with the title.

One of the most prominent differences between US–Native American and Australian-Aboriginal relations is the decentralized nature of the Australian system. Unlike the United States after 1800, where the federal government oversaw indigenous affairs throughout American territorial claims, in eighteenth- and nineteenth-century Australia individual states conducted their own Aboriginal affairs with only some guidance from the

British Colonial Office. Due to the recognized legal basis of British occupancy of Australia, no treaties were officially signed with Aborigines. Individual state governments directed relations, imposed directives, and began assimilation programs that included rations.

Unlike the earlier Australian settlements, such as Sydney and Melbourne, South Australia was not a penal colony. The 1834 Foundation Act granted the lands that make up present-day South Australia and the Northern Territory to a private company who arranged for the establishment of the colony. While the Foundation Act declared that the territory was an unoccupied wasteland, experiences in the other colonies had proven that South Australia would have to deal actively with an Aboriginal population. "legal and illegal deeds"

Parliamentary debates in the years preceding the establishment of South Australia acknowledged the negative effect of colonization on Aboriginal peoples and the assertion that there should be attempts to ameliorate those effects.[5] The first report of the Colonization Commission of South Australia in 1836 suggested steps to ensure humane treatment of Aborigines, which included protection "in the undisturbed enjoyment of their proprietary right to the soil, wherever such right may be found to exist."[6] However, the South Australia Colonization Act declared the lands assigned to the colony to be "waste and unoccupied lands which are supposed to be fit for the purposes of colonization."[7] By acting as though the inhabitants of the new colony had no government, no law, and no property, eighteenth-century international law permitted the British to lay claim to Australia and in the process to declare that the indigenous peoples had never held sovereignty—developing a "doctrine" of dispossession.[8] Aborigines under Australian legal doctrine had no property rights. The British government therefore felt under no obligation to negotiate treaties with the inhabitants or to compensate them for lands acquired by the Crown.[9] Despite the early realization of settlers that there was some social organization among Aboriginal groups, and the belief by a few humanitarians and practical settlers that the colonies had a moral obligation to compensate Natives for lost lands and food supplies, this pattern of dispossession remained the basis of Australian policies until the late twentieth century, creating problems that stretch from the early nineteenth century through the present day.

Although they often worked in concert, the government and humanitarians frequently had different objectives. The South Australian government's first goal with rationing was to prevent theft and control frontier violence.[10] Humanitarians, on the other hand, were more concerned with the moral and spiritual well-being of Aborigines. Alan Lester argues that the spread of British settler colonization in the early nineteenth century pushed humanitarians to look for new ways to "cure" the problems of the world. Those who labeled themselves as humanitarians believed it was their duty to instill the virtues of humanity, civilization, and Christianity in those around the world whom the British Empire touched.[11] These beliefs—that Aborigines had similar natural rights and desires as other peoples, that they simply needed to be shown better ways of living—drove much of the humanitarian push for ration distributions.

While some aspects of the South Australian civilization process, such as the removal of children, were directed at only some Aborigines, other aspects of the forced or coerced acculturation, including rationing, affected most Aboriginal tribes at one point or another. Like the United States, the use of food in Australian Native policy became integral to colonial-indigenous relations. Rations were distributed in part to try to alleviate the starvation of those Aborigines who resided near colonial population centers. Many recognized that settlement had disrupted traditional food supplies. It became increasingly difficult for Aborigines to sustain themselves in their home territories, although as with the arguments enunciated by Michigan Territory Governor Lewis Cass in the United States,[12] much of the force behind early rationing involved a desire to maintain good relations and hopefully prevent attacks, especially on isolated settlers as they spread across the land.

Since there were no approved treaties stipulating how much Aborigines would receive rations and when, issues varied greatly between locations, as did the requirements for receiving the goods. As with rations distributed in the United States, the foods that Aborigines received tended to be nutritionally poorer than their much more varied traditional diet. Quantity and quality were also perennial problems. This created issues with malnutrition and increasing Aboriginal susceptibility to disease, which when combined with an increasing dependence on new stimulants like tobacco, tea, and sugar, created many more problems, some of which continue to the present day.[13]

With the foundation of South Australia occurring during the height of the British antislavery movement and an evangelical revival, stories of Aboriginal massacres coming from Sydney and Melbourne strongly influenced the mind-set of the Commissioners.[14] From his first proclamation in 1836, South Australia's Governor John Hindmarsh established the official state position regarding Aborigines:

> [T]ake every lawful means for extending the same protection to the Native Population as to the rest of His Majesty's Subjects, . . . who are to be considered as much under the Safeguard of the law as the Colonists themselves, and equally entitled to the privileges of British subjects. I trust therefore, with confidence to the exercise of moderation and forebearance [sic] by all the classes, in their intercource [sic] with Native Inhabitants, and that they will omit no opportunity of assisting me to fulfill His Majesty's most gracious and benevolent intentions towards them, by promoting their advancement in civilization, and ultimately, under the blessing of Divine Providence, their conversion to the Christian faith.[15]

The position of the South Australia Colonization Commissioners regarding Aboriginal relations was further clarified in their 1836 letter to Resident Commissioner James Hurtle Fisher and other officers:

> You will see that no lands which the natives may possess in occupation or enjoyment be offered for sale until previously ceded by the Natives to yourself. . . .
>
> On the cession of lands you will make arrangements for supplying the Aboriginal proprietors of such lands not only with food but with shelter and with moral and religious instruction. With this view you will cause [a] weatherproof shed to be erected for their use and you will direct that the [A]borigines be supplied with food and clothing in exchange for an equivalent in labour.[16]

In order to facilitate colonial-Aboriginal relations, the South Australian government created the position of Protector of Aborigines. The protector, and those under his direction, was charged with enforcing the Colonial Commissioners' provisions as set out in the Letters Patent. However, as the economic viability of the colony was of utmost importance to its investors, and the acquisition of land for farming and ranching paramount, the protector of Aborigines had no control over the sale of land, denying him the power to protect Aboriginal property rights. As practiced in the colony, Aborigines only had rights to land used by them in a special way. It was left up to government officials to define what uses qualified and what did not.[17] Therefore, the primary means at the disposal of the protector of Aborigines for fulfilling his duties—promoting friendly relations, educating, civilizing, converting, encouraging adoption of labor—was the use and distribution of rations.[18]

Unlike the United States, South Australia generally did not use a centralized distribution of rations purchased, transported, and distributed by government officials to a specified number of people in particular locations. Rations were predominantly supplied by missionaries, settlers, pastoralists, and farmers (who were compensated by the government), as well as directly by the South Australian government through Aboriginal protectors and the police. In fact, much of the colonization process depended more on local conditions, economics, and individual settler views than any consistent or systematic application of policy.[19] Part of the reason for this decentralized system was the vast distances between both Aboriginal groups and the isolated settlements of the outback. The South Australian system of rationing also opened the door for those distributing the food to have more control over who received the food, the quantity that was provided, and the stipulations made on the people receiving the rations. While there were regulations and guidelines created by the government, the isolated nature of many ration depots made them extremely difficult to enforce on a regular basis.

The South Australian government ignored the official stated policy of Aboriginal equality as British subjects with reference to Aboriginal rights to land and food, and the citizens of the colony also acted counter to the Letters Patent. As ranchers moved farther from the settlements on the coast, appropriating Native lands, conflicts grew in number and bloodiness. One means used by some settlers to gain control over land while avoiding raids that threatened their own herds was to offer small amounts of food, especially flour, to Aborigines. Once this flour had been given a few times, and some sort of trust had been established, the flour supply would be poisoned. Historian Fay Gale noted the effect of this practice on later contact with more distant tribes:

But other settlers preferred "blue pills" as the arsenic put into ration flour was called. Dough made from such flour caused excruciating pain and subsequent death. . . .

. . . The tribal people to the north, who had not previously been contacted by whites, had been forewarned by the experiences of their brothers in the south. . . .Thus when ration flour was handed out it was taken away and buried for fear of poison.[20]

While not widespread, the poisoning of Aboriginal peoples by individual settlers ran the risk of increasing tensions between South Australia and Aborigines, as well as increasing the potential for violence between Aborigines and settlers—circumstances that South Australian officials preferred to avoid. One way to potentially forestall increased tension and violence was to increase systematic distributions of food and goods by the government and government-compensated agents.

The first ration distributions in South Australia consisted of flour or biscuits, rice, and oatmeal. Aborigines objected strongly to oatmeal, refusing to eat it, and referred to rice as *pindiparti* or maggots.[21] Protector William Bromley encountered problems almost immediately, writing in 1837,

I feel it my duty to inform you that the Natives tasted the oatmeal yesterday for the first time which was well boiled but they manifested such a dislike to it that they left half of it in the pot, and I am sorry to say, that this morning they have rejected it altogether.[22]

Except for special occasions, such as the Queen's birthday, South Australian rations rarely included meat. It was expected that Aborigines would still hunt for their meat, even after much of the wild game had been slaughtered or run off by pastoralists and their herds. As meat became more difficult to procure for Aborigines, the rations, which had originally been intended as a supplement to hunting and gathering, served as little more than a starvation diet.

During the early years of the colony, Aborigines in South Australia were given occasional gifts of food and clothing, primarily to maintain peaceful relations and prevent starvation. In 1839 Governor George Gawler initiated the practice of hosting feasts at Government House for Kaurnas living near Adelaide celebrating the Queen's birthday.[23] The purpose for the gathering was to gain Aboriginal confidence and to try to ensure Aboriginal understanding of government policies and laws. Food as a successful tool for conveying these messages was well understood by government officials. The protector of Aborigines believed that "beef and pudding, blankets and clothing were convincing and tangible induce- ments to loyalty."[24] Nevertheless, despite the altruistic motives of some for distributing food, Christobel Mattingley and Ken Hampton argue:

> [R]ations had a drastic effect on health and morale. They under- mined the active independence of a hunting and gathering lifestyle and created sedentary dependence. . . .The traditional healthy diet of game, fish and plant products was replaced by flour, usually second grade, sugar and tea, which often led to malnutrition.[25]

In 1841 an expedition led by South Australia Protector of Aborigines Matthew Moorhouse that set out to capture Aboriginal leaders for trial in Adelaide highlighted the increasing potential for violence as the colo- ny grew. In the battle that ensued near the Rufus River, between twenty and fifty Aborigines were killed. Later that year, in response to the Rufus River Massacre, the South Australian government of Governor George Grey began to gather Aborigines into semi-permanent settlements away from cities like Adelaide. Grey appointed Edward Eyre to occupy an area on the Murray River near present-day Blanchetown, gain the trust of lo- cal Aborigines, suppress attacks on overland travelers, and encourage the civilization process among his charges. Eyre believed that the best, most expedient method to achieve these goals was through the distribution of rations. While he believed that Aborigines were entitled to rations because of their loss of lands and their means of subsistence, Eyre acknowledged another reason to distribute food, blankets, and clothing:

> I believe that the supplying them with food would gradually bring about the abandonment of their wandering habits, in proportion to the frequency of the issue, that the longer they were thus depen- dent upon us for their resources, the more binding our authority would be; . . . by supplying the wants of the natives . . . a security and protection would be afforded to the settlers which do not now exist. . . .[26]

He recommended monthly rations be distributed at locations he set up— such as Moorundie on the Murray River—of four pounds of flour per adult and two pounds per child.[27] The rations actually distributed often fell short of the recommended amounts, especially as more tribes began coming in to the depot to receive the food.

By the middle of the nineteenth century, the blankets, bread, and roast beef being distributed were reduced in amount and quality as more and more Aboriginal groups came into contact with settlers and little desire was shown for increasing the budget for the annual demonstration of Her Majesty's good will.[28] The decrease in food offered at the Queen's birthday celebrations and the apparent cause (the succession of Grey to the governorship) was not lost on the attending Kaurnas. William Anderson Cawthorne, an early settler who wrote on South Australian Aborigines, recorded one Aborigine's opinion of the situation in his diary:

> Cockatoo man [Gawler] very good—long time ago came here— give lanty [plenty] tuckout (feast)—lanty blanket—lanty Bullocky (beef)—lanty sheepy (mutton)—lanty very good. This man (the present Governor) no good, give picanniny meat . . . picanniny bullocky, pickanniny blanket, Gubnor Gay no good, Gubnor Gay bloody rogue!![29]

For South Australia rationing served many purposes. Initially, the main concern was preventing theft and discouraging violence. Distribution points were established in ways to influence Aboriginal movement. By locating depots at distances from the colony's Anglo population centers, the South Australian government was able to encourage Aborigines to create semi-permanent settlements away from the corrupting influences of lower-class city life while at the same time protecting the upper classes from contact with begging and starving Natives. When the government attempted to restrict those receiving rations by location, it was trying to destroy freedom of movement and encourage the abandonment of traditional migration patterns.

The rations were also used to attempt to control Aboriginal behavior. European foods and eating habits were seen as "civilizing" influences. Additionally, government officials used a reward-and-punishment system with ration distributions to evoke certain behaviors. Food was often granted to parents who allowed their children to attend school, and in 1844 the Governor of South Australia sanctioned the issue of one pound of flour to each Aboriginal adult who attended church services.[30] Conversely, rations were withheld as punishment or to induce certain behaviors. Often an entire tribe's rations were withheld until wanted persons were captured or turned in.

When the first full-time protector of Aborigines, Matthew Moorhouse, attempted to introduce a labor requirement, he faced serious challenges. He observed:

> At the location we never distribute rations until an equivalent of
> work is done, and then the food is of an inferior quality to that
> obtained from the town. Bread, for instance, is preferred much
> before biscuit, and fresh meat before salt; and unless the number
> of natives be so great that the town cannot supply them, we get no
> work done at the location.[31]

Historian Robert Foster argues that the main obstacle to implementation of the labor-for-rations policy in the first half of the nineteenth century was that rations were not yet a necessity for Aborigines. Enough land remained unclaimed by settlers for traditional methods of hunting and gathering to continue successfully.[32] However, as more land was taken over by settlers and more restrictions were placed on Aboriginal movement within the established areas, it became more difficult for them to find sufficient food. Ranchers and farmers forbade hunting and gathering on their lands, the herds of cattle and flocks of sheep decimated the natural vegetation, and settlement blocked access to the best coastal fishing areas. With so little fertile land, most settlers believed there was no room for themselves and Aborigines to coexist, and colonial efforts to remove or at least isolate the indigenous population were increased.

The focus on labor in exchange for rations, as in the United States, grew out of a fear that if food was simply gifted to Aborigines they would never develop the work ethic that British colonists found so important. The desire to avoid the "pauperization" of Aborigines was evident at both government depots and mission stations, where only the ill and elderly received rations without work. However, there was often very little work to be had, especially after the shortage of white labor ended in the second half of the nineteenth century, and what jobs there were required Aboriginal men to travel long distances from home for low-paying (payment was almost always in the form of rations) seasonal work. The contradiction of the colonial government actively working to increase Aboriginal dependence on rations in order to gain more control in the first half of the 1800s versus fears of pauperization and the continual need for welfare by the end of the century established a precedent in South Australian–Aboriginal relations that continues up to the present.

Under the administration of Governor Grey (May 15, 1841–October 25, 1845), the South Australian government began using rations "as a means of gaining control over the Aborigines on the frontiers of pastoral settlement."[33] By this time the native food supply had been greatly affected by the spread of settlement. In fact, it was not unusual for settlers wanting to claim Aboriginal lands to destroy native sources of food, forcing them to either move or work for small amounts of food.[34] According to the Report of the Sub-Committee on Australia made by the Aborigines' Protection Society in 1838:

> The kangaroo disappears from the cattle runs, and is also killed by stockmen merely for the skins; but no mercy is shown to the natives who may help themselves to a bullock or sheep. Such a state of things must infallibly lead to the extirpation of the aboriginal natives, as in Van Diemen's Land, unless timely measures are taken for their civilization and protection. . . . I]t would only be an act of justice towards the aborigines to prohibit white men by law from killing these creatures, which are essential to the natives as cattle are to Europeans.[35]

The overriding humanitarian and philanthropic focus in the creation of Aboriginal policy, if not practice, that started the century faded by the end of the 1850s. A combination of decreases in government spending on Aboriginal programs and popular belief in the dying race theory helped change the focus of policy—and ration distribution—from one of humanitarian goals to one of economic expediency. While the distribution of rations to those settled on missions and working on outstations continued, often in payment for labor, government ration depots were reduced to distributing food and clothing only to the aged, ill, and orphaned.[36]

For most of the second half of the nineteenth century, the majority of ration distributors away from Anglo population centers were pastoral stations. This further decentralization—government depots, missions, and pastoral stations—was designed to keep outlying Aboriginal tribes away from cities like Adelaide and to provide the stations with a ready work force.[37] By the end of the 1850s, rations had become a form of social welfare for many Aborigines near the most settled areas of South Australia.

In the 1860s, however, the South Australian government faced an Aboriginal crisis. Due to increasing cases of chronic disease, destitution, and starvation, the government greatly expanded ration distributions throughout South Australia and the Northern Territory. The quantity of rations increased along with the number of depots distributing them, although not necessarily the percentage of Aborigines receiving them.[38] The recommended rations rose from four pounds of flour per adult per month, as suggested in 1847, to a daily ration distributed to the elderly, ill, and destitute that included one pound of flour or rice, 2 or 4 ounces of sugar (depending on whether the staple was flour or rice), and one-half ounce of tea.[39]

Again, however, the full amount of rations was not always available, particularly in the closing decades of the century when government support of mission stations distributing food dwindled and charitable donations, the lifeblood of the institutions, dramatically decreased. Nevertheless, by 1884 an Australian newspaper was able to report that

> nearly the whole of the surviving [A]boriginal inhabitants have gone under their [mission stations] control, the blacks preferring to have a comfortable home and a regular supply of food to the hand to mouth existence of former days.[40]

Despite the official increase in rations, it is doubtful that Aborigines would have felt the same way in regard to their condition in 1884. Many mission stations and ration depots were overcrowded, with few and poorly built European-style cottages, devoid of any means of improvement or escape. Disease, malnutrition, and depression remained constant problems throughout the nineteenth century and into the twentieth, as Aboriginal frustration with their situation increased. In some areas of Australia, rationing continued into the 1960s, when it was replaced by the welfare system. The rationing policies of South Australia, first implemented in the 1830s, continue to have an impact on state-Aboriginal relations. Systemic problems, resulting from more than a century of poor diet, overcrowding, and economic disadvantage, remain for many Aboriginal communities.

One of the responses to the colonial distribution of food was the attraction of Aborigines from the surrounding areas to the areas where those distributions took place. In many areas of Australia, Aborigines began to come in to European settlements soon after contact had been made, while in other locations groups were decimated long before continuous colonial settlement existed. Aboriginal reasons for coming into colonially settled areas included military defeat, starvation, disease, and curiosity. In the 1980s and 1990s Richard Baker studied the history of Yanyuwas in the Northern Territory. Although Yanyuwas did not move into continuous contact with Australians until the early twentieth century, when they began to come in to the town of Borroloola, the oral histories that Baker collected about that process and why people chose to make this change provide a foundation from which to consider the general process as it occurred during the nineteenth century in the central areas of Australia.

Similar to Native American tribes on the Great Plains, Aborigines were not a completely isolated people before the Anglo settlement of Australia. A vast trade network existed across the continent, disseminating goods and knowledge throughout Australia. Aborigines also had contact with Southeast Asians, Polynesians, Chinese, and European sealers and whalers prior to the British invasion in 1788. So the idea that Aboriginal people had had no outside contact prior to British settlement and had no basis for dealing with newcomers is a fallacy. However, what was different about British contact after settlement began in 1788 was its sustained nature, including the regular distribution of food.

If Aboriginal groups had the vast continent at their disposal, temporarily disregarding territorial boundaries, why did they begin congregating near colonial settlements in ever increasing numbers? From the Yanyuwa oral histories that Baker compiled, he identified seven main reasons for Aboriginal people to move closer to Anglo settlements, a process the Aborigines termed "coming in." Many were motivated to move because of concerns about their food supply and out of economic necessity. They longed for stimulants or desired staple foods. Some developed a curiosity about Europeans, or perhaps surrounding groups and relatives had already "come in." Still others feared disease or sought security.[41] While these were reasons underpinning Yanyuwa migration to Borroloola in the 1920s–1940s, similar reasoning may have influenced Aboriginal movements in the nineteenth century.

After the initial introduction of potentially addictive stimulants, such as tea and tobacco, the resulting desire for more led some in search of greater, more consistent supplies. Obtaining a steady supply of staple goods like flour and sugar was another strong draw. These introduced goods could replace native ingredients, reducing the long hours of labor-intensive work needed to harvest and prepare food from traditional sources. This became even more important as the spread of colonial settlement, with the accompanying herds of cattle and sheep, drove off native game and decimated the often-meager vegetation. As increasing numbers of Aborigines settled somewhat permanently near ration depots, communal, social, and ceremonial responsibilities drew others in, to hold gatherings where the majority of people were and where the most abundant food supply was.

While the South Australian government viewed rations as a humanitarian mission or as economically expedient, Aborigines had quite a different view of the worth and purpose of ration distributions. Aborigines fit the gifts of flour and other foods into their existing cultural framework of reciprocal relationships.[42] Since the new settlers were using Aboriginal lands and reducing the native food supply, it was correct and expected for them to give something in return. The settlers also had an overabundance of food, in Aboriginal eyes, and as such it was perceived as their responsibility to share with those who had none. Gathering at ration depots, missions, and outstations fit into existing Aboriginal patterns of moving to areas where food was in abundance.

The goods themselves also came to have different meanings within Aboriginal culture from those prescribed by settler Australians. Aboriginal society was not static—as new materials and goods were introduced, Aboriginal societies selectively adopted those that made life easier. Some goods were adopted in place of more traditional materials because they were more readily available, less labor intensive, or more suitable for the job. The uses these goods were put to did not always conform to European ideas. Other goods, such as wheat flour, were used in traditional methods of preparation, producing a damper type of bread made from European ingredients, rather than leavened bread. Neither did Aborigines always adopt the expected European habits that were associated with food preparation and eating, choosing to continue dining in more traditional ways.[43]

While South Australia never really had a unified rationing system, ration distributions affected most South Australian Aborigines in significant ways. Pastoralists distributed food, subsidized by the colonial government, encouraging Aborigines to live in semi-permanent settlements and ensuring a ready labor pool for the stations. Missionaries also distributed government rations, particularly to the elderly and infirm, congregating Aborigines into mission settlements where Anglo culture, including Christianity and work ethics, could be taught.

By the end of the nineteenth century, concern over Aboriginal welfare, even by "humanitarians," had ebbed. Between 1890 and 1912 every Australian state, including South Australia, began taking over administration of the remaining mission settlements. By making Aborigines wards of the state, the government was able to more closely control the continuing process of forced cultural change, gradually trying to incorporate Aborigines into the lowest rungs of Australian society and eliminating the need for mission settlements.

Periodic ration distributions continued in South Australia, particularly in the more remote areas, well into the twentieth century. However, starting in the 1960s the South Australian government began passing legislation that gradually eased legal restrictions on Aborigines (although they still faced heavy social discrimination). By the end of the 1960s, the distribution of Aboriginal rations had ended and was replaced by inclusion in the larger South Australian welfare system. Similar to commodity foods on Indian reservations in the United States, welfare foods generally came from surplus supplies and were not intended to be the sole means of subsistence.

Despite the best efforts of South Australian government officials in the nineteenth and early twentieth centuries, Aborigines receiving rations did so within their own cultural and social frameworks, creating their own definitions and understandings of the rationing process. Ration goods were used in traditional applications, rather than matching European expectations. The rations were also incorporated within Aboriginal systems of reciprocity, as expected payments as South Australians took land and reduced the availability of traditional subsistence. As with the United States, stated South Australian ration policy and the desire or ability of those responsible for distributions to adhere to those policies were often different. Environment, social conditions, and the individuals involved all impacted the effectiveness of rationing. The effects of rationing in South

Australia will be explored in more detail with case studies of the Moo-rundie ration depot and the Point McLeay (Raukkan) mission, as well as an examination of the ways in which Aborigines adapted the system and goods distributed to fit their cultural and social ideals.

- Missions
- Rations
- Anti-blackness & Aboriginality
- settler violence & proximity a movement
- 'we want to destroy God'
- addictive substances...

Chapter 4

Rationing on the Pawnee Reservations, 1857–1891

The indigenous rationing policies of the United States, while often set out in treaties with individual Native nations and regulated by periodic issuances of the Bureau of Indian Affairs, were piecemeal in practice. Indigenous peoples were caught in the middle of rival political factions within the Indian Service and the government at large. The needs of the people were superseded by bureaucratic requirements and political red tape, resulting in requests for rations appropriations being delayed or not approved at all.

Native nations receiving rations were also at the mercy of unscrupulous traders, many of whom held a near monopoly on annuity goods and ration supplies. Traders and transporters were often able to charge inflated prices for substandard products with little fear of consequences. This was especially troubling during periods of extreme hardship, when tribes were on the verge of starvation, their agents trying to get any supplies possible.

Competing views of humanitarian groups and the believed cultural superiority inherent in settler colonialism also affected the rationing policies of the United States. The focus on "civilizing" efforts and the ways to go about creating cultural and social change involved setting future goals with little consideration of the current needs of the people the humanitarians were purporting to help. These humanitarians often campaigned against the continuation of semi-annual buffalo hunts, believing this would encourage—or coerce—tribes into adopting farming. Unfortunately, this change was forced before reservations were self-sustaining, resulting in a total dependence on government rations for subsistence. The problem was even graver on reservations that lacked adequate arable land, contributing to the problems of hunger, malnutrition, and disease.

Native peoples of the United States were encouraged, or coerced, into changing their social, political, and cultural structures by the policies and actions of the United States government. An integral component of those policies was the control and manipulation of food—restricting access to traditional food sources through removal and relocation and restrictions on hunting, as well as the issuing and withholding of the rations on which people had come to depend. However, the rations issued by the government were never enough for a people to subsist upon completely. The rations were meant to supplement first the hunt and later the transition to self-sufficient farming. Unfortunately, most indigenous peoples became completely dependent on government rations, leaving them in an almost constant state of hunger, struggling to survive on increasingly embattled reservations.[1] In order to appreciate the profound physical, social, and cultural impact that rationing had on indigenous peoples, an examination of rationing practices in microcosm is necessary. The Pawnee and, in the next chapter, the Osage reservations will be our microcosms.

The Pawnees were a confederation of four related but distinct bands (Skidi, Chaui, Kitkehahki, and Pitahawirata) rather than a single, unified political entity. As with many Native American nations, when the United States government came into contact with Pawnee bands, they viewed the people as a single entity, choosing the individuals they would deal with and through gifts and influence maneuvering those individuals into positions of power with little regard to Pawnee desires or existing political frameworks.

The Pawnees, located in the nineteenth century on the Great Plains near the Loup and Platte Rivers in east-central Nebraska, experienced early contacts with Europeans during Spanish expeditions north from Mexico, such as those of Francisco de Coronado in 1541 and Don Pedro de Villasur in 1720. The goal of the Villasur expedition was to discover whether the Pawnees had become military allies with France, which could pose a threat to the New Mexico colonies. When Pawnees and Otos on the Loup and Platte Rivers attacked the expedition, over thirty, including

Villasur, were killed, resulting in Spain leaving the central Great Plains area and retreating to Santa Fe.[2] However, regular contact with European populations did not develop until the eighteenth century when Pawnee villages became regular stops for French traders. When France lost control of its lands in North America in 1763, trade with Europeans diminished until the 1803 Louisiana Purchase brought new waves of American traders, settlers, and soldiers onto the Plains.

The development of contact between Pawnees and the United States followed patterns similar to those experienced by other Great Plains tribes—but with some uniquely Pawnee elements as well. During the early nineteenth century, facing more sustained contact with United States government agents and settlers, members of many Native nations fell prey to unscrupulous traders who trapped them in cycles of debt and introduced large amounts of alcohol into their societies. The alcohol trade not only benefited the traders but also had a negative effect on Indian culture. Unlike most Native nations, the Pawnees maintained a ban on alcohol for a sustained period of time.[3] They were, however, subject to the same pattern of contact—gifts of food to entice friendly relations and certain behaviors—as Major Clifton Wharton stated in his speech to the Pawnees recorded in the journals of his 1844 military expedition through Kansas and Nebraska:

> I give you here a small quantity of flour [and] pork as an evidence
> of the kindly feelings of your white brethren [sic]. . . .
>
> Accept, Pawnee Loups, each of you, this Blanket and Tobacco,
> as a mark of the respect in which your late conduct is held.[4]

Pawnee leaders participated in the fur trade but did not become dependent on European goods until well into the nineteenth century; they were thus able to maintain their traditional power and social structures for a longer period of time. Historical geographer David Wishart described the problems that Pawnees and other Native peoples on the Great Plains faced in the nineteenth century: increased warfare and disease, continued depletion of resources and resulting hunger, population decrease, and government involvement all served to decrease the ability to maintain self-sufficiency.[5]

Several factors contributed to the Pawnees' growing dependence on the United States government. Damage to traditional hunting grounds, noticeable as early as the 1830s, and successive crop failures reduced the available food supply. In addition, the Pawnees faced increasing military pressures from Lakota Sioux, their longstanding enemies, and to a lesser degree the Cheyennes, who had pushed onto the Plains from the north. Lakotas, armed with guns and ammunition provided by the United States as part of negotiated peace settlements, frequently raided Pawnee villages and attacked Pawnees while they hunted. Cheyennes often stole Pawnee horses, making hunting even more difficult. Despite treaty promises and pleas made by chiefs and agents, Pawnees never received arms with which to protect themselves, making them even more vulnerable to attacks.

In addition to the frequent raids and a decreasing food supply, disease also began to take a toll on the Pawnee population. In the early nineteenth century, the Pawnee population was estimated to be between 20,000 and 25,000. Although they faced periods of disease and drought that severely affected their food supply, until the 1830s the Pawnee population remained at least 10,000 strong. However, waves of epidemic disease, especially smallpox, combined with crop failures, enemy raids, and increased competition with white settlers in the mid-nineteenth century took their toll, affecting the ability of the Pawnee population to rebound. By the 1870s the Pawnees numbered approximately 3,000, and by the turn of the twentieth century, their population was less than 1,000.[6]

Problems with disease, food supply, and increased competition in the mid-nineteenth century were compounded by the establishment of the Pawnee reservation, first in Nebraska in 1857, and then in the Indian Territory in 1876. Long before the establishment of the reservations, however, Pawnees entered into a series of treaties that sold most of their lands south of the Platte River to the United States.[7] The 1833 treaty obligations to the Pawnees included a $4,600 annuity in goods for a period of twelve years and $1,000 a year for schools for ten years, as well as farmers, oxen, and horses for the use of the tribe for four years.[8] While the bands received their annuity payments from the treaty, none of the other obligations were fulfilled because the Pawnees refused to remain in villages on a year-round basis, and by 1844 their annuity payments had expired, leaving the tribe in a very difficult position.[9]

On September 24, 1857, the four Pawnee bands signed a treaty with Commissioner James W. Denver establishing a reservation near Genoa in south-central Nebraska. In the treaty, the Pawnee gave up all their lands with the exception of a thirty-by-fifteen-mile tract along the banks of the Loup Fork of the Platte River. In exchange for the cession of land, the Pawnee were to receive a $40,000 annuity for a period of five years and a $30,000 annuity thereafter with one-half paid in goods.[10] Annuity goods included items ranging from blankets and clothing to mirrors and axes. They also occasionally included food items (in addition to the regular rations) such as dried apricots, nutmeg, ground ginger, ground mustard, and syrup.[11] Also included in the treaty was the statement that a breach of any of the treaty stipulations by any Pawnees would result in the withholding of annuity goods and payments to either individuals or the entire tribe.[12] The withholding of goods, including food, served as a blanket threat to discourage a wide range of behaviors the United States government deemed harmful, dangerous, and "uncivilized."

The restrictions of living within the boundaries of the reservation limited the options available to the Pawnees to cope with their increasing problems. While they were permitted to hunt off the reservation, the decimation of the bison herds and the encroachment of American settlers meant longer distances had to be traveled to find game. The loss of horses in raids and Lakota attacks further hampered Pawnee hunts. Fewer horses meant fewer hunters and less capability to carry back bison meat and hides. Attacks by Lakota also prevented slain bison from being cleaned and dressed, further depleting Pawnee food supplies.

Compounding the problems created by unsuccessful hunts were Lakota attacks on Pawnee villages that destroyed crops and raided food caches and crop failures due to weather. The attacks on the villages and fields made it difficult for crops to be cultivated and harvested. The fields were generally at a distance from the villages, making the women who tended the plants easy targets for attacks. A secondary problem the Pawnees faced was the theft of wood from the reservation. Nearby settlers frequently stole large amounts of the precious resource from the Pawnee reservation, leaving the Pawnees with few alternatives for fuel for cooking and heating. Although the US government outlawed the stealing of timber by settlers, there was little done to enforce the law. The Pawnee Council was forced to leave warriors on the reservation during hunts to attempt to prevent the thefts, resulting in even fewer people to participate in the increasingly difficult bison hunts.[13]

Although agents at the Pawnee reservation repeatedly reported the worsening conditions and submitted requests for government rations, the situation continued to deteriorate. When food was delivered to the reservation for distribution, it was usually far less than what was needed, and the beef and flour were of an inferior quality. Distributions to the entire tribe were generally made monthly, bimonthly, or weekly, depending on the supplies available, conditions, and changing Bureau of Indian Affairs policy. Food was regularly distributed by the agent to those he deemed to be destitute. This became increasingly important as growing subsistence problems affected the ability of the tribe to care for those people through traditional means. The regular distribution of rations also greatly affected the Pawnees' use of time. Since many lived at a distance from the distribution site, a considerable amount of time was needed to travel to and from the weekly issuance of rations. John Dunbar, a missionary among the Pawnees, remarked,

> It is no unusual occurrence at agencies to find a very considerable proportion of the Indians, through no fault of their own, centering their thought and activity apparently upon receiving and devouring the weekly stipend of rations doled out to them.[14]

The problems with subsistence relief and the method used to distribute rations continued to develop throughout the 1870s. In January 1872 Agent Jacob Troth reported to Superintendent Barclay White that the number of Pawnees requiring rations to survive was increasing.[15] Even though the Pawnees were becoming more dependent on government rations, they preferred to incorporate the rationing process into their existing cultural framework. In July 1872 Troth reported that the Pawnee Council wanted to distribute their annuity goods themselves, allowing them to follow cultural practices, rather than have the superintendent conduct the distribution.[16] This type of debate became a common element in the rationing process in the United States. Tribal leaders wanted to control the distribution of goods and services on their reservations, maintaining traditional cultural and social mores. US government agents, on the other hand, viewed that form of distribution as inequitable, preferring instead to have an even distribution of goods but also recognizing the political control they might exercise.[17]

Periods of hunger were a common occurrence, particularly in the winter when low hunt yields and difficulty in transporting rations were at their worst. The winter of 1873 was especially harsh. Beef rations were inadequate, with Agent Troth reporting widespread destitution by late February. Pawnees were forced to resort to begging for food in March. These conditions contributed to a lethal outbreak of measles on the reservation during the spring months. By July, however, special federal funds were made available to purchase flour, bacon, potatoes, sugar, and coffee for distribution to the heads of lodges on the reservation.[18]

The Pawnees' rationing problems continued into 1874, with Agent William Burgess reporting insufficient supplies throughout the first nine months of the year. The situation was made even graver by a grasshopper invasion.[19] In February Burgess wrote that most Pawnees only had the flour, cattle, sugar, and coffee that were distributed on a monthly basis, and those supplies did not equal full rations for more than a brief period of time.[20] The desperate conditions continued through August, resulting in many Pawnees pledging their entire annuity payment to traders to obtain food.[21] By October and November the ration situation had somewhat improved, with rations being issued on a weekly basis (see table 4-1). From the last week of October through the end of November, the average weekly issue consisted of six pounds of beef and ten pounds of flour per person, along with an occasional small issue of beans, salt, and coffee. Rations were also given to a group about to leave for the Indian Territory. The increased quantity of rations, however, did not last, and the Pawnees were again quickly faced with hunger in 1875.

Despite the poor quality and quantity of rations from the Pawnee agents and the frequent requests for more food, Superintendent White pressed Washington to withdraw permission for the Pawnees' semi-annual buffalo hunts. The Pawnees' near starvation conditions failed to dissuade White from arguing that the continuation of the hunts was a barrier to civilization efforts among the Pawnee.[22] This demonstrated the importance that the US government placed on changing native behavior, trying to force a change in subsistence patterns even before alternate means of survival had been established. The subsequent malnutrition, and the disease that followed, combined with other changes and challenges in the Pawnees' world, created a powerful sense of depression and a loss of the will to live among some.[23]

Table 4-1. Per-Capita Weekly Rations, Pawnee Reservation,
23 October–20 November 1874

Date Issued	Beef (pounds)	Flour (pounds)	Beans (bushels)	Coffee (bushels)	Sugar (gallons)	# of Persons
23 Oct.	6.67	10	0	0	0	600
1 Nov.	3.77	8.3	5	0.005	0.185	600
6 Nov.	7.22	11.1	0	0	0	360
13 Nov.	6.54	11.1	5	0	0	360
20 Nov.	6.72	11.1	0	0	0	360

Source: William Burgess, agent, to Barclay White, superintendent, November 21, 1874, US, Records of the Northern Superintendency, 1851–1876, RG74 (M1166), National Archives.

Pawnees, like many Native peoples, had faced periods of hunger and strife throughout their history and had persevered, maintaining their social and cultural mores in the process. The Pawnees' situation in the mid-nineteenth century, however, proved to be especially difficult to overcome. Edmond Dounias and others have noted that "drastic modification of resource availability, and invasive influence of modernity intervene so rapidly that they compromise the adjustment of social, cultural, economic, and political systems."[24] Pawnees were faced with challenges, some familiar and some never before experienced, from every direction. European weapons, supplied by the United States government, magnified competition with other indigenous peoples over increasingly scarce resources. While Lakotas and Cheyennes received guns and ammunition from government agents trying to negotiate peace with the tribes, the Pawnees, due in part to their Quaker agents, did not receive arms, despite repeated requests by chiefs for some means to protect their people from attack. This hastened the shift in the balance of power among Native nations away from the Pawnees.

In addition to competition with indigenous neighbors, the Pawnees also faced increased competition from encroaching American settlers. As more settlers arrived in Nebraska, Pawnee lands became more and more coveted. Along with arable land, the reservation contained the best supply of firewood in the area. As a result, the Pawnees constantly battled squatters to keep them off their lands and to prevent their precious wood supply from being exploited.

Historian Richard White believes that the Pawnees, using traditional means, could have succeeded in overcoming any one of the crises they faced in the 1870s, but they were not able to defend against the pressures they confronted from multiple directions.[25] In the face of the disintegration of their way of life and the disruption of their means of subsistence, the Pawnees turned to a traditional method of saving their society: moving to a new location and reestablishing the villages. This time, however, the move was negotiated and dictated by the United States government, and the Pawnees' means of subsistence during and after the move became a significant point of conflict.

The primary goals of the United States in their rationing policy in regard to the Pawnees shifted over time. Prior to the 1857 treaty the government used gifts of food and goods to maintain goodwill and peace with the tribe. With the establishment of the reservation near Genoa, Nebraska, the government's focus moved more towards its "civilization" program. Rations were to be provided to supplement the people as they made the transition from biannual bison hunts to farming. In order to allay the fears of many humanitarians—that the provision of rations would slow the Pawnees' development of a work ethic—the ration amounts were kept purposefully low. As white settlement expanded on the Great Plains in the mid-nineteenth century, the purpose of the rationing policy took on an additional element—removal.

By 1870 the number of settlers in Nebraska had increased at a substantial rate, surrounding the Pawnee reservation with white settlement. As the best, most fertile lands were claimed, the reservation, with its timber, water, and fields, became property more and more coveted by Nebraskans.[26] Most settlers viewed the reservation as wasted land, unjustly withheld from settlement. The goal of the civilization program, transforming the Pawnees from a hunting-horticulture society into yeoman farmers, was intended to end this problem. Additionally, the reasoning followed, if the Pawnees, and other Native peoples, became farmers and personal property owners, they would need less land, opening much of the reservation to white settlement. To the frustration of Nebraskan settlers (as well as humanitarians and government agents), however, the desired changes in Pawnee society were slow in coming, increasing the tensions between the reservation and surrounding communities.[27]

Initially, most Pawnees preferred to remain in Nebraska, unwilling to sever ties to their homelands, sacred sites, and graves of their ancestors. As early as 1873, however, some Pawnees began expressing their desires to move to the Indian Territory, where they would be safe from Lakota raids and encroaching settlers.[28] By 1874 the external pressures on the Pawnees caused many to start considering a move to the Indian Territory, where they believed they could successfully hunt and subsist, living close to their Wichita relatives. Despite the growing belief that migration might be the best chance for their people to survive, many remained reluctant to leave their homelands permanently.

Nonetheless, on October 8, 1874, the Pawnee Council met with officials from the Office of Indian Affairs and agreed to move to the Indian Territory, selling their Nebraska reservation.[29] By the spring of 1875, parts of several Pawnee bands had begun their move, temporarily residing on the Wichita reservation while their new reservation was established. Other groups left periodically throughout 1875. The remaining Pawnees reached the Indian Territory in 1876, completing the nation's move away from their homelands.

The act providing for the sale of the Pawnees' Nebraska lands and the survey and purchase of suitable lands for the establishment of a reservation in the Indian Territory passed Congress on April 10, 1876. The act stated:

> That there be, and hereby is, appropriated out of any moneys in the Treasury not otherwise appropriated, the sum of three hundred thousand dollars, out of which not more than one hundred and fifty thousand dollars shall be used in defraying expenses already incurred for the subsistence of said Pawnee tribe of Indians and for their removal to the Indian Territory, and other necessary expenses connected with their establishment and settlement therein. . . . And the residue of said three hundred thousand dollars . . . shall be applied to defray the expenses of appraisement and sale of the [Nebraska] lands . . . and to the settlement of said Indians, and to their further subsistence, until they can become

self-sustaining. . . . And provided also, That so much of the residue
of the three hundred thousand dollars aforesaid as may be needed for the immediate necessities of the aforesaid Pawnee Indians
may be expended in the purchase of supplies therefore in open
market.[30]

The proceeds from the Nebraska land sale were to be used to repay
the US Treasury for moving expenses with the surplus, minus any needed
for immediate subsistence, held as a credit by the Treasury Department.[31]

For those Pawnees who remained in Nebraska into the late summer of
1875, rations were distributed on a weekly basis (money for which would
be provided by the act passed on April 10, 1876). Despite the lack of successful hunts during past seasons and the reduced population (due to the
periodic move of groups to the Indian Territory), which hampered any
new hunt efforts, the rations reported distributed in July, August, and September included no beef or bacon, and the issue in June was small (see
table 4-2).

The June rations included a weekly issue to each individual of approximately seven pounds of flour,[32] slightly more than one pound of sugar,
and one-half pound of coffee. Beef was issued only the first two weeks,
equaling about five pounds per person each issue. During each week in
July, each person received a ration of approximately 8.3 pounds of flour,
one-half pound of sugar, and one-quarter pound of coffee. In August the
weekly ration of flour decreased to 5.5 pounds per person. In September,
flour was issued only once, during the third week, equaling eleven pounds
per person. This diet was supplemented with what vegetables could be
gathered in the wild and what could be harvested from the fields after Lakota raids. Dependence on the small quantity of these rations, combined
with subsistence problems encountered on the road to the Indian Territory, resulted in many Pawnees arriving at their new home in desperate
condition.

Pawnee removal was carried out in stages with parties ranging from
forty families to several hundred at a time. Some supplies were provided
for the journey; however, it was expected that the men would hunt for
buffalo on the way to provide food and hides, and supplies of grain would
be carried from Nebraska. The parties also had a government voucher to

purchase food, if need be, from merchants along the trail. Unfortunately, most white merchants would not accept the voucher, and the only food they were able to purchase was poor-quality flour from a merchant in Great Bend, Kansas, and Texas longhorn cattle in fair condition from a man on Medicine Lodge River at exorbitant prices.[33]

Table 4-2. Per Capita Weekly Rations, Pawnee Reservation,
July–September 1875 (issues made to 360 persons)

Date Issued	Beef (in pounds)	Flour (in pounds)	Coffee (in pounds)	Sugar (in pounds)
3-Jun.	5.17	6.94	0	0
10-Jun.	5.1	6.94	0.56	1.11
19-Jun.	0	6.94	0.56	1.11
26-Jun.	0	6.94	0.56	1.11
3-Jul.	0	8.33	0.25	0.5
10-Jul.	0	8.33	0.25	0.5
17-Jul.	0	8.33	0.25	0.5
24-Jul.	0	8.33	0.25	0.5
31-Jul.	0	8.33	0.25	0.5
7-Aug.	0	5.56	0.25	0.5
14-Aug.	0	5.56	0.25	0.5
21-Aug.	0	5.56	0.25	0.5
28-Aug.	0	5.56	0.25	0.5
4-Sep.	0	0	0.25	0.5
11-Sep.	0	0	0.25	0.5
18-Sep.	0	11.11	0.25	0.5
25-Sep.	0	0	0.25	0.5

Source: William Burgess, Agent to Barclay White, superintendent, June 30, 1875, August 2, 1875, and September 30, 1875, Records of the Northern Superintendency, 1851–1876, RG75 (M1166), National Archives.

The lack of food on the plains, due to increased usage, drought, and other natural disasters, extended to vegetation for the Pawnees' packhorses as well. The increasing numbers of settlers, and their livestock, over the preceding several decades had taken a toll on the environment, severely affecting the natural vegetation of the area.[34] There was little grass to feed the horses, resulting in the use of bark for fodder. The bark was a poor substitute for grass, resulting in weaker horses and slower travel, which in turn put added pressure on the group's food supplies.[35] Pawnee bands were also harassed by townspeople during their journey. It was common for individuals to make claims against the groups as they passed, accusing the Pawnees of stealing horses, food, or wood.[36]

As travel continued slowly, the first groups to leave encountered worsening winter weather. Adding to the increasingly more desperate situation was the lack of buffalo and other game. While the government plan had been for the Pawnees to hunt to provide adequate meat during their removal, there was no sufficient plan if game was not found. Thus, starvation was a looming prospect.

The difficulties experienced by the parties of Pawnees on the trail to the Indian Territory, including the knowledge that they were leaving behind their homelands and the lands of their ancestors, only increased once they reached their destination. Despite the formal agreements with the United States government and the arrangements set forth in the "Act to Authorize the sale of the Pawnee Reservation," the situation in the Indian Territory was disorganized and little had been accomplished before the arrival of the Pawnees to provide for their establishment at their new reservation or for their immediate subsistence after their long journey.

The first large group of Pawnees arrived at the Wichita Agency, in the Indian Territory, on February 16, 1875. The long, difficult trip had exhausted most of the Pawnees' supplies, and although the Wichita agent issued a weekly beef ration, it was barely sufficient to feed 1,760 Pawnees, especially with no additional means of subsistence.[37] In March 1875 E. P. Smith, the Commissioner of Indian Affairs, reported that the Pawnees had "but a small annuity fund of about ten dollars per capita with which to be maintained for a whole year."[38] Even after the survey and establishment of their new reservation, between the forks of the Arkansas River and Cimarron River east of the 97th meridian, subsistence was something of a problem as the first Pawnees to arrive came too late in the season to plant crops.[39] In December 1875 the situation had still not been resolved, as the Pawnee agent informed the people that their annuity could not be distributed because some were not yet at the new reservation and the annual census could not be finished in time for Congress to make the necessary appropriations.[40]

During the first months of the new reservation, while some Pawnees remained in Nebraska, at the Wichita Agency, on the trail to the Indian Territory, as well as on the new reservation, subsistence was a particular problem. John Williamson, the Pawnee subagent, wrote about Pawnees trading anything they could for food or old grease to make fry bread.[41] Failed crops and hunts prior to removal added to the crisis, leaving them with no caches to fall back upon. Then the bill providing for the appropriation of funds for Pawnee subsistence failed to go to a vote before the end of the session, which left the Pawnees with nowhere to turn. They had no supplies, and it would be months before the first possible harvest on the new reservation. In 1876 Commissioner Smith reported to Secretary of the Interior Zachariah Chandler:

> [H]undreds of Pawnees had been compelled to abandon their agency, to live by begging or stealing in southern Kansas. In numerous other instances, notwithstanding the passage of several relief bills, the funds at the disposal of this office have been so limited as to make it a matter of the utmost difficulty to keep Indians from suffering with hunger.[42]

By June and July of that year Agent William Burgess was still reporting on the lack of ration supplies, writing that there was little flour remaining and that he "sent to Coffeyville for 100 sacks of flour pledging my private means in payment if not allowed to purchase."[43] When Frank and Luther North visited the new Pawnee reservation in 1876, to enlist scouts for a campaign against the Sioux, Frank remarked on the condition he found many Pawnees in: "Shaken by ague and fever, the Pawnees tell an awful story of destitution, disease, and death. These people have only been here two years, a third of them only a year."[44] Despite the tremendous hunger facing the Pawnees in the Indian Territory in 1875 and 1876 due to the lack of rations, the United States government wanted to restrict their movement off the reservation. Barclay White recorded in his journal that he informed the Pawnees' agent that he

> must allow no one to leave the reservation for that purpose [hunting]. The Commissioner says in his letter that the number of cattle to be sent to you will furnish meat sufficient for the tribe.[45]

Starvation had become an official policy for those in charge in Washington, DC.

The new environment was also a problem. The people could not find many of the medicinal herbs and edible plants they were familiar with, leaving them without traditional recourse against disease made worse by malnutrition. Once established on their new reservation, the Pawnee population declined rapidly, with a simultaneous increase in disease and destitution. It was a vicious cycle that the Pawnees could not escape. Restricted from hunting buffalo off the reservation, the smaller game on the reservation was soon exhausted, leaving them dependent on government rations, which more often than not were lacking in both quality and quantity.[46] Without a sufficient food supply, the Pawnees were forced to trade their other annuity goods for food, but the general poor quality of those goods meant that they were once again at a disadvantage.

The year 1877 was typical of the experience the Pawnees had with the rationing process. Problems existed with the quantity, and sometimes quality, of the supplies held at the agency for distribution. The Pawnees told stories of slabs of pork that were mostly fat and green with mold. The bacon was often so bad that it was reportedly used as stepping-stones in the river.[47] There were also ongoing discussions between the Pawnee agent and the superintendent regarding ways in which to cut the rations, to extend the stores as far as possible, and reduce the amount of money (from the tribe's own accounts) spent on subsistence. At one point the coffee ration was reduced to a level where families repeatedly shared used coffee beans.[48] In December of the previous year, Acting Superintendent G. Nicholson had informed Agent Burgess that the "Commissioner of Indian Affairs fixes the ration of hard bread at 25 lb. with each 100 rations in lieu of 50 lb. of flour," and that the "fresh beef issue of 3 lb. gross is believed to be sufficient. . . . [T]his ration is 4 ounces larger per day than the army ration."[49] On February 7, 1877, Burgess wrote to Superintendent Nicholson:

> If we do alternate weekly issues of bacon and beef, with 1250 Indians at present and probably 1560 part of the time, up to 1 May . . . less will be required than if issued to full amount. . . . I think that instead of expending $2000 more or less for an extra amount of bacon, that one half the amount expended for good corn meal on

the alternate weeks would do more good to the tribe, and would prove satisfactory, though important to have a small amount of bacon for cooking purposes as there is no lard. The hard bread ration, when there is no flour is entirely too scant, and objected to mainly on that account.[50]

Burgess wrote again later that month that changing the weekly ration to an alternating distribution of beef and cornmeal "would be much cheaper [and] do quite as much good."[51]

With the emphasis on reducing the amount distributed each week, particularly in regard to beef, the supply of meat (either in beef or bacon) became a somewhat lesser administrative concern, with rations distributed for only forty-one of the fifty weeks for which receipts exist.[52] This did not mean the end of the problems with the rations. Occasionally, the agent reported supplies on hand, but none were distributed, such as coffee on March 17 and flour on March 31.[53] However, the most common problem was that the supply of food goods was often unpredictable. Beef cattle stampeded or died, contractors did not fulfill the terms of their contracts, and goods were lost during transport. This resulted in a complete lack of particular foodstuffs for weeks at a time, as with the bacon and beef supply throughout the entire month of April.[54] Many goods listed in the standards for weekly distribution, such as beans and rice, were not available for the entirety of 1877.

The plans to save money and ration stores by issuing bacon and beef on alternate weeks lasted less than two months (February 10–March 31) when the supply of both goods ran out. Throughout April and the first week of May, neither form of meat was issued, as the agency reported no supplies were available.[55] In fact, in a February 2 letter, Superintendent Nicholson directed Agent Burgess to issue all the available stores of bacon and beef within the next ten to twelve weeks and to reduce the issue of fresh beef to the absolute lowest amount possible.[56] It was also reported during that spring that the agent was having difficulty getting the contractors to ship the remainder of the agency's flour supply.[57] Superintendent Nicholson then approved the issue of cornmeal during the meat shortage, although there was only enough of that staple for one week's rations.[58] On many weeks hard bread, or hard tack, was issued either in lieu of another staple item, such as meat or flour or corn, or when supplies of the other items fell well below normal ration amounts.[59]

When the amounts of foodstuffs issued each week is examined on a per capita basis, the rations are not consistent with the instructions set out in the 1876 circular by Commissioner John Q. Smith. The circular, also discussed in chapter 2, provided for weekly rations of 0.1 pound bacon, 3 pounds beef, 0.5 pound flour, 0.5 pound corn, 0.08 pound sugar, and 0.04 pound coffee for every person. The list of goods in the circular also included beans, rice, corn, and tobacco, but these goods were not distributed to Pawnees in 1877. According to the ration receipts for that year, completed by the Pawnee agent, there was little regularity to the amounts of most goods issued week to week, with excesses of some goods issued to make up scant amounts of others and the complete replacement of some goods by hard bread and cornmeal.

The average amount of beef, when issued, exceeded the mandate established in the circular, usually ranging between eighteen and twenty-one pounds per person (see table 4-3). However, many weeks during the first four months of the year no beef was issued, including all of April, and once only 2.6 pounds per person was issued. When averaged out over the entire four-month period, the amount issued was slightly more than seven pounds per person per week. The issue of bacon for the first five weeks of 1877 was approximately 0.7 pound per person. From the second week of February through the end of March, during the period of alternating beef and bacon rations, the amount of bacon issued ranged from 3 to 3.5 pounds. No bacon was issued during April. When averaged over the four-month period, slightly less than one pound of bacon per person per week was issued. The amounts of flour (2.57 pounds), coffee (0.23 pound), salt (0.1 pound), and sugar (0.458 pound), with the bacon and beef, in the Pawnees' rations all exceeded the amounts indicated in the 1876 circular. The Pawnees also received a ration of hard bread, or hard tack. However, they received no rice or beans and were only issued cornmeal once during the first four months of the year.

Table 4-3. Average Weekly Ration per Person, Pawnee Agency, January–April
1877 (weight in pounds)

Date Issued	Beef (gross)	Bacon	Coffee	Corn-meal	Flour	Hard Bread	Salt	Sugar	# of People
6 Jan.	21	0.7	0.3	0	3.5	0	0.06	0.56	1567
13 Jan.	21	0.68	0.3	0	3.5	0	0.06	0.55	1567
20 Jan.	0	0.7	0.3	0	2.6	0.8	0.08	0.56	1250
27 Jan.	2.6	0.69	0.3	0	0.6	2.3	0.12	0.56	1250
3 Feb.	0	0.7	0.3	0	0	2.8	0.06	0.56	1250
10 Feb.	0	3.5	0.3	0	0	2.4	0.06	0.56	1250
17 Feb.	20.5	0	0.3	0	2.8	1.7	0.06	0.56	1250
24 Feb.	0	3	0.24	0	2.8	2.1	0.06	0.53	1250
3 Mar.	19.7	0	0.26	0	3.5	1.75	0	0.56	1250
10 Mar.	0	3.4	0.26	0	3.5	1.75	0	0.56	1250
17 Mar.	20.2	0	0	0	3.5	1.75	0.06	0	1250
24 Mar.	0	3.4	0.26	0	3.5	1.75	0.06	0.56	1250
31 Mar.	18	0	0.26	0	0	2.8	0.06	0.56	1250
7 Apr.	0	0	0	0	3.5	1.75	0.06	0	1250
14 Apr.	0	0	0.26	0	3.5	1.75	0.06	0.56	1250
21 Apr.	0	0	0	3	3.5	0	0.07	0	1360
28 Apr.	0	0	0.28	0	3.5	1.75	0.07	0.56	1500

Source: Compiled from Weekly Ration Reports, Pawnee Agency, January–April
1877, Records of the Central Superintendency of Indian Affairs, 1813–1878,
RG75 (M856), National Archives.

Despite the increase in the ration amounts issued the Pawnees, exceed-
ing the instructions of the circular in some instances, it was not enough to
sustain a people completely dependent on government rations. Combined
with repeated crop failures in Nebraska and the Indian Territory, and government restrictions on buffalo hunts and the lack of success when hunts
were allowed, the ration diet resulted in systemic widespread malnutrition. The conditions on the Pawnee reservation in Oklahoma grew worse
as 1877 wore on, as some goods became more scarce and disease continued to attack the nation.

The difficulties with the rations and supplies continued through the spring and into the summer. In May and June hard bread was issued in lieu of first beef and then other goods, including corn and flour. There was no bacon issued in June, July, or August. At the beginning of June, Charles H. Searing, the new Pawnee agent, reported that he had not been able to issue the standard ration of flour and the agency was "down to hard bread every week and sugar and coffee every other week until other supplies come."[60] Fresh supplies of both beef cattle and flour arrived at the agency during the last week of June and the first week of July, once again allowing for the somewhat regular issuance of rations of these staples for the remainder of the year, with the exception of two weeks without beef and six weeks without flour—although there were instances when flour was on hand but none was issued. The acquisition of the beef and flour supplies ended the issue of hard bread, which was probably a relief to the people.

As with the issuance of rations during the first four months of 1877, the amounts issued to the Pawnees in May through August tended to average more per person per week than instructed by the 1876 circular (see table 4-4). The issuance of bacon, averaged over the entire four-month period (0.15 pound), more closely relates to the orders contained in the circular, but the issue was only made four weeks during this period. The issues of beef (7.5 pounds), flour (1.7 pounds), and coffee (0.12 pound) continued to be inconsistent with orders. Many goods instructed to be issued were not available at the Pawnee Agency, which provides some explanation for the larger average issues. However, the use of cornmeal as a replacement for corn and/or rice was not effective, as it was only issued four times during the four-month period.

The discrepancy between established guidelines and actual ration distributions illustrates the differences between the federal policy, and the application of that policy in Indian Territory, as well as the difficulty that agents had in obtaining supplies through a bureaucratic system that required closed bids to be sent to New York and that resulted in exorbitant transportation costs and little fresh food. The intentions of the Commissioner of Indian Affairs and humanitarians in the East did not always reach fulfillment in the West. The quantity of food available for distribution was not always sufficient to replace the necessity of the hunt.

Table 4-4. Average Weekly Ration per Person,
Pawnee Agency, May–August 1877 (**weight in pounds**)

Date Issued	Beef (gross)	Bacon	Coffee	Corn Meal	Flour	Hard Bread	Salt	Sugar	# of People
5-May	0	0	0	0	3	1.75	0.07	0	1500
12-May	0	0.7	0.28	0	3.5	1.75	0.07	0.56	1561
19-May	0	0.7	0	0	3.5	1.75	0.1	0	1569
26-May	0	0.7	0.28	0	3	2.05	0.07	0.56	1574
2-Jun.	0	0.52	0	0	0	2.8	0.03	0	1606
9-Jun.	0	0	0.28	0	0	2.8	0	0.56	1665
16-Jun.	0	0	0	0	0	2.8	0	0	1700
23-Jun.	13.58	0	0.18	0	0	2.3	0	0.56	1700
30-Jun.	13.36	0	0	0	2.73	0	0	0	1700
7-Jul.	13.36	0	0.18	0	2.8	0	0	0.56	1700
14-Jul.	14	0	0	2.5	0	0	0	0	1700
21-Jul.	0	0	0.18	0	3.5	0	0	0.56	1700
28-Jul.	0	0	0	1.5	1.75	0	0	0	1510
4 Aug.	18.21	0	0.18	3.5	0	0	0	0.33	1510
11 Aug.	18.21	0	0.18	0	3.25	0	0	0.33	1510
18 Aug.	18.17	0	0.18	0.7	2.1	0	0	0.33	1513
25 Aug.	18.75	0	0.17	0	0	0	0	0.33	1513

Source: Compiled from Weekly Ration Reports, Pawnee Agency, May–August
1877, Records of the Central Superintendency of Indian Affairs, 1813–1878,
RG75 (M856), National Archives.

However, local agents attempted to fulfill many of the goals of the rationing policy with the resources at hand. Distributions, or the threat of
withholding those foodstuffs, were used to shape life on the reservation
as much as possible—school attendance, proximity to the agency, willing-
ness to work. Even though distributed rations were often not adequate to
sustain an entire population, the dependence on the government for those
goods gave the agents substantial influence over the reservation population.

At times, supplies of some goods were adequate, or even abundant.
The beef supply during the final four months of 1877 was much more

consistent than earlier in the year (usually between fourteen and sixteen pounds); however, bacon was only issued once and cornmeal only on three instances. The supply of flour was also more consistent, ranging between 2.5 and 3.5 pounds weekly, allowing the agent to end the issue of hard bread.

During this four-month period, with the exception of October 27, when the agent issued the extra rations to those leaving on a buffalo hunt, the ration amounts remained fairly consistent. The beef issue averaged approximately 15.3 pounds, and flour averaged 2.7 pounds per person per week. While the average amount of the beef and flour issued increased during the final four months of the year, the variety of rationed foodstuffs, already extremely limited, was cut with the exclusion of bacon and cornmeal.

Despite the resupply of the agency with cattle and flour during June and July, in September the Pawnees requested permission to leave the reservation for a winter buffalo hunt. The people were well aware of the possible ration shortages that could occur during the winter months and the difficulty that government agents had in getting emergency supplies purchased and transported to the reservations. Superintendent Nicholson approved the request and ordered Agent Charles H. Searing to issue four weeks' rations to those going on the hunt.[61] The additional rations were issued to 740 Pawnees on October 27[62] (see table 4-5). The hunt, however, went against the official "civilization" efforts of the government, and when Commissioner of Indian Affairs Ezra A. Hayt was informed, he chastised the Pawnee agent:

> [R]elating to departure of some 740 Pawnees on a buffalo hunt, [I] have to state that such expeditions are not very conducive to the welfare and advancement of the Indians, and should not be permitted except in rare instances, as when there is a scarcity of subsistence supplies etc. and then the application should be made to the office for approval with a statement of the facts in connection therewith.[63]

The winter hunt of 1877, like so many in recent years, was a failure and proved to be one of the last involving Pawnee participation.

The end of the bison hunts signaled a transition lamented by the Pawnees and welcomed by the government. With the end of the hunts, Pawnees were even more dependent on rations for their meat supply, as well as for those goods that used to be supplied by the hunts. Once the Pawnees were established in the Indian Territory, the federal government used the rationing program to help force the completion of their "civilization" program—allotment. The Office of Indian Affairs began instructing agents to further limit the recipients of rations—forcing most males to labor in order to receive issues—and the amount they could receive. It was hoped that by doing this the Pawnees would submit to allotment, where their reservation was divided into individual plots, owned and worked by single families. Once this was accomplished, the government could finally end its rationing policy and open "excess" Pawnee lands to white settlement. This final process, like much of the rest of the government's Indian policies, did not go smoothly.

Table 4-5. Average Weekly Ration per Person,
Pawnee Agency, September–December 1877 (weight in pounds)

Date Issued	Beef (gross)	Bacon	Coffee	Corn-meal	Flour	Hard Bread	Salt	Sug-ar	# of People
1 Sep.	18.16	0	0.17	3.3	0	0	0.07	0.33	1513
8 Sep.	18.16	0	0.17	0	3.2	0	0.07	0.33	1513
15 Sep.	16.66	0	0.18	3.5	0	0	0.07	0.33	1513
22 Sep.	16.07	0	0.18	2.2	0	0	0.07	0.33	1517
29 Sep.	16.03	0	0.18	0	3.5	0	0.07	0.26	1521
20 Oct.	14.63	0	0	0	2.6	0	0.07	0	1529
27 Oct.	31.52	0	0.19	0	6.4	0	0.13	0.63	1529
3 Nov.	14.16	0	0	0	2.9	0	0	0.06	790
10 Nov.	14.16	0	0.13	0	3	0	0.06	0.51	790
17 Nov.	14.16	0	0	0	3.5	0	0	0	790
24 Nov.	13.98	0	0.13	0	3.5	0	0	0.5	800
1 Dec.	14.78	0.61	0	0	3.5	0	0	0	815
8 Dec.	15.74	0	0.25	0	3.5	0	0	0.55	820
15 Dec.	14.12	0	0	0	3.9	0	0	0	853
22 Dec.	13.67	0	0.17	0	3	0	0	0.51	881
29 Dec.	14.31	0	0	0	3.6	0	0	0	842

Source: Compiled from Weekly Ration Reports, Pawnee Agency, September–December 1877, Records of the Central Superintendency of Indian Affairs, 1813–1878, RG75 (M856), National Archives. The receipts for the first two weeks of October are missing.

Although the average per-person daily ration exceeded the amounts established by the 1876 circular, at least in certain goods, it did not translate into abundance on the Pawnee reservation. Rather, the discrepancy illustrates the differences and problems that existed between the bureaucracy of the Office of Indian Affairs in Washington and the application of policies on reservations in the Indian Territory and beyond. Government rations were devised to supplement the food supply during what was hoped would be the brief transition from hunting to agriculture. Pawnee dependence on their ration diet, increased by repeated crop failures, the lack of small game on the reservation, and the often poor quality of ration goods, resulted in years of malnutrition and increased susceptibility to disease.

One of the bleakest situations facing the Pawnees on their new reservation in the Indian Territory was poor health, disease, and malnutrition. The problem was caused in large part by their ration diet. The Pawnee population had been in decline since the 1840s, and the move to the Indian Territory did little to reverse this trend. On February 13, 1877, Agent Burgess reported that at the last census the Pawnee population numbered 1,667.[64] At the next census, taken June 27, 1877, the population was only 1,508.[65] By October of the same year, Agent Searing reported that the general health of the Pawnees was "terribly bad" and that "deaths [are] getting to be quite frequent."[66] By the turn of the twentieth century, the Pawnee population had dropped below 700.[67]

The different climate, environment, and endemic diseases, combined with the ration diet and malnutrition, created the high death rate at the new reservation. Suicide, resulting from depression caused by regrets at leaving their homelands, and the large number of deaths, especially among children, became a new facet of Pawnee life in the Indian Territory.[68] Wichita Blaine, who made the journey from Nebraska, described early life in the Indian Territory:

> When we first moved here we had little to eat. We'd get a bag of flour and make fry bread day after day. Sometimes I would go out and bring home a deer, but we got little of it. . . . After awhile the deer were gone and we had to hunt prairie chickens and that's what we ate for awhile. Then they were gone.[69]

In November 1877 a new agency clerk, Joseph Hertford, reported that the Pawnees were in a state of starvation, including one family, suffering from illness and without food, which put one of their starving children on the woodpile because they had no food and knew the child was nearly dead.[70] Hertford also substantiated that the amount of rations the Pawnees received was often less than what was recorded on the ration receipts and that agency traders charged higher prices for fewer goods to the Pawnees than to white agency workers.[71]

The persistent malnutrition suffered by the Pawnees affected their ability to procure needed food. People were often too weak and ill to break ground, tend plants, and harvest crops. Their ability to hunt what little game remained was also reduced. Malnutrition also affected men's ability to work for their family's rations, as mandated by the federal act passed March 3, 1875, which required all capable Indian men to labor on the reservation in exchange for their rations. The situation was made worse for the Pawnees when drought or insects destroyed crops, as happened in May 1879. Throughout the late 1870s and 1880s the Pawnees frequently were forced to go to nearby towns and sell their annuity clothing and blankets to obtain food or were forced to kill cattle belonging to whites on the reservation or drovers to avoid starvation.

The situation the Pawnees faced with the government's rationing policy, from the establishment of their first reservation in 1857 to their removal to the Indian Territory, continually worsened. The federal government's failure, supported and encouraged by Quaker agents, to fulfill the 1857 treaty obligations providing the Pawnees with arms and ammunition to protect themselves from Lakota and Cheyenne raids, while at the same time arming the Pawnees' enemies in attempts to negotiate peace, effectively made the Pawnees dependent on government rations. This increasing tribal dependence on ration supplies gave the government additional leverage in its plans to "civilize" the Pawnees and reach their ultimate goal of allotment and the opening of reservations to white settlement.

The government's removal of the Pawnees to the Indian Territory, made easier by the dire food situation on the Nebraska reservation, was another step in reaching its final goal. The move opened highly coveted lands in Nebraska to settlement and placed the Pawnees in an even more dependent situation on their new reservation. Moving the people to a new environment guaranteed that their traditional subsistence methods were even less likely to be successful.

The Pawnees' methods of cultivation did not work in their new home, and the supply of game was quickly exhausted. The government turned this situation to its own benefit. By continuing ration policies that en-sured inadequate and unpredictable supplies with no way to enforce re-quirements of good quality, the government hoped to force the Pawnees to abandon their culture and become self-sufficient farmers. When the Pawnees did not change quickly enough, many humanitarians argued that it was the government's rationing policies themselves that were to blame. Although the government was reluctant to completely and immediately end the issuing of rations, policies were changed to limit who could re-ceive rations, forcing most men to labor for their issues, in essence making them pay again for goods that had already been purchased by the sale of their treaty lands. Through this manipulation of the food supply, the gov-ernment coerced the Pawnees into giving up what federal officials viewed as undesirable behaviors and adopting ones that fit into the desired view of American society.

By the 1890s the Pawnees, like many other Native nations, began fight-ing to receive their entire annuity in cash instead of half in goods, includ-ing food. The Pawnees believed that they could purchase higher-quality goods at lower prices than what the government was supplying them. By amending their treaty in this way, the Pawnees hoped to be able to ensure the quality and quantity of their food supply, as well as gain the power of choice over which goods they wanted and end the government's control over their subsistence. On August 29, 1891, a petition drawn up by the Pawnees was sent to Washington stating:

> We the undersigned, Pawnee Indians, in council assembled in their council house at Pawnee Agency, do this 29th day of August, 1891, pray that the Honorable, the Secretary of the Interior, will ask the Congress of the United States to amend Article 2 of their treaty of September 24th, 1857, in such a manner so that they can have all the $30,000 annuity per annum issued to them in cash instead of $15,000 in cash, and $15,000 in goods, or other such articles as may be deemed necessary for them.[72]

The Pawnees succeeded in their petition—but at the cost of accepting allotment and being forced to sell the tribe's "surplus lands" to the federal government. In an agreement with the Pawnees, passed by Congress on March 3, 1893, Section 12, Article III stated:

> It is further agreed that article 2 of the treaty between the United States and the chiefs and headmen of the four confederate bands of Pawnee Indians, viz, Grand Pawnees, Pawnee Loups, Pawnee Republicans, and Pawnee Tappahs, and generally known as the Pawnee tribe, proclaimed May 26, 1858, so long as the same shall be in force, is hereby amended so as to read as follows:

> "The United States agrees to pay to the Pawnees the sum of thirty thousand dollars per annum, as a perpetual annuity, to be distributed annually among them per capita, in coin, unless the President of the United States shall from time to time otherwise direct. But it is further agreed that the President may, at any time in his discretion, discontinue said perpetuity by causing the value of a fair commutation thereof to be paid to or expended for the benefit of said Indians in such manner as to him shall seem proper."[73]

Thus, even in the negotiations to end rationing, the government used the system to further its goals of ending the tribe as a political, cultural, and property-owning entity.

Despite the phasing out of the United States government's rationing policies for Native American nations and the Pawnees in particular, begun in the last decade of the nineteenth century, the consequences of those policies continued to be felt by Native peoples. In addition to becoming an element in twentieth-century legal battles between the Pawnees and the federal government, which played out in the Court of Claims and Indian Claims Commission, rationing policies continued to affect Pawnee social and cultural life as well as health. Poor nutrition, commodity food programs, and nutritional diseases like diabetes plague reservations into the twenty-first century.

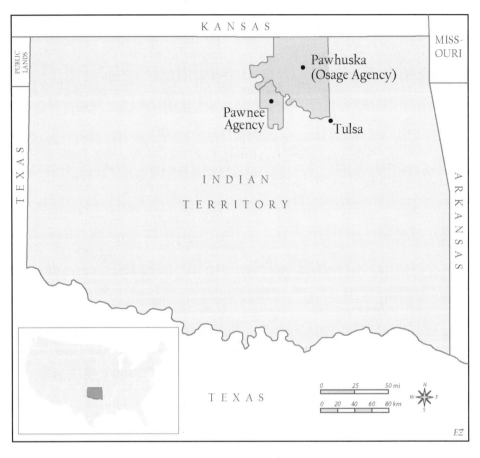

Map 1. Indian Territory. Map by Ezra Zeitler.

Chapter 5

Rationing and the Osage Nation, 1839–1879

As with the Pawnees and many other Native nations, the United States government used the distribution of rations as part of its policies in dealing with the Osage. Due in part to the size of their lands and their early military prowess, the Osage (or Wahzhazhe) experience with rationing differs from that of the Pawnees. Osage relations with Europeans, and later Americans, differs from many other Native nations. By not attacking European settlements and remaining on peaceful terms, the Osage were able to achieve relatively favorable trade relations and autonomy through the eighteenth century. When the United States gained control, the Osage lost the ability to play the imperial powers against one another and were forced to rely on Americans for the goods upon which they had become dependent.[1] The initial desire of the US government was to gain access to Osage land, and the means to achieve that goal was removal and "civilization." Rationing was one of the tools used to achieve these ends. Again, the actual implementation of rationing and distribution of necessary foodstuffs to the Osage deviated from the policies established in Washington. An examination of the process on the Osage reservations will reveal more about the immediate, and lasting, impact that rations had on the people themselves.

The Osage, originally a part of the Dhegiha language group that included Quapaws, Omahas, Poncas, and Kansas, migrated into the eastern plains from the Ohio Valley, first settling in present-day Missouri at least as early as 1500. By the early nineteenth century, there were three distinct bands: Great Osage (Pahatsi), Little Osage (Utsehta), and Arkansas

Osage (Santsukhdhi), living on the Osage and Arkansas Rivers. The vast expanse of Osage territory, ranging from woodlands to prairie, afforded the people a highly diversified diet.[2] Similar to the Pawnees, the Osage led a semi-mobile lifestyle, living in permanent villages part of the year, where they cultivated maize, squashes, and beans, and going on buffalo hunts in the spring, fall, and winter.[3] Prior to contact with European fur traders, the Osage lifestyle was more semi-stationary, with only limited amounts of time spent on bison hunts. However, with the introduction of the fur trade into Osage economics in the eighteenth century, the people began focusing more on the hunt.[4]

The wealth and diversity of the Osage territory made the group a powerful people within the Native political and economic landscape, as well as in early relations with European nations in North America. In addition to the abundance of vegetation and game, Osage lands contained tremendous mineral wealth. Most important to the Osage was calcite, gypsum, and salt. The abundance of minerals and the agricultural potential of Osage lands attracted European powers, but the Osage nation maintained power and dominance over its lands into the eighteenth century.

The Osage had long and direct contact with Europeans, whom they were able to deal with on their own terms through the end of the eighteenth century. The first Europeans encountered by the Osage were probably members of the expeditions of Hernando de Soto or Francisco Coronado. Sustained contact did not begin, however, until French and Spanish explorers and traders entered Osage homelands in the early eighteenth century. The Osage developed closer ties to the French than any other European power in America. In addition to trading their own goods, they acted as middlemen between the French and other tribes to the west and south.

Osage relations with the Spanish, on the other hand, were neither as profitable nor as amicable as with the French. When they gained control of Louisiana, Spanish authorities attempted, unsuccessfully, to control trade with the Osage and other Native nations. The Spanish government's alternating desire to curb Osage power while maintaining an "Indian barrier" between its colonies and British and American expansion caused unstable relations both with the Osage and settlers who continued to trade in violation of Spain's new regulations.[5]

The Osage were successful in preventing France and Spain from creating trails through their territory, effectively limiting, at least temporarily, European expansion across the southern plains. Despite Osage success in controlling their lands during the eighteenth century, theirs was not a static culture. Historian Willard H. Rollings noted,

> The eighteenth century was a time of dramatic change for the Osage. The increased raiding, hunting, and trading created new opportunities for wealth and prestige which were not always recognized by Osage society. Increased wealth and status challenged Osage social, political, and economic systems, and in time the Osage changed to meet the new challenges. The changes were never uniform or consistent, but they were always shaped according to the familiar patterns of Osage culture.[6]

As the European powers fought for dominance over North America, the Osage developed new trade contacts with each power, and ultimately with the United States. Although they had been able to keep the French and Spanish out of their territory while maintaining a brisk trade with them, they were unable to do the same with the United States. Changes in Osage society combined with the swiftness of the new invasion made a united front against Americans extremely difficult. Following the Lewis and Clark expedition in 1804–1806, American settlers and eastern tribes began invading Osage territory, creating a very tenuous situation. After initially resisting this invasion, in 1808 the Osage signed the first in a long line of treaties ceding portions of their lands to the United States government.[7]

While food gifts had been a part of Osage diplomacy with French and Spanish traders, the use of rationing as a tool of forced cultural change had not. It was not until the Americans began expanding into Osage territory that those people faced a power determined to take their land that was strong enough to accomplish that goal. Part of the difference was in the desired use of the land. The French had primarily been interested only in trade, and as long as good relations were maintained with their Indian allies, France saw no benefit in attempting to seize Osage lands or change their culture. Spain had treated the Louisiana Territory more as a buffer zone than anything else, to protect its Texas and New Mexico colonies from American expansion. Although Spain had wanted to end Osage dominance, it had lacked the manpower to overcome Osage numbers, and so posed little threat.

The Americans, however, had a completely different goal for Osage lands—permanent settlement. While the first Americans to enter Osage territory—fur traders, explorers, and mountain men—were not interested in seizing the lands, others who were soon followed. As the eastern seaboard of the United States became more crowded, Americans and new immigrants pushed westward in search of affordable land on which to establish farms. It was this desired use of the land that was at the heart of Osage-American tensions. Trade and exploration did not conflict with Osage use of the land; farming, however, did. The American farms altered the Osage environment, limiting native game and destroying native plant species, thereby reducing the Osage's subsistence base and forcing gradual cultural changes.[8] The settlers viewed Osage use of the land as wasteful and believed the way to seize that land was through treaties and the "civilization" of the Osage.[9]

American settlers, moving westward at an accelerated pace following the Louisiana Purchase and the Lewis and Clark expedition, sought clear title to lands on which to establish farming communities. Although the initial Osage reaction was to avoid these new settlements, and thus avoid conflict, this approach soon became more and more difficult.[10] The situation was made more precarious when the pace of settlement outstripped the expansion of American law. The rapid pace of change made it impossible for the Osage to adapt to their new circumstances, resulting in a more tenuous situation.[11] In 1808 the United States government, in an effort to maintain peace and extend legal control to the new settlements, negotiated the first in a series of treaties with the Osage people.

The first treaty negotiated between the United States and the Osage nation focused on trade and civilization efforts in exchange for land; it had the appearance of accommodating the wishes and best interests of the Osage. In addition to establishing the factory trading system, where the Osage were able to trade furs for goods at a fair exchange rate, and promising protection of the remaining Osage lands from intruders, the treaty guaranteed an annuity of goods worth $1,000 to the Great Osage Indians and $500 to the Little Osage Indians.[12]

The treaty also partially protected Osage hunting grounds at a time when there was still an abundance of land:

> And the United States agree that such of the Great and Little Osage
> Indians, as may think proper to put themselves under the protec-
> tion of Fort Clark, and who observe the stipulations of this treaty
> with good faith, shall be permitted to live and to hunt, without
> molestation, on all that tract of country, . . . on which they, the said
> Great and Little Osage, have usually hunted or resided . . . until
> the United States may think proper to assign the same as hunting
> grounds to other friendly Indians.[13]

This portion of the treaty, however, eventually became a source of tension between the Osage and the United States. In addition to the assertion
of the United States of its right to reassign Osage hunting grounds when-
ever it saw fit, the two sides interpreted the language of the article differently. When the Osage began protecting their hunting rights from intrusions by tribes being forced out of the east, particularly Cherokees, these
misunderstandings of the treaty article accentuated the conflict between
the Osage and emigrant tribes.[14] The Osage were punished for protecting
their lands from intruding tribes, while the United States refused to prevent the illegal intrusions in the first place. Thus, even with the appearance
of protection, the traditional Osage means of subsistence was placed in
jeopardy, and the people's quality of life began to deteriorate.

The Osage Treaty of 1818 similarly compromised Osage hunting
grounds, and thus their access to food, to the benefit of other tribes and
the United States. In the treaty, the Osage agreed

> to cede to the United States, and forever quit claim to, the tract of
> country included within the following bounds, to wit: Beginning
> at the Arkansaw [sic] River, at where the present Osage boundary
> line strikes the river at Frog Bayou; then up the Arkansaw and
> Verdigris, to the falls of Verdigris River; thence, eastwardly, to the
> said Osage boundary line, at a point twenty leagues north from the
> Arkansaw River; and, with that line, to the place of beginning.[15]

This cession included some of the most fertile remaining Osage lands.
Cherokees and others also used it as an outlet to the plains for buffalo
hunts.

Despite the efforts of the United States government to turn the Osage
into yeomen farmers, the change never fully took place. In the early nine-

teenth century, while the fur trade was still flourishing, the government's attempts at "civilizing" the Osage were undermined by economic forces at every turn. The Osage, who could easily trade a handful of furs for a year's supply of food, had no incentive to adopt farming. Traders, who were making large profits from the trade, actively encouraged the Osage to continue hunting. While the economic and environmental factors remained conducive to their traditional lifestyle, the Osage had no reason to give up their culture or their way of life. Unfortunately for them, this balance could not be maintained indefinitely.

In 1825 the Osage were again forced to cede major portions of their territory, including the area that became known as the Cherokee Outlet.[16] The treaty reduced the once-expansive Osage territory to an eleven-million-acre reservation near the Kansas-Oklahoma border known as the Osage Diminished Reserve. This further limited Osage means of subsistence, reducing their hunting grounds, increasing their dependence on government rations, and leaving them at the mercy of Kansas settlers. In this environment, the Osage faced increasing problems and an ever-bleaker future.

In exchange for their ceded lands, the Osage were promised a twenty-year annuity of $7,000 in money, goods, and provisions.[17] In addition, they acceded to a greater focus on "civilization" efforts by the Americans. Article 4 of the 1825 treaty promised to provide the Osage with

> six hundred head of cattle, six hundred hogs, one thousand domestic fowls, ten yoke of oxen, and six carts, with such farming utensils as the Superintendent of Indian Affairs may think necessary, and shall employ such persons, to aid them in their agricultural pursuits, as to the President of the United States may seem expedient, and shall, also, provide, furnish, and support for them, one blacksmith.[18]

All of this was paid for out of Osage funds held by the United States Department of the Treasury. The Osage, who still maintained their right to hunt on the plains portions of their territory, had little need or use for the farming implements. They saw no benefit to adopting the culture of the invaders, especially one they saw as hypocritical and inferior to their own.

In this treaty the United States government also continued its practice of building the power and influence of the Native people it chose to work with, rather than with existing Indian leadership. The Osage political structure changed dramatically during the nineteenth century. Traditionally, the Osage political power resided in two principal (hereditary) chiefs. Power then flowed through the chief's soldier assistants and the tribal council. However, due to their own political history, when Europeans began political relations with the Osage, they were not prepared to deal with more than one leader.[19] When they encountered the two-chief system of the Osage, the United States began cultivating its own point of contact for the Osage nation. Included in the provisions of the treaty, the government promised to "build, for each of the four principal chiefs, at their respective villages, a comfortable and commodious dwelling house."[20]

In the face of increasing American settlement, Osage independence began to erode by the 1830s. In addition to white encroachment, the Osage were also forced to deal with the settlement of other tribes that had themselves removed from areas east of the Mississippi River. Major Paul Liguest Chouteau, a member of a prominent St. Louis–based fur-trading family, who often worked as a negotiator and interpreter for government dealings with Indian tribes, wrote about the Osage situation in 1832:

> They are surrounded by Various tribes of Indians Upon whom they look with a jealous eye. These Indians are now overrunning the former hunting grounds of the Osages; the Osages are cramped in their means of subsistence, in fact hunting has become so laborious, that the privations and dangers they suffer in pursuing the Chase is not compensated by the sale of their skins, and as their annuity is small (only 8500 per annum to upwards of 6000 souls) they have become a poor people.[21]

The cultural and social impact of the process at the source of Chouteau's observations, of outside encroachment and land cessions, had wider implications than simply a loss of territory. Each loss was compounded by reduced access to sacred animals and the disruption of essential spiritual traditions tied to specific locations. These changes left the Osage increasingly vulnerable to continued encroachment.[22] With the increasing pressure on Osage resources, from both encroaching white settlement and relocated Native tribes, and the continued weakening of their tribal power structure, the Osage were forced to make more and more concessions to the United States at increasingly less favorable terms.

Another treaty, this time in 1839, continued this process. In return for agreeing to leave the lands of other tribes (who had been removed by the US government to lands originally controlled by the Osage), the Great and Little Osages received another twenty-year annuity of $12,000 in money and $8,000 in goods and provisions designed to encourage their adoption of "civilization."[23] This cession, in which the Osage lost most of their winter hunting grounds, served to facilitate further Osage dependence on government rations. The result was to make the Osage even more vulnerable to the coercive policies of the United States government.

In addition to supplying goods such as farming implements and furnishing grist- and sawmills, the government continued its policy of influencing Osage internal politics by granting treaty goods to "chiefs."[24] Unlike earlier Osage treaties, however, where additional goods were bestowed on unnamed "chiefs," Article 2 of the 1839 treaty specifies individuals, declared by the government to be chiefs, to receive additional treaty goods:

> To furnish the following named chiefs, viz: Pa-hu-sca, Clermont, Chiga-wa-sa, Ka-he-gais-tanga, Tawan-ga-hais, Wa-cho chais, Ni-ka-wa-chin-tanga, Tally, Gui-hira-ba-chais, Baptisté Mongrain, each with a house worth two hundred dollars; and the following named chiefs, viz: Chi-to-ka-sa-bais, Wa-ta-ni-ga, Wa-tier-chi-ga, Chon-ta-sa-bais, Nan-gais-wa-ha-qui hais, Ka-hi-gais-stier-de-gais, Man-haie-spais-we-te-chis, Chow-gais-mo-non, Gre-tan-man-sais, Kan-sais-ke-cris, Cho-mi-ka-sais, Man-cha-ki-da-chi-ga, each with a house worth one hundred dollars, and to furnish the above named chiefs with six good wagons, sixteen carts, and twenty-eight yoke of oxen, with a yoke and log chain to each yoke of oxen, to be delivered to them in their own country, as soon as practicable after the ratification of this treaty.[25]

It has been suggested that the increasing payments to Osage chiefs indicated a growing discontent among the remainder of the tribe and the need for the United States government to keep its designated chiefs in positions of power.[26] This is certainly a possibility, especially as conditions on the Osage Diminished Reserve deteriorated.

The distribution of goods through chiefs, and later in the name of chiefs, was also important to the Osage. This can be seen in an 1875 letter from Joseph Paw ne no pa she:

Complaints have been made to me that Agent Gibson has issued rations to "Beaver's" Band in the name of R. Choteau as chief of said Band instead of in the name of Beaver himself, who is the lawful chief of his said Band. . . . I respectfully ask that you cause Agent Gibson to issue the rations due Beaver's Band in the name of Beaver himself as chief of his Band, as in doing otherwise Beaver will be greatly wronged and the rights of the people of his Band, as secured by the laws and customs of the Osages will be ignored.[27]

Arguments over whose name rations were issued in were not the only problems arising from US policy. The federal government and religious missions established on the Osage reservation did little to ensure the health, well-being, or success of the Osage. In spite of the government's and reformers' stated goal of "civilization," the Osage people were settled in small villages close to the agency, more convenient for government agents but detrimental to the people. Even if the missionaries and agency farmers had been successful in teaching the Osage how to farm, the established settlement pattern would have proved a tremendous obstacle to success.[28]

Another problem made worse by the settlement of the Osage in small, close villages was the deteriorating health conditions of the tribe. The close quarters of the villages put an additional strain on the local food supply, increasing Osage dependence on rations. The poor quality and limited quantity of the rations combined with the depletion of available native foods to cause widespread malnutrition. Malnutrition, periods of starvation, and poor sanitation left the Osage more susceptible to epidemic diseases. In 1849 John R. Chenault wrote to the Office of Indian Affairs that the Osage were destitute and suffering from cholera. Their condition also made it difficult to get enough hides on the hunt to trade for needed goods.[29] Osage population numbers during this period fluctuated widely. Epidemics took a heavy toll, especially among the elderly and very young. Periods of high birthrates followed the epidemics, only for many of those young children to be claimed by the next outbreak of disease.

The Osage treaty process, from 1808 through 1839, resulted in the loss of the majority of Osage territory to the United States. This loss had a profound effect on the Osage in many different ways. First, their power—political, military, and economic—was substantially affected. They lost access to natural resources and thus began to lose their advantage with traders as well as their remaining subsistence base. These losses, and interference in internal tribal matters by the United States government, also began to affect their political structure. Culturally and spiritually, the Osage began to lose their base. They were pushed off the majority of their lands, severing important cultural and religious bonds ranging from the loss of sacred locations to the disruption of food taboos. Following the changes in Osage power structures and culture, traditional Osage society started to weaken. Old patterns ceased to work. While the United States government did not achieve its goal of complete assimilation, with the integration of the nation into the lower rungs of American society as Christian farmers, tribal Osage society was forever changed.

By the time of the 1865 Osage Treaty, the last ratified treaty between the Osage and the United States, much had changed for both parties. For the United States, the concept of Manifest Destiny was in full force. The Homestead Act, passed in 1862, provided 160 acres of western land to settlers who occupied, improved, and cultivated it for five years and paid a small fee. Much of the best land was quickly claimed, making Osage lands very desirable. The act successfully drew increasing numbers of people from eastern cities into the West. The flow of westward settlement increased again following the Civil War as displaced veterans and former slaves moved west in search of affordable land. Once again, the Osage felt the effects of increasing encroachment.

The pressure to open Indian lands to white settlement was at the heart of the 1865 treaty. Many Kansas settlers, encouraged by their state government, had already illegally established themselves within the bounds of the Osage reservation. The powerful railroad companies were also pressuring the federal government to open lands for their use. The United States government used white encroachment and increasing stresses on traditional Osage subsistence methods, along with the coercion of the rationing system, to take Osage lands and to advocate their complete removal from Kansas. Believing the Osage had been given plenty of time and opportunity to become self-sufficient farmers, the government argued that much of their lands were now "surplus." The government arranged for the sale of these surplus lands for $300,000 paid in money, clothing, provisions, and other goods.[30]

All additional profit made on the sale of Osage lands, in excess of the

$300,000, was placed in the Treasury as part of the "civilization fund."[31] Instead of that money being available for use by the Osage, or on their behalf, the "civilization fund" was used "under the direction of the Secretary of the Interior, for the education and civilization of Indian tribes residing within the limits of the United States."[32] By directing the distribution of land-sale proceeds, the government denied the Osage the full benefit from their lands and created a system by which other tribes benefitted from Osage removal.

Evidence of the problems and failures of the rationing system established by the United States government is also found in the 1865 treaty. Article 5 states:

> The Osages being desirous of paying their just debts to James N. Coffey and A. B. Canville, for advances in provisions, clothing, and other necessaries of life, hereby agree that the [S]uperintendent of Indian [A]ffairs for the [S]outhern [S]uperintendency and the agent of the tribe shall examine all claims against said tribe, . . . and the Secretary may issue to the claimants scrip for the claims thus allowed, which shall be receivable as cash in payment for any of the lands sold in trust for said tribe.[33]

The incurring of debts to traders for provisions is an indication of the inadequacy of government-distributed rations. Regardless of Indian Bureau instructions, the proscribed amounts of foodstuffs were rarely on hand, let alone issued to the people. The Osage, continually deprived of traditional subsistence methods and sources of food, and increasingly harassed when off their reservation, were forced to purchase on credit the food necessary to survive. Meanwhile, traders, especially the less scrupulous ones, made sure they charged the Osage high enough prices to ensure a continuing pattern of Osage debt and profit for themselves.

The final removal of the Osage from Kansas was a period of tremendous turmoil for those people. Louis Burns, comparing it to the Cherokees' removal, stated that "Osage removal from Kansas was equally unjust, equally full of suffering, and, on a percentage basis, equally costly in lives."[34] Osage removal was part of a larger effort by the state of Kansas to remove all Native peoples from its borders. While the Osage received more for their Kansas lands than many other tribes ($1.25 an acre, established in the Treaty of 1865), government bureaucracy costs and placement of that money into the "Civilization Fund" left the Osage in a very precarious position during and immediately after their removal to the Indian Territory.

The campaign for Osage removal was led primarily by illegal settlers within the Osage Diminished Reserve. When another treaty, this one directly providing for Osage removal, was not ratified, these settlers, supported by the state government, drafted a resolution to Congress calling for passage of an Osage removal bill so they could buy the land they were living on.[35] The state of Kansas and the federal government did little to prevent white intrusions onto Osage lands, nor did they protect the Osage from depredations made by those intruders. As a result, Osage living conditions quickly deteriorated, making it easier for the government to force them to move.

The years prior to removal were a time of increasing tensions and difficulties for the Osage. Most of the tribe was spending increasingly longer periods of time on buffalo hunts on the plains, away from their villages and fields on the Diminished Reserve. Several factors worked to create this situation. Many Osage preferred to remain on the plains rather than return to their reservation and live in close proximity to the white intruders. Another factor was the increasing scarcity of bison herds on the plains. The Osage and other Native nations were forced to travel farther to find fewer animals. In addition, as the bison food supply became more scarce, more time and manpower was needed to protect hunting parties from attacks by other tribes. This meant that fewer people were actively hunting, slowing down the process even more.

Less productive hunts affected Osage food supplies, leaving the people more dependent on government rations. In November 1858 Osage ration vouchers included flour, beef, sugar, and coffee.[36] The poor quality and low quantity of the rations, designed to prod the Osage into becoming self-sufficient farmers, had profound physical and psychological effects on the people. Their dependence on a food source lacking the nutrition of traditional foods, combined with larger villages, led to a high mortality rate among the Osage, especially the full-blood population. The mixed-blood Osage population, predominately Osage-French, fared better than their full-blood relations since many had started farming and ranching as a means of subsistence. This adoption of "civilization," however, did not protect them from the invaders. Although certain mixed-blood families were permitted to remain on their farms in Kansas after removal, the terror tactics used by white settlers made it virtually impossible for them to stay in their homes, and they too moved to the Indian Territory.

The push of settlers, railroads, and the state of Kansas for the complete removal of the Osage from their lands came to fruition in 1870. The purchase of a new Osage reservation of 1,500,000 acres within the Indian Territory was made possible by the Act of 15 July 1870:

> That whenever the Great and Little Osage Indians shall agree thereto, in such manner as the President shall prescribe, it shall be the duty of the President to remove said Indians from the State of Kansas to lands provided or to be provided for them for a permanent home in the Indian Territory.[37]

Not all Osages agreed with the act, however, and several requests for changes were made. They requested more land than 160 acres per person, to avoid forced allotment, and to continue to be permitted to go on buffalo hunts, all of which were granted at least to some degree. Other requests, including access to their annuity moneys when they desired (rather than the annual or semi-annual distributions that were invariably late or short), as well as a guarantee against future encroachment by settlers and a concrete way to deal with those who invaded the reservation, were rejected.

The removal act also included an appropriation of $50,000 to be used to finance Osage removal and provide subsistence for the first year on their new reservation. After payment, the money was to be reimbursed to the United States Treasury from the proceeds of the sale of the Diminished Reserve. The appropriation was essential to the Osage. Between weak hunt results and tensions with whites, they were in desperate need of support. Dependence on government rations, with constant problems concerning quality and quantity, had greatly weakened both the physical health and spirit of the people. However, not all the removal money was used for its stated purposes, and once again the Osage became the victims of the negotiation process.[38]

In addition to owning their new reservation in fee simple,[39] the Osage also retained the right to hunt on the Diminished Reserve and other public lands on the plains as long as there were buffalo to hunt. While humanitarians and Indian agents increasingly discouraged buffalo hunts, seeing them as impeding progress toward "civilization," the Osage were completely prevented from hunting off the reservation only during United States–Cheyenne conflicts in the 1870s.[40] However, despite the retention of their hunting rights, removal and reestablishment in the Indian Territory resulted in continued periods of hunger and high mortality rates.

One of the reasons the Osage agreed to removal from Kansas was to distance themselves from American settlement. Unfortunately, they were forced to deal with the same situation on their new reservation as well. Prior to Osage removal from Kansas, the United States military canvassed the new reservation and removed illegal settlers across the Kansas state line. However, there was no way to prevent the settlers from returning once the troops had left the area. One possible way the Osage hoped to avoid problems with intruders on their new reservation was the type of land the reservation encompassed. They had fought for land in excess of 160 acres per person in exchange for moving even farther west, leaving the more arable lands to the American settlers already established there.

Similar to the removal of the Pawnees from Nebraska, Osage removal from Kansas was accomplished in a piecemeal fashion. Approximately 3,150 Osage made the move. The majority left Kansas following the long winter hunts in 1870–1871. Hunting parties departed from their Kansas villages following the signing of the Removal Act and returned to the area of their new reservation in the spring of 1871. The remaining Osage (approximately 300), physically unable to join the hunt, were led to the Indian Territory by Agent Isaac Gibson. The small number of mixed-blood Osage who attempted to remain in Kansas had fled to the Indian Territory by 1872.

After several survey mistakes and negotiations with the Cherokee nation, confirmation of the purchase of the new reservation was completed by the Act of 5 June 1872.[41] Owning the title to their reservation lands placed the Osage in a unique position.[42] Most tribes did not own the lands they were removed to; the Osage did. Possession of the title to their reservation exempted the Osage from the 1887 Dawes Severalty Act that forced the division of reservations into allotments. While they did not avoid allotment forever, through tribal ownership of the land, the Osage were able to negotiate the terms of allotment on their reservation and maintained communal ownership of their mineral rights.[43] The removal itself, however, was a difficult process for all Osages.

The Osage experiences highlight the importance that the control of food can have in influencing behavior. Rations on the Osage reservation were used as a tool to encourage and coerce the people to adopt "civilization." The coercion exerted on the Osage took two forms: reward and withdrawal. One form of that coercion included the attempt to limit rations to those families who were considered "civilized," that is, those who were making attempts to live in houses and establish farms.[44] In his 1876 annual report to Superintendent William Nicholson, the new agent Cyrus Beede reported that many of the traditional Osage complained that during distributions larger portions went to those exhibiting more inclination toward adopting civilization.[45] This attempt at coercion also found support in the decision by the Bureau of Indian Affairs to make Indians work to receive their rations. Because there were so few job opportunities, the agent counted the labor of those who did work on their own individual farms. Those who did not at least attempt to adopt farming found it even more difficult to meet the labor requirement to receive their needed rations. In October 1874 Agent Gibson reported what he believed to be the success of this coercive tactic:

> That provision in the appropriation bill requiring service for food
> is working admirably. All the leading men of the tribe have now
> given up their opposition to civilization.[46]

Another method used by agents to coerce Indians to comply with "civilization" policies was through the threat of withholding needed rations. This form of coercion was used to ensure school attendance:

> The Secretary of the Interior may in his discretion, establish such
> regulations as will prevent the issuing of rations or the furnishing
> of subsistence either in money or in kind to the head of any Indian
> family for or on account of any Indian child or children between
> the ages of eight and twenty-one years who shall not have attended
> school during the preceding year in accordance with such regula-
> tions. . . .
>
> The amount and value of subsistence so withheld shall be
> credited to the tribe or tribes from whom the same is withheld,
> to be issued and paid when in the judgment of the Secretary of
> the Interior they shall have fully complied with such regulations.[47]

The threat of stopping the supply of needed goods was also used to pressure the Osage to sign the Drum Creek Treaty in 1868.[48] Commissioner of Indian Affairs Nathaniel Taylor, pressed by the state of Kansas, demanded that the Osage accept the terms of the treaty or their rations would be withdrawn and their lands opened to white settlement.[49]

The two coercive strategies of reward and withdrawal of rations was an exceptionally effective combination in the federal government's attempts to influence the behavior and culture of the Osage peoples. Through the control of the primary means of subsistence, the government was able to maintain steady pressure, forcing the Osage to accept government decrees and cede territory or face starvation. The established pattern of alternating rewards and withdrawal of food rations followed the Osage to their new reservation in the Indian Territory.

The first years on their new reservation were difficult for the Osage nation. In addition to the trauma of forced removal from Kansas, and despite the funds from the Removal Act that were supposed to provide for subsistence, the Osage population declined during their first year in the Indian Territory. Louis F. Burns calculates that approximately 1,083 Osages died in 1872. The longer-than-normal buffalo hunt before removal and one soon after arriving in the Indian Territory could signify a shortage of foodstuffs. The situation was made worse by crop problems. Most of the crops planted in 1870–1871 had been destroyed by intruders, leaving the Osage with no supply of corn and other vegetables during their removal and establishment in the Indian Territory.

Osage subsistence for the first year, promised in the Removal Act, appears to have been problematic. Agent Gibson was not aware of the amounts of rations to be issued each week, delaying the distribution to people in desperate need.[50] The government may have unrealistically been depending on the Osage to have successful hunts and first harvests and therefore not been prepared for the amount of rations that were needed. There were also problems with the quality of foodstuffs the agency received for distribution. Gibson wrote to Central Superintendent Enoch Hoag:

> The late purchase of tobacco . . . is worthless . . . little has been
> issued. The Indians throw it away in disgust. . . . The Indians also
> complain that some of the barrels of sugar are badly mixed with

rat manure, and [covered with] clean sugar in each end, evidently a willful fraud.[51]

He also remarked on the effect the bad rations were having on the reservation:

> These things are used and magnified by the half breeds to induce the full bloods to insist on their annuities and subsistence being paid in money and they protest against their funds being expended for such articles.[52]

While Gibson correctly reported that the poor quality of the rations being issued was a cause of protest among the Osage, his belief that mixed-blood Osage were the instigators may not have been completely correct. The Osage, well aware that the poorly made annuity goods and rancid food they were receiving was being paid for by themselves through treaties ceding their land, had pushed for their payments in cash rather than goods for years, if not decades.[53] It seems unlikely that the protests in 1871 were not a continuation of their years-long fight for more control of their money and goods.

Compounding the difficulties were tensions between Osage leaders and Agent Gibson over how rations were to be distributed. Traditionally, goods were given to the chiefs, who then divided them among their people according to Osage cultural precepts. However, as Native nations became less of a threat to the United States, the government's need to maintain influence over its chosen "chiefs" became less important. Instead, the focus moved to the breaking of tribal social forms, among them the power of traditional chiefs. One of the ways that humanitarians, reformers, and agents saw to break up tribal society was to issue rations and annuity goods directly to the heads of families, thereby cutting off some of the power base of the chiefs. In 1871 Agent Gibson stated his views in a letter to Superintendent Hoag: "The issuing of subsistence to the chiefs is certainly a bad practice. I wish to issue to each head of family by weight on measure."[54]

Subsistence problems on the Osage reservation in the Indian Territory continued well past the first year. Agent Gibson regularly reported shortages of food and medicine.[55] Even when the majority of the tribe was away on a hunt in January 1873, there was not enough food to support the elderly and sick who remained. They were forced to dig for potatoes in the frozen ground. While Gibson issued "small quantities of flour, sugar, coffee, salt, and corn in most extreme cases of necessity," it was barely enough to keep starvation at bay.[56]

Conditions continued to deteriorate in 1874. The Osage faced a nearly total crop failure. Gibson noted:

> They planted more corn and vegetables than ever before, but the drought made a short crop, and the grasshoppers ate up most of that. They are thus made to depend on their Government funds for support.[57]

Making conditions worse, 1873 was the last successful buffalo hunt for the Osage, leaving the people with fewer supplies of dried meat and tallow, as well as hides to trade for more provisions.[58] The shortages of food and subsequent starvation forced many Osage to steal cattle from the Chisholm Trail to survive. Three Osage families began stopping Texas cattle drovers, demanding a toll paid in food to cross Osage lands.[59] In addition to contributing to the food shortage, the unsuccessful hunts had an adverse effect on Osage spiritual traditions, for which the buffalo was integral.

In the fall of 1874, due to increasing tensions caused by the Red River War, all hunting off the reservation was halted, increasing reliance on government stores. The Indian Appropriation Bill required labor to be performed in exchange for rations. However, because they were not able to hunt and there was little work to be done on the reservation, as well as the fact that they viewed the requirement as forcing them to pay twice for inferior goods, knowing that the money from the sale of their lands bought the goods, the Osage felt it appropriate that they be released from the labor requirement. As reported by Agent Gibson,

> The Osage Council has just adjourned, having decided with great unanimity that all their people should remain on the Reservation until the troubles with the Plains Indians are settled, . . .
>
> They earnestly request the Hon. Secretary of the Interior to relieve them (the Osages) from the conditions of Section 3 of the Indian Appropriation Bill of June 22nd 1874, as they claim to be willing to work, and will do all in their power to develop their

country by labor without compulsion. They say many of their people regard the law as a great burden and oppressive, and they sincerely request that all persons may have rations issued to them; and to heads of families whether they labor or not as provided in Section 7 of said act.[60]

Finding work to meet the labor requirement was difficult, however. Even when there was work for the men to perform on the reservation, the shortage of supplies was a continual problem. In his monthly report for September 1874, Gibson wrote:

> I issue flour and beef to them for herding their own ponies and coffee, sugar, dried fruits, etc. for manual labor. I have also allowed them to anticipate an additional sum on their annuities as I had not all the necessaries of life to give them for their labor.[61]

Because of the shortage of rations, Gibson was occasionally forced to buy needed goods on the open market, rather than through the bid system established by the Bureau of Indian Affairs, in order to prevent hunger and starvation on the Osage reservation.[62]

The goal of assimilation was never far from Gibson's mind. Although he was granted permission in 1875 to exempt the Osage from the labor requirement for rations, he did not inform the tribe:

> The telegram of the 1st Inst., exempting Osages from the requirements of Sec. 3 of [the] Appropriation Act was received in due time, but as the question of labor has not been brought up by the Osages since receiving it, I have not informed them of the action of the Sec. of the Interior. . . .
>
> A little pressure will bring all of them to obedience and nobody will be hurt, and the growth of civilization maintained and prospered.[63]

By not informing the tribe, Gibson hoped to continue to push them toward the adoption of "civilization," a key element of which, in the eyes of reformers, agents, and the government, was labor. They believed the best way to encourage Native nations to adopt a work ethic was to manipulate their food supply. If rations were tied to labor performed, the government reasoned, the Osage would not remain in idleness but learn to desire to work.

Despite the problems with subsistence in 1874, and the malnutrition it caused, Agent Gibson discussed with the Commissioner of Indian Affairs the possibility of prohibiting all further buffalo hunts and the benefits of doing so:

> I am impressed daily with the importance of holding the Osages on their Reservation hereafter if their funds can be obtained to aid them in making a support for themselves; this cannot be done while such a vast hunting ground is reserved for them and other Indians in close proximity to their Reservation. Remove this temptation and there would be no grounds left them to hope for opportunity in the future to continue their nomadic habits.[64]

Again, government agents were considering using their control of Osage access to food to elicit a desired change in behavior—in this case the complete acceptance of a sedentary lifestyle and the adoption of "civilization." Although Gibson desired the end of the buffalo hunts, he was forced to allow them to return to the plains when funds for ration supplies ran out at the end of February 1875.[65] At the end of March, Gibson described the subsistence situation on the reservation:

> No provision having been made to subsist the Osages and carry on the work of civilization the remainder of the year, the situation is somewhat embarrassing. . . .
>
> After reserving a small portion of sugar and coffee for the school, the balance will be entirely exhausted by the close of this month. It will then require about ten thousand dollars worth to subsist them the coming quarter.[66]

The lack of adequate supplies became a problem again in October and November 1875. Although Gibson reported that the goods purchased in New York were on hand, most Osage were already in desperate need of the supplies.[67] By early November the agency was out of beef cattle and requesting additional funds to purchase supplies.[68]

Another issue concerning rations, in addition to the persistent problems with quality and quantity, was distance. Initially, rations were distributed from three locations around the reservation. These locations corresponded to the main villages established by the different bands. In January 1876, however, Agent Gibson reported that the issuing of rations at the remote locations, Salt Creek and Hominy Stations, was discontinued. The result was to make distributions easier on the agent, but more difficult for many Osages. People were forced to travel twenty to thirty miles from their homes to the agency buildings, many walking, in order to report their labor and receive their flour, sugar, and coffee rations. In an attempt to make the situation easier for Osages traveling the greater distances, Gibson issued two weeks' rations at each distribution.[69] Despite this attempt to decrease travel time, the difficulty remained of carrying two weeks' rations—which occasionally included pounds of raw beef—thirty miles home. When Gibson left the agency soon after, ration issues returned to a weekly basis, but the single distribution location was maintained.

In March 1876 the Osage were again facing a food shortage. Their new agent, Cyrus Beede, in reporting the situation to Superintendent Nicholson, wrote:

> I also may state my convictions, that surrounded as these Indians are on all sides, their former source of living entirely cut-off, a failure on the part of the Government to grant the needed relief, is simply to invite depredations and plunder on the part of the Indians, to prevent starvation, hostilities on account of depredations, and an Indian War as a legitimate result of our own unfaithfulness.[70]

The small quantity of rations issued must have been galling to the Osage. Being forced to travel thirty miles to receive substandard rations that were barely enough to keep a family alive gave them plenty of reason to distrust and push for a change in the system.

The supply of rations on the Osage reservation continued to be a problem throughout much of 1876. Agent Beede continually wrote to Superintendent Nicholson about the lack of supplies and the desperate conditions the Osage were living in.[71] A flood in June created more problems:

> Their life, since the occurrence of the flood on the 28th of June last, has been of intense anxiety, crops gone, fences washed away,

farms destroyed, . . . relying upon the honesty of the Government to give them a portion of their own ample means to aid them in the effort. The flood wasted their first years efforts, and Congress has failed to render them any relief on their own earnest petition, from their own funds, locked up in the US Treasury, and this people . . . are left destitute even of means of subsistence, to starve, flee to the plains, or become vagrants.[72]

The situation was such that in June the Osage agent suggested issuing the work oxen as a beef ration.[73] At the end of July, Superintendent Nicholson informed Agent Beede of the purchase of supplies for the Osage and Kaw agencies. The supplies included flour, sugar, coffee, bacon, and beef cattle.[74] Although Beede reported receipts for goods received on August 31, on October 15 he noted that the agency had been out of sugar, coffee, and tobacco for over a month.[75] Beede occasionally postponed ration issues in an attempt to wait until adequate supplies arrived, but often he had to distribute whatever was on hand, which did not constitute a full ration.[76]

As with the Pawnees' rations, issues for the year 1877, for which the surviving record is the most complete, can serve as a case study of Osage rationing experiences. By examining the weekly ration returns for that year in detail, many of the problems with the system become apparent. The quality of the ration supplies, as evidenced by previous reports of bad sugar and continual problems with beef cattle, also remained an issue. There were additional reports of poor-quality flour, despite advertisements for bids specifically stating the desired quality. Unlike Pawnee rations, however, when quality and quantity were short, the Osage agent did not have hard bread or cornmeal to add to the issues. With the exception of the sporadic distribution of beans, this limited the Osage ration diet even further.

There were also directives from the Superintendent of Indian Affairs designed to save money and to stretch the existing supplies as far as possible. The Superintendent suggested that bacon and fresh beef not be distributed at the same issue.[77] This was hardly a problem on the Osage reservation, as the agency rarely had supplies of both bacon and beef at the same time. Only twice in 1877 were bacon and beef issued in the same week (June 9 and June 16), and then the beef ration was miniscule. During the first four months of 1877, beef was only issued twice, on March 10 and

March 17. In response to the insufficient supply of beef, other goods were issued in excess. The supply of bacon was slightly steadier, with issues being made half of the weeks between January 6 and April 28.

Table 5-1. Average Weekly Ration per Person,
Osage Agency, January–April 1877 (**weight in pounds**)

Date Issued	Beef (gross)	Bacon	Coffee	Flour	Beans	Salt	Sugar	Tobacco	# of People
6 Jan.	0	1.01	0.25	0	0	0	0.5	0	1913
13 Jan.	0	1	0.25	3.5	0	0	0.5	0	1825
20 Jan.	0	0.5	0.25	0.05	0	0	0.5	0.31	1917
27 Jan.	0	1.02	0.62	4.46	0	0.03	0	0	1871
3 Feb.	0	0	0.25	4.77	0	0	0.5	0	1963
10 Feb.	0	0	0.25	2.37	0	0	0.51	0	1931
17 Feb.	0	0	0.25	0	0	0	0.51	0	1611
24 Feb.	0	0	0.25	0.13	0	0	0.49	0	2065
3 Mar.	0	0	0.25	5.67	0	0	0.5	0	2008
10 Mar.	6.97	0	0.25	0.84	0	0	0.5	0	1936
17 Mar.	4.87	0	0.25	0.05	0	0	0.5	0	2129
24 Mar.	0	0.31	0.25	3.34	0	0	0.49	0	2485
31 Mar.	0	1	0.24	3.38	0	0	0.5	0	2392
7 Apr.	0	1	0.25	3.45	0	0	0.5	0	2219
14 Apr.	0	0	0.25	1.91	0	0	0	0	2041
21 Apr.	0	0.98	0.25	0	0	0	0.5	0	2098
28 Apr.	0	1	0.25	0	0	0.28	0.5	0	1970

Source: Compiled from Weekly Ration Reports, Osage Agency, January–April 1877, Records of the Central Superintendency of Indian Affairs, 1813–1878, RG75 (M856), National Archives. Report for April 14 is torn at either end, only center portion remains.

While the supply of coffee, flour, and sugar was maintained and issues made, the same is not true for salt and tobacco. Despite its necessity, salt was only issued twice during the first four months of the year (January 27 and April 28). Tobacco was only issued once, on January 20. However, it was a larger amount than on any other occasion. This over-issue of tobacco may have been due to deficiencies of most other ration goods that week. When the amount of rations each person received on a weekly basis is averaged out, it becomes apparent that the guidelines for ration distributions established in 1876 were not met (see table 5-1). From January 6 to April 28, when bacon was distributed, it usually amounted to one pound per person. When averaged over the entire four months, each person received approximately 0.459 pound per week. While this exceeded the amount stated in the circular (0.1 pound), when the near total absence of beef is considered (specified to equal 3 pounds per week, the amount distributed averaged only 0.696 pound), the amount of meat distributed on a weekly basis fell significantly short.

To make up for the lack of meat in the rations, coffee, flour, and sugar were over-issued on a regular basis. While the bureau circular set the amounts of these goods to be issued at 0.04 pound coffee, 0.5 pound flour, and 0.08 pound sugar per person, the rations on the Osage reservation generally far exceeded those amounts. However, there were weeks when little or no flour was distributed, and the agency had neither cornmeal nor hard bread to make up the difference. When the agent was forced, by necessity, to issue extra amounts of flour, sugar, or coffee, the Superintendent, Commissioner, or Secretary of the Interior often questioned the act. Beede explained,

> I think a careful examination of the over issues of a given article
> of supplies during a given quarter will be found fully counterbalanced by deficit in other articles. This may not always appear on
> a given weekly report, as we are not at all times able to render an
> equivalent for an article, the supply of which is exhausted and are
> obliged to pay in promises, but these promises must necessarily be
> fulfilled when a supply arrives.[78]

During the four-month period from May 5 to August 25, the quantity of rations distributed shifted slightly. Bacon was only issued seven of seventeen weeks, but beef was issued six times (an increase from the first four months). Despite the additional supply of beef, a June 15 letter from Beede to Superintendent Nicholson illustrates some of the problems that surrounded the purchase of ration supplies. Beede informed Nicholson of the "inferior quality of Texas beef delivered as far north as the Osage and Kaw Agencies during a large portion of the year" and "purchase of better quality cattle even at extra cost."[79] He also proposed that the cattle be fed with corn if there was not enough grass. If the agency started with better cattle, and they were fed corn through periods of drought, the cattle would still be of good quality by the time they were slaughtered. In this way he hoped to improve the quality of beef issued to the Osage.

The coffee ration, with the exception of May, continued to be in excess of the amount set out in the circular. During this same period, however, the flour issue fell off dramatically. On July 17, Beede reported the receipt of 24,100 pounds of flour at the Osage agency.[80] However, ten days later he wrote that the agency had no cornmeal or flour on hand, as well as being nearly out of beef.[81] There is no explanation of what happened to the flour received on the seventeenth. Beans were also included in the rations on three occasions. The amounts conformed to the circular, but with no beef or flour those weeks the ration was so small as to be of little help.

The weekly average of goods issued per person during the period May–August 1877 again did not completely conform to the guidelines established by the Bureau of Indian Affairs (see table 5-2). The amount of bacon, issued on seven occasions, averaged 0.3 pound per person per week for the four-month period. The beef distributed averaged approximately 2.5 pounds per person per week, but the majority was issued in July, so most of that amount was not available during May and June. While the meat distribution came closer to the regulated amount overall, the fact that the majority was issued over a four-week period, rather than throughout the four months, created another problem. The Osage faced weeks of hunger followed by brief periods of abundant beef rations. So much fresh beef was issued during July that much of it had to be dried or go to waste.

The amount of flour issued during the May–August period generally fell below the amount called for in the circular. Only twice did the ration amount to more than 0.5 pound per person. When flour was issued, only on six of seventeen weeks, it equaled less than 0.1 pound per person. Again, with this lack of flour, the agent had no cornmeal, hard bread, or rice with which to compensate.

The final four months of 1877 were generally better in terms of the quantity of rations issued. Although no beans or bacon were issued, like the Pawnee rations, the beef supply was more consistent than during the previous eight months. However, the lack of beef rations during September prompted Superintendent Nicholson to grant permission for a limited number of Osages to leave the reservation on a hunt. The party was to be given a military escort to protect against depredations on settlements and to protect the Osage from hostile settlers and other tribes.[82] Despite permission to go on a hunt, the number of people receiving weekly rations on the reservation did not decrease, indicating that the Osage either did not go on the hunt or did not leave before the beginning of January 1878.

Table 5-2. Average Weekly Ration per Person,
Osage Agency, May–August 1877 (weight in pounds)

Date Issued	Beef (gross)	Bacon	Coffee	Flour	Beans	Salt	Sugar	Tobacco	# of People
5 May	1.69	1	0.21	0	0	0	0.48	0.03	1992
12 May	0.72	0	0	0	0	0	0	0	2391
19 May	0	0.29	0.08	0	0	0	0.17	0	2391
26 May	0	0.13	0.02	0	0	0	0.03	0	2391
2 Jun.	0	0	0	0	?	0	0	0	?
9 Jun.	0	1	0.25	0	0.08	0	0.5	0	1825
16 Jun.	0	1	0.25	0	0.11	0	0.5	0	1890
23 Jun.	0	1	0.25	0	0	0	0.49	0	1778
30 Jun.	0	0.79	0.25	0.06	0	0	0.49	0	1958
7 Jul.	13.37	0	0.25	0	0	0	0.5	0	1885
14 Jul.	12.35	0	0.25	0	0	0	0.5	0	2070
21 Jul.	7.47	0	0.26	0	0	0	0.54	0	1880
28 Jul.	6.39	0	0.25	0.06	0	0	0.5	0	2052
4 Aug.	0	0	0.26	3.49	0	0	0.51	0	2050
11 Aug.	0	0	0.25	0.06	0	0	0.5	0	2015
18 Aug.	0	0	0.26	0.1	0	0	0.5	0	2133
25 Aug.	0	0	0.24	3.46	0	0	0.49	0	2131

Source: Compiled from Weekly Ration Reports, Osage Agency, May–August 1877, Records of the Central Superintendency of Indian Affairs, 1813–1878, RG75 (M856), National Archives.

Rations of coffee, flour, and sugar during the last four months of the year continued to exceed regulations (see table 5-3). The coffee and sugar rations averaged 0.25 pound per person, and the flour ration averaged approximately 3.5 pounds per person. The distribution of salt and tobacco, however, continued to be negligible. Salt was only distributed twice during this period (only four times the entire year), and while each issue was in excess of the weekly amount, it was not enough to equal the proper amount for the year.

From a breakdown of the Osage agency ration reports for 1877, it becomes clear that the Osage faced an almost feast-or-famine situation. While on the whole for the year there were over-issues of bacon, flour, coffee, and sugar, beans and salt were under-issued, and no rice or corn was issued at all. The beef and tobacco issues were close to Bureau of Indian Affairs regulations, but as with all of the goods, the issues tended to be made in bulk on a few dates rather than spread evenly throughout the year. As other agents had done with the Pawnee rations, the Osage agents were forced to make do with whatever goods they could obtain, regardless of Bureau of Indian Affairs regulations and any attempts made to ensure better quality and quantity of goods.

In spite of the centralized government policy of "civilization" through reservations and rations, the reality of Osage rations in 1877 did not conform to the guidelines established by the United States and the Bureau of Indian Affairs. The abundance, at times, of certain goods belied the problems faced by the Osage. Ration quantity was often hit-and-miss. The agents had little control over the quality of the goods they received, and the people receiving the goods had no control at all. The Osage—at the mercy of unscrupulous merchants and traders who charged excessive prices for substandard goods—were left in a spiral of malnutrition, starvation, and disease.

A comparison of the distributions on the Osage and Pawnee reservations in 1877 reveals the disparate nature of rationing policies when put into practice. Certain trends emerge from an examination of the ration receipts and agent correspondence. There was a consistent effort to find ways to stretch supplies and cut expenses, such as the attempt, on both reservations, to issue beef and bacon on alternating weeks. Agents for both nations also express repeated concerns over the quality of cattle for the beef issue. The over-issue of certain goods in lieu of other core supplies was a common practice. Another similarity between the two reservations was the feast/famine cycle—the issuance of excessive amounts of an item followed by weeks or even months of little or none, such as with the beef issues.

Table 5-3. Average Weekly Ration per Person, Osage Agency,
September–December 1877 (weight in pounds)

Date Issued	Beef (gross)	Bacon	Coffee	Flour	Beans	Salt	Sugar	Tobacco	# of People
1 Sep.	11.42	0	0.25	3.45	0	0	0.49	0	2153
8 Sep.	9.06	0	0.24	3.34	0	0	0.5	0	2130
15 Sep.	0	0	0.25	3.38	0	0	0.5	0.07	2110
22 Sep.	0	0	0.25	3.38	0	0	0.5	0	2084
29 Sep.	0	0	0.25	3.33	0	0	0.25	0	2096
6 Oct.	0	0	0.25	3.35	0	0	0.25	0	2135
13 Oct.	11	0	0.24	3.31	0	0.06	0.25	0	2295
20 Oct.	11.26	0	0.24	3.36	0	0	0.25	0.03	2375
27 Oct.	9.34	0	0.25	3.42	0	0	0.25	0	2284
3 Nov.	11.99	0	0.25	3.49	0	0	0.25	0	2339
10 Nov.	0	0	0.25	3.42	0	0	0.25	0.03	2256
17 Nov.	13.31	0	0.25	3.48	0	0.07	0.25	0.03	2113
24 Nov.	8.82	0	0.25	3.5	0	0	0.25	0.03	2035
1 Dec.	9.65	0	0.25	3.38	0	0	0.24	0	1935
8 Dec.	7.73	0	0.25	3.5	0	0	0.25	0	1857
15 Dec.	0	0	0.25	3.49	0	0	0.25	0.03	2013
22 Dec.	13.26	0	0.25	2.49	0	0	0.26	0	1772
29 Dec.	0	0	0.25	2.49	0	0	0.25	0	1496

Source: Compiled from Weekly Ration Reports, Osage Agency, September–December 1877, Records of the Central Superintendency of Indian Affairs, 1813–1878, RG75 (M856), National Archives.

The list of supplies on hand during any given week, and the amounts issued, however, show the difficulties in the government contract system. Despite having neighboring reservations in the Indian Territory, the Pawnees received large rations of beef and flour on the same weeks that the Osage received little or none. The Pawnee agent also had access to corn-meal and hard bread as alternate rations when other supplies were low, a luxury not enjoyed by the Osage. This indicates a failure of suppliers to provide the necessary goods in appropriate quantities. It also suggests that the ration system was not flexible or that there was a reluctance on the part of the Bureau of Indian Affairs to share supplies, even when the people of one nation were near starvation. The rationing system was created in such a way that it was impossible for policies to adapt quickly to changing conditions and the needs of the people. However, since rations were only supposed to be a temporary solution on the path to "civilization," many felt the deficiencies in the system would encourage swifter cultural change.

One of the most pressing problems facing the Osage during the 1870s–1890s, as with most Native people, was malnutrition and disease. Although ration issues may have averaged higher than the amounts set out in the 1876 circular, the feast-and-famine nature of the distributions and the poor nutritional quality of the food had serious consequences. The Osage suffered a large number of fatalities during their final removal from Kansas, and their continued dependence on government rations made a population rebound difficult. The Osage population steadily declined from the late seventeenth century, when it totaled about 17,000, through 1870, when it had dropped to 3,000.[83] Louis F. Burns's study of the Osage annuity rolls of 1878 indicated that most of the tribe's children died between 1870 and 1875. He found the same pattern for the 1822–1827 removal as well.[84]

After 1877 rationing on the Osage reservation came under more fire from both Osages who believed they could purchase better goods on their own and humanitarians who believed that as long as rationing continued the Osage would not adopt "civilization." The Osage Council expressed its desire to end rationing in January 1878. Governor Joseph Paw ne no pah she argued that the people did not want many of the goods purchased by the government and that the Osage were better able to care for themselves when they raised corn in the traditional manner, rather than depending on rations. Augustus Captain argued that rationing was especially difficult in the winter when pony herds had to be taken further out to find grass since the herders then had to travel the extra distance to receive their rations. Wah-ti-anka argued that the Osage were too poor, the rations were too bad, and the distance to the agency was too great for the practice to continue.[85]

E. C. Watkins, in an 1878 inspection report, presented a view of the rationing system aimed at ending the practice. He reported that the Osage fought against the government purchase of their food. He also stated that issues were made at all times during the week, not in the orderly weekly issues indicated by the agents. He continued:

> This system of forcing food onto Indians living in a good farming country, or feeding them if they ask it, for any extended term of years, I consider radically wrong, and only productive of idleness, shiftlessness, and vice among the Indians. It makes vagabonds of them and beggars of the worst class; and would doubtless produce the same effect on an average community of white people.[86]

Watkins also suggested that rationing on the Osage reservation be halted at the end of the fiscal year, with only the ill and indigent continuing to receive support.

In August 1878, again, Osage leaders expressed their desire to end rationing on the reservation:

> We spoke to the General Inspector that was out here last winter in reference to the rations and told him that we positively did not want any more rations bought with our money after the 1st of July 1878. . . . We think our reasons are good for not wanting rations bought with our money.[87]

Osage leaders listed their reasons for wanting the end of rationing, including the quantity issued each week and the great distances that people had to travel on a weekly basis for such small rations. The leaders argued that if they were compelled to accept the rations, they should be issued monthly rather than weekly, to make the forced travel worth it.[88]

After decades of fighting to end the practice of government rations purchased with their own money, in July 1879 the Osage became the first tribe to receive their entire annuity, including rations, in cash.[89] An Act of Congress passed in 1892 cemented this move:

> That when in the judgment of the Secretary of the Interior any Indian tribe, or part thereof, who are receiving rations and clothing under this act, are sufficiently advanced in civilization to purchase such rations and clothing judiciously, they may commute the same and pay the value thereof in money per capita to such tribe or part

thereof, the manner of such payment to be prescribed by the Secretary of the Interior.[90]

By the time the Osage began receiving their subsistence in money instead of rations much of their old way of life had been eroded. The last moderately successful bison hunt occurred in 1873. The final large hunt in 1876 was completely unsuccessful due to the decimation of the bison herds and the enclosure of the plains. The end of the hunts and the coming of cash annuities continued to change Osage society, a process that had begun with their first contacts with French traders. Despite the efforts of the United States government, however, these changes continued to be made on Osage terms. Removal, the end of bison hunts, and the high mortality rates caused by malnutrition and disease forever altered Osage ceremonial life. Many who died were the very old and the very young, leaving the tribe with few people to teach the ceremonies to the next generation and few new initiates for the secret societies. In spite of this devastation, however, the Osage maintained much of their ceremonial life, altering or adapting the meanings of many of their ceremonies to their current situation.

The Osage were also able to adapt to allotment and life at the end of the nineteenth and beginning of the twentieth centuries according to their own desires. Taking advantage of their abundant grazing lands, in the 1880s the Osage began leasing pastures to cattle drovers who passed through their reservation. They also were able to cope with allotment in their own way, by leasing the farmsteads to white tenant farmers while maintaining the style of living they desired. The Osage people's new prosperity continued in the early twentieth century with the discovery of oil on the reservation, making them one of the wealthiest Native nations in the United States.

The rationing system implemented by the United States government was partially successful in achieving its desired goals. The government's control of food was a major factor in the cession of the majority of Osage lands, particularly in their complete removal from Kansas. The policies also worked to induce many to attempt farming and to send their children to school, either on the reservation or to boarding schools. However, the government failed in its attempt to replace Osage culture with that of Euro-America. The Osage maintain their cultural identity and important connections with their past. Although the rationing system did not attain its desired goals, it continues to affect Osages in the twenty-first century. Many of the health problems experienced on the reservation, such as diabetes, are the result of poor diets started by rationing and continued through the distribution of commodities. Through it all, however, the Osage people persevered.

Chapter 6
Moorundie Ration Depot, South Australia, 1845–1856

With a common origin in English settler colonialism and a similar frontier mythos, Australia is a popular and constructive subject for comparison with the United States. Like the government of the United States, the colonial government of Australia incorporated elements of assimilation, "New Colonialism," into indigenous relations. To secure access to land, ensure peace, and—in the case of Australia—obtain labor, efforts at "civilizing" Aborigines were made. A people who adopted Christianity and the other characteristics of Anglo-Australian society better fit the ideals of the colonial structure. As in the United States, part of the strategy used by Australian governments to instill this cultural change was the control and distribution of food.

While both governments utilized rationing, the structure of their policies differed greatly. South Australia created a much more decentralized system and utilized both government agents (Aboriginal protectors and police) and civilians to distribute the food. The South Australian government also determined the content of rations based on the idea that the Aborigines would continue to hunt. Thus, rations in South Australia, as in the United States, were not intended to become the sole source of subsistence, though for very different reasons. Despite the differences in the structure of indigenous policy, the similar goals of both governments—"civilization," access to land, etc.—highlight the common threads of settler societies. There are also similarities in the reaction to rationing by the Aborigines and Native Americans, as well as in the lasting impact of the system itself. As in the case of the Pawnee and the Osage, a study of

Australian ration policies and their implementation at specific locations will reveal the broader aims of the government and how actual ration distributions differed from stated regulations, as well as how rationing impacted the people involved.

Established as a British colony in 1836, South Australia, like the rest of the Australian colonies, faced immediate conflict with the Native population of the area. When the British first arrived, the land was home to over forty different Aboriginal nations, including Bungandidj, Dhanggagarli, Kaurna, Nawu, Ngadjuri, Ngangurugu, Ngarinyeri, Ngayawung, Ngintait, Pitjantjatjara, Wangganguru, Yankuntjara, Yaraldi, and Yawarawarga peoples.[1] Each Aboriginal nation had its own religion, language, territory, and culture. Each utilized the region's natural resources and well-developed trade networks, and each created strong physical and spiritual ties to the land. As European settlers invaded their territories, Aboriginal ties to the land were disrupted and their survival was threatened.

The establishment of the colony had a profound effect on the Aboriginal population of South Australia. Some groups faced swift destruction through disease and violence. Others were far enough away from European settlement to survive another century nearly free from direct contact, though the diseases brought by colonization often affected them. However, all eventually faced an invading culture that wanted their land and used violence, assimilation, and manipulation to obtain it. Observed Ken Hampton,

> They robbed us of our laws, languages and religion and imposed their own upon us. They destroyed sacred places of the Dreamtime and introduced their own religion. They took our children and educated them in their ways, deliberately teaching them to forget the ways of the Old People. They took away our peoples' freedom. They took away our land. They eroded our economy with handouts. They reduced us from independence to the lowest rank in their capitalist society.[2]

South Australia's position as the first noncriminal settlement in Australia and the founders' (at least superficially) humanitarian interests created a dilemma within the administration of the colony. While the documents founding the colony provided for the protection of Aborigines under crown law, the orders were left vague, with no consequence to those who ignored them. There were also differences between the outlooks of those establishing laws and policies in Britain and Adelaide, the capital of South Australia, and those colonists pushing settlement farther into the bush. Ultimately, the founders and settlers of South Australia sought a financially stable and profitable colony and had little real interest in preserving the humanitarian ideals set forth on paper.

Aboriginal nations in coastal South Australia, particularly in the Adelaide area, were no strangers to European contact. They knew of the conditions that Aborigines faced in New South Wales and Victoria through long-established trade networks. The coastal nations also had long and direct contact with European whalers and sealers who traveled along the Australian coast. These ships often anchored in the harbors of South Australia to obtain food and fresh water, trade with local Aborigines, and kidnap slaves (usually women). After 1836, however, a new form of contact began to occur. With the establishment of a permanent colony at Adelaide, conflict between Aborigines and Europeans developed. Permanent European settlement on the Adelaide Plains meant not only cultural conflict but competition over the area's scarce natural resources as well. The colonists' use of the land, for cattle and sheep runs and mining, was in direct conflict with Aboriginal uses and became the source of many of the conflicts.

Edward John Eyre, an explorer and first sub-protector[3] of Aborigines at Moorundie ration depot, who had traveled throughout South Australia during exploration expeditions in 1839 and 1840–1841, developed strong views concerning the Aborigines and the settlement of the colony:

> Without entering upon the abstract question concerning the right of one race of people to wrest from another their possessions, simply because they happen to be more powerful than the original inhabitants, or because they imagine that they can, by their superior skill or acquirements, enable the soil to support a denser population, I think it will be conceded by every candid and right-thinking mind, that no one can justly take that which is not his own, without giving some equivalent in return, or deprive a people of their ordinary means of support, and not provide them with any other instead. Yet such is exactly the position we are in with regard to the inhabitants of Australia.[4]

Eyre's views paralleled many humanitarians of the day, both in Australia and Britain: a paternalistic desire to protect Aborigines while guiding them toward a European definition of civilization. Nineteenth-century definitions of "civilization" generally included the goals of Christianization and Europeanization. The humanitarians sought to encourage the adoption of European habits—foods and their method of preparation and consumption, work habits, and seasonal patterns of life—even as most believed the Aborigines were a dying race. Christianization was also a primary goal, particularly for those groups in closest contact with colonial society and the increasing numbers of mixed-heritage individuals.

Despite their altruistic words, however, the true objective and scope of the humanitarians' intent should not be overlooked. While they espoused the need for the Aborigines to be compensated for their loss of land, they never acknowledged Native title but rather focused on the loss of subsistence. Humanitarians, in their arguments for "saving" the Aborigines, did nothing that endangered British imperial rights or the ability of the colony to grow economically. The views of the humanitarians, however coercive their motives were, acknowledged some of the suffering that the Aborigines underwent at the hands of colonization. This sentiment was not shared by the vast majority of South Australian settlers nor by those financing the colony, to whom survival and financial stability were most important and who had little concern for the welfare of the Aborigines.[5] The South Australian government needed to strike a balance between the position of the humanitarians and that of the settlers and financiers; rations played a significant role in accomplishing this goal.

The ultimate objective of rationing for the government of South Australia was control over and "civilization" of indigenous populations. While specific goals of the policies were adapted to fit changing circumstances, general trends remained fairly constant. Easy access to and control over ever-larger amounts of territory was particularly important to settlers on the edges of the frontier. Christianization and Europeanization of Aboriginal peoples were important to the various humanitarian groups in South Australia and Britain. As the Aboriginal population became more "civilized," it became a potential labor force for both manual and domestic service. The ultimate desire was for Aborigines to fade away, culturally at the very least.

Through rations, the government hoped to gain and maintain control over the land, with as little expense and warfare as possible. The key to achieving the goal was the destruction of the indigenous culture, including language, religion, political structures, economies, and food ways. The Aborigines were to be eventually assimilated into the lowest levels of white society. Eyre summarized the Australian government's goal in 1840:

> We must adopt a system which may at once administer to their wants, and at the same time, give to us a controlling influence over them; such as may not only restrain them from doing what is wrong, but may eventually lead them to do what is right. . . .
>
> It appears that the most important point, in fact almost the only essential one, . . . is to gain such in influence or authority over the Aborigines as may be sufficient to enable us to induce them to adopt, or submit to any regulations that we make for their improvement.[6]

South Australia quickly adopted the use of rations as a control mechanism over the Aborigines, and the process of rationing (where, when, and how the food was distributed) became a tool to achieve that goal. Historian Robert Foster summarized South Australia's rationale for the use of rationing. It became "a means of providing support for a people whose traditional economy had been undermined . . . a system of control . . . [and] a political tool."[7]

The colonial government took a three-part approach in relation to controlling Aboriginal patterns of movement and behavior. The first goal in distributing rations was to prevent theft and attacks by Aborigines on fledgling settlements in order to procure food. The second goal, particularly as white settlement increased, was to draw Aborigines away from large towns and induce them to adopt a more sedentary lifestyle. This would allow government agents to keep closer watch over Aboriginal populations and reassure settlers as they expanded into the bush. South Australia believed the best, most expedient way of accomplishing this was through the continued distribution of food, particularly flour. In 1842 the clerk to the Resident Magistrate at Port Lincoln, Nathaniel Hailes, wrote:

> I am decidedly of the opinion that the stomach is the organ which should first be attempted as the medium of civilization. Full and

regular meals gradually disqualify them for the precarious life of
the bush. . . . Boiled wheat and sugar, or bread and milk . . . are
most effective civilizers.[8]

Both of these goals were somewhat difficult to achieve across all of South
Australia, initially because of the smaller European population and later
because Aborigines were not yet restricted to reservations and were free
to travel where they wished (although they were discouraged from staying
near large settlements).

The third purpose for rationing in South Australia was to maintain a
ready and inexpensive source of labor. As the pastoral industry expanded
into the bush, it was often difficult to obtain enough white laborers to
fill needed positions at the wages that station owners were willing to pay.
However, if a station was located near a government ration depot or mission, or if the owner himself issued rations to the Aborigines, they could
maintain a population of low-wage workers who were familiar with the
environment and well suited to survival out on the range.

The adoption of Christianity, agriculture, English language, and other
European habits furthered the goals of the South Australian government.
Settlers often found such "civilized" Aboriginal settlements less threatening and better sources of potential laborers than those who maintained
more traditional lifestyles. Pushing these goals not only increased governmental control but gradually reduced a perceived deterrent to the attraction of new settlers to the colony.

In order for the colony to survive and become successful, the South
Australian government needed to assure its citizens that they were safe
and protected from the indigenous population. Only by doing such would
they be able to attract the numbers of settlers needed to become financially stable. The colonial government established schools to teach Aboriginal children English and European ways and manners, and they used
food to induce parents to allow their children to attend. Once the colony
had attracted enough settlers for people to begin pushing into the bush,
the colonists needed to be able to acquire land and be assured of a cheap
source of labor for their sheep and cattle stations. The government used
its control over rations and the process of rationing, combined with the
new pressures placed on the Aborigines' original means of subsistence, to
achieve many of its goals.

The act of rationing was often a point of cultural breakdown, with each participant viewing the rations and the reason behind the distribution differently. The Aborigines viewed rations as part of a reciprocal relationship with European settlers in their area. If the Europeans used up or cut off the Aborigines from their traditional means of subsistence and maintained what to the Aborigines appeared to be an abundance of food, it was expected that they would share their food with those who had none. The rations were also sometimes seen as payment for European use of the land. The government, on the other hand, viewed rations as a type of contract with the Aborigines to prevent the hunting of station sheep and cattle or the theft of flour and other supplies. Rations were also distributed to prevent violence and facilitate the spread of settlement. The distributions were a way to attempt the creation of a common ground between two disparate groups.

Rations in South Australia—generally including flour, rice or sago, sugar, tea, and tobacco—represented a drastic change from the Aborigines' traditional diet. Mutton was occasionally issued when flour or rice was in short supply. Early rations also included oatmeal, biscuits (similar to hard tack), and on the Queen's Birthday bread and roast beef. The adoption of these European foods was not immediate, especially when the Aborigines did not recognize the goods as edible. The introduction of European foodstuffs, in a story told by Harry Palada Kulamburut of the nearby Northern Territory, gives an indication of how South Australian Aborigines may have reacted to these new foods:

> They took the tea and looked at it. "What's this? It (must) be leaves!" they said. They threw it away (over there). Next they took the sugar and looked at it. "This is (surely) sand!" they said. They threw it away. (Then) they took the tobacco and smelt it. "Rotten!" they said. They got the treacle, opened it and had a look. "Ah . . . sugarbag!" they said. "This is sugarbag; this really is sugarbag." They cut open the flour and looked at it. "This surely must be white clay," they said.[9]

The rejection of particular goods was not the only issue the government had to face concerning the use of food as a mechanism of control. Rationing policies in South Australia were not strictly structured. The first ration depots established in South Australia, in and near Adelaide, were run by government officials, police, and the protector of Aborigines. As settlement expanded and more Aboriginal groups came into contact with Europeans, the practice of rationing expanded beyond Adelaide to areas further from white settlement. By 1845 four ration depots had been established: the Aborigines Location, a specific depot in Adelaide; and stations at Moorundie, Encounter Bay, and Port Lincoln. By 1866 fifty-seven depots existed across South Australia and another twenty-one in the South Australia–administered Northern Territory.

The government preferred to provide rations in ways that kept the Aborigines in their own territories rather than congregating large numbers in one location. This meant colonial choices of depot locations depended more on achieving an even distribution rather than on addressing the particular needs of any one area or taking seasonal movements into account.[10] In addition to depots administered by police and sub-protectors, religious missions and a few individual settlers began issuing rations, often subsidized by the government. As a consequence of the more decentralized nature of South Australia's nineteenth-century rationing program, the number and location of depots or stations continually fluctuated, particularly among those issued by private citizens.

Initially, rations were distributed piecemeal in return for labor or as gifts to establish friendly relations to those living around Adelaide. As the Aborigines' access to traditional food sources was diminished by European settlement, the necessity of regular ration distributions to prevent theft, attacks, and starvation became apparent. The *Adelaide Gazette* summarized:

> [I]t has been a principle of the Government, fully acted upon, that in localities in which the ordinary means of subsistence of the [N]atives have been diminished by colonization, all deficiency of food beyond what they could procure by other reasonable means should be made up from the Government stores—that, in consequence, daily rations of biscuit have been liberally issued.[11]

The Aborigines, however, were not expected to quit hunting native game. Their rations rarely included meat. Even when local fauna was depleted through sport hunting or driven away by Europeans or when access to waterways was restricted, the rations did not change. The quantity of rations distributed by the government did not rise above a level meant to supplement traditional means of subsistence. This left many Aborigines with few choices. The increasingly desperate situation the Aborigines found themselves in was commented upon by Eyre in the 1840s:

> The Game of the Wilds that the European does not destroy for his amusement are driven away by his flocks and herds. The waters are occupied and enclosed, and access to them is frequently forbidden. . . .
>
> The fields are fenced in, and the natives are no longer at liberty to dig up roots.[12]

Despite the hardships and dependence created through the ration system located at depots, missions, and pastoral stations in South Australia, the Aborigines resisted government policies in a variety of ways. They were not passive victims of colonial policy; rather, Aboriginal Australians adapted to the system of rations through their own cultural and social understandings. In doing so, South Australia's indigenous peoples undermined part of the government's goals, particularly those pertaining to "civilization"—they did not accept rations with the same understanding and expectations as the government had in distributing them.[13] While the Aborigines took rations based on reciprocity, the South Australian government distributed rations as a tool of manipulation.

As it became clear that the two sides approached rationing with different perceptions, and as the government began asking for more in return for the meager supplies of food it distributed, many Aborigines physically began to resist. Some left the stations rather than be forced to work in exchange for rations. When the government built communal dining rooms at Aboriginal stations to encourage the adoption of European eating habits, the Aborigines refused to use the silverware provided and brought the food outside to eat in a more traditional manner.[14] Rations were also adapted to fit into traditional food preparations. Flour, sugar, and other goods were cooked in ways that reflected Aboriginal culture and understandings, rather than in the European ways anticipated by the government. Flour, for example, replaced ground wattle seed in the preparation of damper, rather than being used to make European-style bread. Rations, thus, were not immediately incorporated into Aboriginal life.

The rations, and all goods distributed to the Aborigines in South Australia, were purchased by funds received from the Sale of Waste Lands Act of 1842.[15] The act provided for the establishment of reserves for the use of the Aborigines in "civilized" pursuits like farming. Few Aborigines, however, ever farmed on these reserves. Instead, most of the benefit the Aborigines saw from the act was the proceeds from the leases and sales of those lands to colonists. Only a very small portion of the funds sent to the Aborigines Office was used on rations and blankets for distribution. The majority of funding went toward salaries for officials and maintaining schools.[16]

Despite the lack or misuse of funding, it was through the distribution of rations and declarations of protection under British law that South Australian officials believed they had more than compensated the local Aborigines for their land. At an 1839 court hearing, Charles Mann, the first advocate-general of South Australia, argued:

> If we have settled in their country, and perhaps scared the animals which in their primitive state formed their food, we have given them better food than they previously had, and we have at the same time conferred on them a recompense of far more importance, by giving them all the advantages of British subjects in this world.[17]

Like the United States, South Australia faced problems with both the quality and quantity of the rations it distributed. In 1847 the government resident magistrate[18] for Guichen Bay, Butler, reported the flour forwarded to this station for distribution to the Aborigines was of extremely bad quality and altogether inferior.[19] Over twenty years later quality remained a problem when an 1869 settler wrote a letter to the *Adelaide Observer* complaining about the flour distributed in his area:

> [A]llow me through your columns to draw the attention of the proper authorities to the cruel fraud practiced upon the aborigines in this neighbourhood by the party or parties holding the contract for supplying flour to be issued to them as rations. This so-called flour is of the vilest description (I speak from ocular inspection); so bad, indeed, that many of the natives who have been compelled by sheer hunger to eat it have been made ill in consequence. It is

a well-known fact that some persons here have given the natives some good flour in exchange for the trash served out to them, and on giving this latter to their pigs could scarcely induce said pigs to devour it.[20]

Problems with the quality of food distributed to the Aborigines extended beyond the outlying areas and distant ration depots. The quality of the food used at the schools established for Aboriginal children was also poor. Victoria Archibald, who attended a school in New South Wales, recalled the food she was served at the institution:

> [W]e were to have a porridge for breakfast, or rolled oats, whatever you like to call it, a little drop of milk on it, a slice of bread and golden syrup. But then again the porridge wasn't what you would call porridge. The porridge was moving while you were eating it because there used to be a lot of weevils in it, little weeny grubs. You had to eat it.[21]

The government also confronted problems of transporting the ration goods over long distances to outlying depots. Not only was adequate transportation difficult to find, it was also expensive. In addition, extremes in weather made travel very difficult, particularly during the wet season when roads and trails were likely to be washed out or under water. The government also faced problems ensuring that the goods reached their destination in adequate condition. For example, the protector of Aborigines determined that the bad flour received at Guichen Bay in 1847 had been exchanged in transit between Adelaide and Guichen Bay, as the flour that had left Adelaide had been of good quality.[22]

Within a few years of the establishment of the colony, it became necessary to expand the ration depots farther into the outback. The movement of colonists farther from the urban centers of South Australia, as well as the development of overland sheep trails to settlements in New South Wales, meant increased contact with different Aboriginal nations. The increasing contact invariably meant more conflict as Aborigines' land and means of subsistence began to constrict. One such confrontation occurred in 1841 near the Rufus and Murray Rivers after Europeans driving sheep overland were attacked by Aborigines protecting their lands from invasion. In retaliation, the South Australian government sent a police expedition to the area to protect the drovers and their flocks. Another conflict arose after an Aboriginal attack, and at least thirty Aborigines were killed. This incident became known as the Rufus River Massacre. Attempting to restore peace to the area after the massacre and in order to forestall additional conflicts between travelers and Aborigines, in 1841 Governor George Grey instructed that a new ration depot be established along the Murray River:

> I have directed [Edward John] Eyre to bring into operation a system of periodical distribution of Flour to the Natives, this distribution being made dependent upon their good conduct—They are to assemble on every other full moon for the purpose of receiving these presents.—Opportunities will thus be afforded them bringing under Mr. Eyre's notice any grievances under which they may be suffering, and he, at the same time, can impart to them any regulations or directions for their guidance.[23]

The new ration depot was established near present-day Blanchetown at a location called Moorundie, named after the local Aboriginal name for the River Murray, Murrundi.[24]

Since Moorundie was initially farther from the large colonial settlements, rations were distributed monthly to the Aborigines who came in from the surrounding areas, rather than daily, as done in Adelaide. The depot drew Aboriginal groups from a relatively wide-ranging area. Thus, establishing the precise groups who received rations there is an impossible task, as the divisions of groups and the names used by early colonists were not accurate and the groups who assembled frequently changed. In many instances clans of the same group were identified as being their own entity.[25]

The predominant language/tribal groups residing in the area around Moorundie were Merus. Danggalis and Barkindjis lived to the north and northeast, Ngargads to the south, and Ngadjuris to the west.[26] Some sources identify some of the Aboriginal tribes belonging to the Meru language group as the Ngintait, Yirawirung, Ngawait, Ngayawung, and Ngangurugu.[27] Neither Eyre nor any of his successors recorded the specific groups that came in to Moorundie, but the Aborigines likely belonged to the Meru language group of the surrounding tribes.

The initial goal of the Moorundie station was to bring the Aborigines into contact with a "civilizing" force, as well as to discourage any attacks on settlers or travelers moving through the area by distributing a token amount of flour. During the 1840s rations in the amount of four pounds of flour per adult and two pounds per child were given to any Aborigines who came to the monthly distributions, together with an annual distribution of a small number of blankets to select individuals.[28] This ration equaled approximately 0.13 pounds of flour for adults and 0.07 pounds per child per day. The Aborigines could obtain additional European foods through labor for whites, barter, and theft. However, there are a few accounts that put the amount of flour distributed monthly at 2.5 pounds per person.[29] The small quantity of the ration was not necessarily a problem while there was still sufficient wild game and other native foods on which the Aborigines could subsist.

Edward John Eyre, at the direction of the protector of Aborigines and the South Australian government, used the distribution of food as an incentive for the Aborigines to begin adopting "civilized" behavior, even if only superficially. An example is seen in an 1844 directive from the government: "His Excellency the Governor sanctions the issue of one pound of flour to each [N]ative adult who attends divine service on the Sabbath."[30] While the practice of distributing food for attendance at church services was later frowned upon, in the early contact history in South Australia it was seen as a legitimate way to begin the Christianization of the Aborigines by both government ration depot officials and early missionaries. The inducement of additional rations was also used to encourage more secular advances toward "civilization" as well. In 1850 at Moorundie, for example, the population of dogs owned by the Aborigines became a nuisance to local whites. To help alleviate this problem, the resident magistrate offered an additional six pounds of flour to be given to any Aborigine who turned over their female dog to be killed.[31]

Within a few months of the first few distributions of flour, the number of people at each issue increased as the Aborigines began trusting Moorundie as a place to obtain flour free from poison. Eyre believed he was quickly earning the trust of the local Natives:

> This plan of assembling the Aborigines once every month and making a distribution of flour to them . . . has been fully carried out and appears to me admirably adapted to bring about a friendly

inter-course in the first instance and subsequently to establish a
controlling influence over them of the most salutary kind. In addition to the above mentioned distribution of food at the monthly musters I have assiduously endeavored to bring the natives as
much about me as possible,—to teach them to do such work as
was adapted to their character and habits or to barter with me
such produce as it was in their power to procure, as fish, game, &c.
On these occasions I give them either flour or rice according to the
reward I think they deserve.[32]

Unfortunately, Eyre was directed to discontinue the issue of rations in
exchange for goods procured by the Aborigines, thus eliminating barter
with government agents as a means for the Aborigines to obtain food.
The government believed that such a program was too expensive and did
not conform to its goals for the rationing system, because it allowed the
Aborigines to maintain their traditional habits rather than adopting "civilized" manners.[33]

In addition to distributing extra rations to those Aborigines he deemed
as exhibiting particularly good behavior or assisting the government, Eyre
also used his control over the rations as a means of punishment.[34] In 1842,
when an Aborigine was found guilty of stealing from the flour supply, his
punishment included twenty-four hours in confinement and the loss of
his next issue of flour.[35] In 1844 Eyre reported the punishment he invoked
for those who persisted in visiting Adelaide:

> [S]everal of the tribes still persisted in deserting their own district
> and crowding into town—upon their return again to the Murray
> it became necessary to fulfill the threat I had held out to them and
> stop that monthly issue of flour which hitherto they had regularly
> received.[36]

The South Australian government did not establish specific regulations
concerning the use of rations as a means of punishment but rather gave
the individuals in charge of the government issues the latitude to withhold rations from individuals or groups in cases of theft and aggression.[37]
This lack of specific regulation allowed sub-protectors and police to give
leniency in certain situations, but it also opened the possibility of harsh
punishments for minor infractions of European law and customs, such as

withholding rations from an entire tribe as punishment for the actions of a single individual.

Despite the apparent success of the Moorundie station in maintaining peace in the region, Eyre was still forced to continuously request additional supplies of flour and blankets to distribute to the Aborigines. Regardless of the stated desire of the government for Eyre to contact and maintain friendly relations with more tribes, he was consistently turned down in his requests for more goods, especially blankets.[38] This exemplifies the contradiction that existed with South Australia's rationing policies. The government desired that peace be maintained and the Aborigines "civilized" as quickly as possible, but it was unwilling to invest more money than the absolute minimum to achieve those goals.[39] As more Aboriginal tribes came into contact with white settlement, the same amount of goods had to be stretched to accommodate additional recipients. As a result, goods of increasingly inferior quality were sought for distribution to the Aborigines:

> I have in conjunction with Mr. Moorehouse made many inquiries in Adelaide and . . . we have inspected many samples of both blankets and rugs which may be purchased at a much lower rate than the estimated price. . . .
> [The distribution should] include Rugs—the latter being much cheaper than blankets and equally good for distribution among the more distant Natives.[40]

During 1842, in its first full year in operation, over 1,000 individuals from the Murray River area, 41 percent of whom were children, attended ration distributions held by Resident Magistrate John Edward Eyre at the Moorundie depot (see table 6-1). If the standard monthly issue of four pounds of flour per adult and two per child was maintained, approximately 3,466 pounds of flour was distributed. Additional amounts of flour, rice, tea, and tobacco distributed in return for labor and service to the government were not regularly recorded, making it difficult to determine the importance the additional foodstuffs had to Aboriginal subsistence at this early date. It certainly would have become increasingly more important as access to traditional food sources was restricted and native game was driven away by the altered landscape.

The average number of Aborigines receiving rations at the monthly issues increased steadily through the first half of the 1840s (see table 6-2). The average number of Aborigines receiving flour at the twelve monthly distributions in 1842 was 94. The following year the average increased to 136 for only ten issues. In 1844 the number again increased to an average of 171 Aborigines attending each of the nine distributions made that year. This early yearly increase was largely due to new tribes coming in from more distant locations, particularly as white settlement spread and native game was driven away.

Table 6-1. Aborigines Attending Monthly Issue of Flour at Moorundie, 1842

Date	Men	Women	Boys	Girls	Infants	Total
26 Jan.	37	41	26	20	6	130
25 Feb.	24	21	21	11	5	82
26 Mar.	14	20	15	9	3	61
25 Apr.	20	28	22	13	0	83
23 May	35	25	25	22	0	107
19 Jun.	60	45	57	25	4	191
22 Jul.	7	11	5	6	0	29
21 Aug.	—	—	—	—	—	[53]
20 Sep.	25	23	13	12	0	73
18 Oct.	37	35	31	14	0	117
18 Nov.	38	39	30	19	4	130
18 Dec.	31	34	27	16	5	113
Total	328	322	272	167	27	1116

Source: Edward J. Eyre to Colonial Secretary, February 7, 1842, reprinted in Eyre, *Report and Letters to Governor Grey from E. J. Eyre at Moorunde* (Adelaide: Sullivan's Cove, 1985), 52. Because August 1842 data is more general, it is not included in the yearly total.

While Moorundie successfully attracted Aborigines, they were still drawn into Adelaide for a variety of reasons, including curiosity and access to liquor and other stimulants. Eyre reported,

At Moorundie the monthly attendance of the Natives has comprised only those to the Northward of the station, the Natives living more Southerly having always gone to Adelaide by the route of Mt. Barker. During the greater part of the past year a considerable proportion even of our more immediate tribes here have also been absent in Adelaide and the numbers attending the monthly issues have consisted principally of the Natives of the river beyond the Great Bend.[41]

The continued migration into Adelaide became a problem for the colonial government. Citizens complained of poorly clothed Aborigines begging or stealing food. Humanitarians complained that Aboriginal contact with the lower classes of white society was retarding any progress toward "civilization." The government also had to deal with periodic clashes between Aboriginal groups meeting in the city, such as an 1849 skirmish between Aborigines from Encounter Bay and a group from the Moorundie area.[42]

Table 6-2. Average Yearly Attendance at Full-Moon Issues, Moorundie, 1841–1844

Year	Average Attendance	Number of Issues
1841	52	2
1842	94	12
1843	136	10
1844	171	9

Source: Edward J. Eyre, *Journals of the Expeditions of Discovery into Central Australia, and Overland from Adelaide to King Georges Sound in the Years 1840–1* (reprint Adelaide, SA: eBooks @ Adelaide, 2004), 192.

As the number of Aborigines assembling for monthly ration issues at Moorundie increased, it became necessary to adjust the method by which food was distributed. Rations were no longer distributed only at the full moon, which allowed for the extended travel time needed by many Aboriginal groups. Unfortunately, those rations issued at times other than the full moon were not necessarily included in the quarterly and yearly reports sent to the government in Adelaide, so the exact number coming in for rations at Moorundie can never be known. In 1843 the resident magistrate reported on two issues that necessitated this change in the method of distribution:

Natives began to assemble at these periodical musters in such very great numbers that I deemed it necessary to curtail in some way or other what would otherwise have formed a very heavy source of expense to the Government. . . . The Governor had given me instructions to use my influence in preventing the tribes of my neighborhood from visiting Adelaide where they were very troublesome to Europeans.[43]

The established rationing policy followed by Eyre was also affected by the increased pace of white settlement in and travel through the Murray River region, forcing larger numbers of Aborigines to come to Moorundie to receive flour each year.

By October 1844, when Eyre was replaced at Moorundie by W. Nation, the delicate balance of maintaining peace with the Aborigines through the distribution of rations was expected to become a much more difficult task. Nation's official instructions stipulated:

The aspect of affairs in the River Murray is daily undergoing considerable modifications. The length of time which has elapsed since the contest took place between the Natives and Police . . . a number of boys must be growing up, and rapidly replacing the men who fell in that encounter, and settlers are rapidly forming sheep and cattle stations, even at remote points upon the river . . . much reason to apprehend that disturbances between the Natives and the Settlers on the River Murray may shortly take place, and that such disturbances can only be avoided by the exercise of great activity and industry upon your part.[44]

Increasing tensions, however, made gaining and maintaining influence over the male elders of Aboriginal tribes in the area increasingly important. Resident Magistrate Nation recognized this necessity, and he used the issues of flour and especially blankets to encourage the continuation of friendly and peaceful relations:

I however succeeded in supplying a few of the old men from the distant tribes with a blanket each as they have generally . . . great influence among their people, and may thus be the cause of maintaining the friendly feeling which at present exists between the Europeans and the Natives.[45]

Still, the continued influence of elders (or "chiefs"), while useful for maintaining peaceful relations, was also recognized by government officials as a barrier to the "civilization" of the tribe. Eyre admitted that

> I cannot persuade myself, that any real or permanent good will ever be effected, until the influence exercised over the young by the adults be destroyed, and they are freed from the contagious effects of their example.[46]

This belief eventually prevailed over contradictory government policies and paved the way for removal of Aboriginal children from families to schools where they were taught English and "civilized" habits and expected to forget or reject their Native language and culture. Rather than using the threat of withholding rations to induce Aboriginal parents to give their children up to the schools, parents received extra rations and blankets as incentives. In terms of schooling in the nineteenth century, South Australia used a carrot instead of a stick.[47]

The numbers recorded for the second half of the 1840s fluctuate, possibly reflecting changing conditions in the area. The total number of Aborigines coming in to Moorundie for the monthly flour distributions in 1845 was 1,946, and from July to December the percentage of children decreased to 26 percent (see table 6-3). Although the all-Aborigine count represents an increase from the full count provided by Eyre for 1842, the average per issue for the year fell to 162 (down from the 171 for nine issues the previous year). This decrease could have several causes. It is possible that a number of Aboriginal tribes spent more time in Adelaide or other towns during that year, although the continued decline in numbers in subsequent years tends to rule out this possibility as a permanent situation. It is also possible that the Aboriginal population coming in to Moorundie was older or that parents hid children from authorities or that the European invasion was already having demographic effects on indigenous childbearing. It is also possible that several of the local tribes moved to areas that were more distant from the white settlements that were growing closer to Moorundie. However, the rapid growth of pastoral stations, which often outpaced the establishment of ration depots, and the strong recognition of territorial boundaries by the Aborigines tends to rule out this possible explanation.

The most likely cause of the decrease in the number of Aborigines re-

ceiving flour at Moorundie on the full moon from 1844 to 1845 is a gradual decrease in Aboriginal population as a whole. The data for the first four
months of 1846 continued the pattern of decreasing issues (see table 6-4).
Only 995 Aborigines came in from January through April in 1846, whereas in 1845 that same four-month period saw 1,041 people receiving flour.

Table 6-3. Aborigines Receiving Flour at the Monthly Issue,
January–December 1845

Month	Men	Women	Children	Total
January	—	—	—	179
February	—	—	—	113
March	—	—	—	346
April	—	—	—	403
May	—	—	—	104
June	—	—	—	191
July	103	90	61	254
August	21	30	40	91
September	10	16	15	41
December	101	81	42	224
Total				1946

Source: Resident Magistrate's Report (W. Nation acting), June 30, 1845, SRSA,
GRG 24/6/1845/752; and Nation to Colonial Secretary, July 25, 1845, September
19, 1845, December 29, 1845, SRSA, GRG 24/6/1845/894, GRG 24/6/1845/1151,
GRG 24/6/1844/1605.

Table 6-4. Aborigines Receiving Flour at the Monthly Issue,
January–April 1846

Month	Men	Women	Children	Total
January	60	46	17	123
February	231	183	190	604
March	46	51	37	134
April	53	46	35	134
Total	390	326	279	995

Source: W. Nation to Colonial Secretary, April 24, 1846, May 5, 1846, SRSA,
GRG 24/6/1846/236, GRG 24/6/1846/497.

Aside from observing gradual decreases in the number of Aborigines receiving rations at Moorundie after 1845, estimating the total Aboriginal population in the region at that time, and its subsequent decline, is a most difficult task. While it was fairly easy to estimate the Aboriginal population in the immediate area of Adelaide, as settlement spread into the outback and more tribes came into unfavorable contact with Europeans, population estimates became less reliable. Many Aboriginal groups traveled significant distances, and so may have been counted by more than one person or not have been accounted for at all. Other groups purposefully avoided contact with Europeans until pressed into the farthest corners of their territory.

Establishing the Aboriginal population before European colonization is extremely difficult, and the estimates vary widely. Historian Richard Broome believes there were approximately 300,000 Aborigines across all of Australia.[48] Other estimates of the precontact Aboriginal population run as high as 750,000.[49] Those numbers decreased rapidly within the first years of contact as new diseases affected the coastal tribes and then spread inland through existing trade networks. The Aboriginal population of South Australia followed a similar pattern. Broome estimates that in the settled regions of the colony, the Aboriginal population went from approximately 11,129 before contact to only 2,203 within twenty years.[50] By the turn of the twentieth century, many of the Aboriginal tribes encountered by the early settlers no longer existed. The primary cause of the population decline was disease, made worse by malnutrition caused by the loss of traditional homeland subsistence areas and replacement with the nutritionally poor ration diet.

In 1843 Moorundie Resident Magistrate Eyre estimated Aboriginal populations in regular contact with Europeans there as well as those who were not. He estimated that 300 Aborigines in the Moorundie area were in regular contact with the depot, while approximately 200 were not in regular contact.[51] His total estimate of the population encompassing an area of roughly eighty miles (130 km) around Adelaide was 1,600. By February 1848 Protector of the Aborigines Matthew Moorhouse reported the estimated Aboriginal population of the settled districts in South Australia (encompassing an area larger than that considered by Eyre) to be 3,680. On the River Murray, in the Moorundie area, the estimated population was 900, whereas five years earlier the estimate listed 500. Similarly Port

Lincoln increased from 400 to 600.[52] These increases are more significant when the high death rates of Aborigines in the immediate area of the coast are taken into consideration. The vast difference between the two population estimates, even though they are only separated by five years, is an indication of the difficulty the government had in accurately estimating indigenous populations.

Despite the increase in the estimated Aboriginal population in the colonized areas of South Australia from 1843 to 1848, the overall Aboriginal population was decreasing. This can be seen in the total number of people who received flour in the eleven-month period between May 1847 and March 1848 (see table 6-5). The number decreased by nearly 900, from 1,946 in 1845 to only 1,096 people in 1847–1848, averaging only 84 for the thirteen distributions made over that period. Children decreased to 14 percent of the population receiving rations. Even missing data for April, this represents a significant drop, in all likelihood reflecting the dropping total population.

Table 6-5. Aborigines Receiving Flour and Blankets, May 1847–March 1848[54]

Date	Men	Women	Boys	Girls	Total
24 May	88	81	15	16	200
30 Jun.	45	36	9	16	106
29 Jul.	16	13	1	1	31
30 Aug.	8	1	2	0	11
15 Sep.	32	25	12	9	78
24 Sep.	20	15	1	1	37
26 Oct.	12	17	4	5	38
2 Dec.	10	13	3	0	26
16 Dec.	46	0	0	0	46
24 Dec.	73	62	9	4	148
25 Jan.	80	54	12	4	150
21 Feb.	82	57	14	6	159
27 Mar.	36	26	3	1	66
Total	548	400	85	63	1096

Source: Reports by Commissioner of Police George Duchwood, included with Colonial Secretary to Commissioner of Police, April 20, 1847, SRSA, GRG 24/6/1848/1486

In 1849 the number who received flour at Moorundie rebounded slightly to 1,341 as did the percentage of children at 17 percent (see table 6-6). This may indicate a year of extreme hardship caused by drought, flood, or conflict, forcing Aborigines who did not regularly come to Moorundie to assemble there for the monthly flour distribution.

The numbers present for the distributions fluctuated according to jobs available in the area of the depot as well as any environmental factors, temporary or permanent, that disrupted normal subsistence. The fluctuating numbers of Aborigines coming in to Moorundie to receive flour each month made difficult the job of predicting the amount of stores necessary. Eyre recorded a steady increase in the average number of Aborigines receiving rations from 1841 through 1844. The averages, however, do not reflect the large numbers (as many as 500) at particular distributions who then left for Adelaide. Distributions such as these would have put a strain on the supplies stored at Moorundie. The averages also do not include those receiving rations at times other than the full moon.[53]

Table 6-6. Aborigines Receiving Flour and Blankets, January–December 1849

Date	Men	Women	Boys	Girls	Total
January	64	51	7	11	133
February	66	59	12	17	154
March	46	50	17	5	118
April	55	45	7	4	111
May	71	71	19	12	173
June	103	106	12	25	246
July	49	49	9	14	121
August	16	15	1	4	36
September	23	33	6	7	69
October	18	18	9	2	47
November	14	11	1	1	27
December	44	45	7	10	106
Total	569	553	107	112	1341

Source: Numerical Return of Natives to whom Flour and Blankets have been distributed at the Police Stations, January 1 to November 30, 1849, and December 1, 1849, to February 28, 1850, SRSA, GRG 24/6/1850/82.5.

The difficulty of transportation to the Moorundie depot, especially during the winter, also posed problems.[55] Estimates of goods needed to be made well in advance to allow time for the government to purchase and arrange for the shipment of ration goods. The inherent difficulties of the rationing system meant that there were periods of scarce supplies, which was not as pressing a problem during the early 1840s as later in the century when traditional sources were even more restricted. At times when the supply of flour was scarce, it was customary to supplement the rations with mutton.[56] However, this also posed a problem. The transportation of meat was even more difficult than flour because there was no practical way to keep it from spoiling. As pastoral stations moved closer to Moorundie, it was easier to get a supply of mutton when necessary, but only if the European station owner was willing to sell his sheep to the government for the benefit of the Aborigines. When the government inquired about the feasibility of substituting wheat when flour was unavailable, Sub-Protector George Mason noted that the Aborigines would not accept the wheat.[57]

The variable number of people receiving monthly rations also meant that on rare occasions a surplus of supplies was accumulated. Rather than store the extra ration supplies until they were needed, the government chose to offer the goods for sale to the public. Such an occasion occurred in October 1847 when 270 pounds of ration sugar, 45 pounds of ration tea, and 84 pounds of soap were offered for sale from Moorundie.[58]

The ration depot established at Moorundie was at least partially successful. While it could not entirely dissuade the Aborigines from traveling to Adelaide, it did succeed in maintaining peace between them and the settlers in the area. Even as the total Aboriginal population in South Australia declined, the monthly ration distributions at Moorundie drew in Aboriginal groups from increasingly farther away. In doing so, the government was able to establish a presence among an increasing number of Aboriginal nations, and it used that presence to try to influence and manipulate Aboriginal behavior and movement.

While the South Australian government hoped the distribution of rations at locations such as Moorundie would encourage the Aborigines to settle permanently in their home territories and not travel into Adelaide or other white settlements, congregating there in large numbers, its goal was never fully realized. Instead of transitioning into the settled farm laborers or rural workforce that the government envisioned, the Aborigines opted instead to include ration depots into their established seasonal migration patterns.

Edward John Eyre recorded a description of part of the Aborigines' seasonal gatherings in his "Manners and Customs of the Aborigines of Australia":

> At certain seasons of the year, usually in the spring or summer, when food is most abundant, several tribes meet together in each other's territory for the purpose of festivity or war, or to barter and exchange such food, clothing, implements, weapons, or other commodities as they respectively possess.[59]

As Moorundie and other depots became known and trusted sources of food, many of these gatherings revolved around these locations. After receiving subsistence at an outlying depot such as Moorundie for a season, the Aborigines often traveled into Adelaide or other towns to obtain more food and stimulants like alcohol and tobacco.

Aboriginal tribes often replaced traditionally gathered foods with rations because they required less effort to procure and prepare, which left more time for ceremonial and community gatherings. To take advantage of the different ration depots, tribes sometimes shifted the time and location of such gatherings. A similar process can be seen in geographer Richard Baker's study of Yanyuwas in coastal Northern Territory. Yanyuwas gradually "came in" to the inland town of Borroloola from their homes in the Sir Edward Pellew Islands, largely through the influence of rationing. Once larger numbers began settling in the Borroloola area, particularly tribal elders, others were attracted, and ceremonies that had once taken place in other locations were moved to where the people now gathered.[60]

In addition to the movement observed by Eyre, a distinct seasonal pattern can be seen in the monthly numbers recorded at Moorundie (see table 6-7 and figure 6-1). Based on the available records for the Moorundie ration depot, the average monthly attendance was highest from December to June. This incorporates the summer and fall months. The average lowers slightly in July and remains low from August to November, essentially from midwinter through spring. This drop probably indicates Aboriginal migrations from Moorundie into Adelaide or one of the other settlements.

It was during this season that a conflict between the Kaurnas, from the Adelaide Plains, and Aborigines from the Moorundie occurred in the Adelaide area.[61]

While there are probably a number of reasons the Aborigines from the Moorundie area chose to spend winter and spring away from the ration depot in the 1840s, availability of food may have been most prominent. Eyre and his successors repeatedly wrote of the difficulty in transporting goods to the depot, especially during the winter months of June, July, and August. If supplies of flour and other goods ran low during this time, it was unlikely the depot would receive more before late spring. It is not unreasonable to believe that, after having experienced this, the Aborigines would have preferred to spend those months in or near settlements like Adelaide, where there were more opportunities to obtain subsistence.

By the 1850s South Australian officials had begun to direct more attention to Aboriginal relations, particularly rationing.[62] Many missionaries and humanitarians in South Australia, as well as in Britain, began to worry about the pauperization of the Aborigines receiving rations. The Aborigines viewed the distribution of rations as part of their reciprocal relationship with the colonists—they were entitled to the food in exchange for their loss of land. Many humanitarians, however, believed that the "free" distribution of rations to the Aborigines was having a deleterious effect, causing them to live in idleness. The expansion of the pastoral industry into the bush provided a convenient solution to this problem.

South Australia's government decided that the best course of action was to encourage Aborigines to find work in the colonial pastoral industry, where they were paid primarily in rations. When private work was not available, the government often tried to arrange for Aborigines to gain jobs through the ration depots like Moorundie. A. W. Sturt noted:

> [W]ith a view to furnish the Aborigines with a profitable employment, suited to their habits, His Excellency wishes to ascertain from you whether you can procure a sufficient number of Natives willing to be engaged . . . to be paid daily or weekly to collect so much lumber or scrubwood as will amount to 80 tons per week.[63]

Table 6-7. Aborigines Receiving Monthly Rations, Moorundie,
1842, 1845–1850

Month	Average Number	Month	Average Number
January	134.6	July	108.75
February	217.3	August	47.75
March	145	September	73.75
April	178.4	October	67.3
May	150.4	November	78.5
June	190.2	December	165.75

Source: Compiled from the information in Tables 6-1, 6-3, 6-4, and 6-6, and "Protector's Report," *Adelaide Observer* (November 9, 1850): Supplement 1BC.

The availability of jobs for Aborigines in the Moorundie area became greater in 1852 as most of the European laborers migrated to the Victorian gold fields. Once their stockmen and other employees left, European station owners had little alternative other than to hire local Aborigines.[64] However, the new opportunities for work and the subsequent increase in rations were not an unmitigated success for Aborigines. The rations distributed by station managers were subject to the same problems of quality and quantity as those distributed at Moorundie. While the work allowed the Aborigines to continue a slightly altered form of traditional life, something much more difficult for those who found themselves on mission stations, the conditions did nothing to improve or even maintain the health of the tribes. The protector of Aborigines wrote:

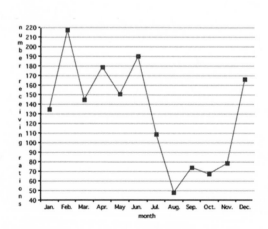

Figure 6-1. Average Monthly Attendance at Moorundie, 1842–1850.

In a slight degree they still continue to work for the squatters—
and although their labour is precarious and variable, yet, in the
absence of European labour, it is of some importance. It is melan-
choly, however, to observe that as civilization advances, and as the
country of the [A]borigines becomes more thickly populated by
Europeans, the numbers of the former decrease.[65]

As the potential of Aborigines receiving employment in the pastoral
industry around Moorundie increased, distributions from the government depot began to decrease. Station owners argued that if the government continued to gratuitously supply the Aborigines with food, there
was no inducement for them to labor on their pastoral runs. The South
Australian government, seeing an opportunity to decrease the amount of
revenue needed for the Aborigines Department, began to scale back on its
distributions. Beginning in 1853, regular subsistence was given only to the
old, infirm, orphans, and women with infants. Aboriginal men could only
receive rations either by laboring at the depot under the direction of the
resident magistrate or when there was not enough work to go around and
subsistence could not be gained through hunting or fishing.[66]

The increase of pastoral stations along the River Murray in the 1850s
also had a profound effect on the Moorundie ration depot and the people it
served. As more Aboriginal men (and some women) received their rations
through employment, the perceived need for the depot decreased. While
the reduced distributions from Moorundie continued for a few years, by
September 1856 the depot was closed, although it reopened temporarily
on a smaller scale a few years later, after an 1860 Select Committee investigation revealed the terrible starvation conditions many Aborigines
faced.[67]

The closing of Moorundie and the withdrawal of widespread regular
rationing in the settled districts of South Australia also marked a shift in
the focus of government policy. When Protector of the Aborigines Matthew Moorhouse resigned in 1856, the position was terminated, and control over Aboriginal Affairs was shifted to the Commissioner of Crown
Lands.[68] The colonial government, and most of its citizens, believed it was
only a matter of time before the Aborigines ceased to exist. They conclud-
ed that the only way for the people themselves to survive was for them to

give up their culture and language completely. This "dying race" theory, used in various colonial societies to rationalize indigenous policies, however, never came to fruition.

By 1857 the situation in which the Moorundie Aborigines, as well as other Aborigines in South Australia, found themselves was increasingly desperate. The withdrawal of regular rations from the depot resulted in heavier dependence on employment at pastoral stations, where rations were not always adequate to support a family, let alone a community, nor could everyone who needed employment find it. Station owners paid Aboriginal laborers for their work in rations and relied on government-subsidized distributions to maintain the remainder of the community on their lands. When these subsidized distributions did not meet the community's needs, the rations provided by those in employment were divided among the entire community. As a result, malnutrition and hunger remained a constant state among most Aboriginal nations. The situation became even more disastrous at the end of the 1850s as European workers began returning from the gold fields and fencing reduced the need for shepherds.[69] In the face of hunger and starvation, the Aborigines were at the mercy of station owners or were forced to travel to towns or the few remaining government depots, such as at Wellington to the south.

The increased malnutrition caused by the reduction of government rations had a debilitating effect on Aboriginal communities, further weakening their resistance to disease. The deteriorating situation in which the Aborigines found themselves led to an increase in begging and thefts of food from white settlements. In 1857 A. Whitefellow, a South Australian settler, asked:

> Is it supposed that the native does not regret the loss of his land, his game, his sport, and, aye, his freedom? . . . Can he visit once-loved spots endeared to him by many remembrances? No; it is fenced and grubbed, not a tree standing; and when its original owner presents himself at the back-door of its present occupier, petitioning for "bit of bread, me bery hungry," the chances are against his obtaining it—oftentimes refused with abuse, and frequently with threats.[70]

Although colonial officials took an interest in Aboriginal rationing in the early 1850s, the end of the decade was a period of extreme hardship for the Aborigines in South Australia. The 1860 report on the condition of the Aborigines by the Select Committee of the Legislative Council found that there was great suffering among the natives from the want of both food and clothing, that "disease prevailed to a fearful extent" during the previous winter, and that "the Government supplies at the depots were insufficient and irregular."[71]

Despite these dire circumstances, those in charge of issuing rations to the Aborigines in 1859 were ordered to give subsistence only to those unable to provide for themselves (elderly, infirm, orphans, and women with infants), and that none should be given to "able-bodied natives, if there is reason to believe they can get work or can obtain a subsistence by fishing or hunting."[72] Despite the admonition that those who could not find work be given rations, the South Australian Parliamentary debates in April 1861 indicated that many Aborigines were not receiving enough to survive:

> Deaths from starvation had actually occurred amongst some of these poor creatures, and there was no provision made for them beyond a mere subsidiary grant for a periodic distribution of a little flour and a few blankets.[73]

As white settlement expanded in the 1850s and 1860s, more government ration depots were established in the north and west of South Australia, and the systematic monthly issues, such as those made early at Moorundie, fell apart into an assortment of different amounts and times. In response to the inconsistency of ration distributions in the late 1850s, and the labor shortage created by the Victorian gold rush, the protector of the Aborigines established a new standard for rationing in 1863 consisting of 1 pound flour, 2 ounces sugar, and 0.5 ounce tea per diem.[74] The protector of Aborigines also specified issues to the old and infirm:

> I do not think it advisable to issue Rice as an ordinary article . . . but would use it rather as a Medical Comfort. When substituted for flour the allowance to be 1 lb. with 4 oz. of sugar. Authority should be given to purchase meat for the sick and infirm when required, and to provide in any serious case whatever is certified to be absolutely necessary by any qualified medical practitioner. The issues should be made daily whenever it is possible.[75]

While this new policy for rationing attempted to make allowances for

those who could not procure subsistence in any other way, the requirements necessary for a person to get a ration of meat were, at best, problematic. Especially for those depots at any distance from a town, finding
a "qualified medical practitioner" was difficult. While there were a few
doctors who traveled to the various ration depots and mission settlements, their small number and the distance between locations meant that
a great deal of time often passed between visits. Therefore, an Aborigine
who needed additional rations may have been forced to wait months for
the necessary medical approval, facing the prospect of starvation in the
meantime. The restriction of ration distributions to the sick and infirm
was also meant to encourage able-bodied Aborigines to find work on local
stations. Pastoralists offered good rations and occasionally wages for work
tending their sheep. This pattern only lasted until South Australians began
returning from the Victorian gold fields.[76]

Rationing at Moorundie greatly affected the Meru-speaking peoples
and their neighbors. Aboriginal tribes around Moorundie who came to
depend on rations as their primary means of subsistence faced malnutrition, starvation, and disease. The Aboriginal population of southern and
eastern South Australia continued to decrease throughout the eighteenth
century and did not begin to increase until the 1920s.[77] By that time, however, many of the tribes who had received the first rations at Moorundie
no longer existed, and those who did had no traditional community and
little left of their previous way of life and culture.

In addition to the physical problems brought on by rationing, South
Australia's policies began to break down traditional Aboriginal culture
and social structures. Ration depots were situated in such a way as to draw
Aboriginal groups away from white settlements. This sometimes forced
them out of their home territories, particularly those who resided close
to the coastline. Even when depots were established within their homelands, settlements and station owners often restricted Aboriginal access
to many important spiritual and cultural sites. Aboriginal culture and religion are closely tied to the land, so the loss of homelands to the invasion
of colonists had a profound effect. In the introduction to a series of Lander
Warlpiri, Northern Territory, women's stories, Petronella Vaarzon-Morel
observed,

> The spiritual benefits of obtaining food from the country are as
> important to people as the taste. The practice of hunting and gath-

ering is not just an economic activity but involves an embodied
relationship with the land. . . . It is a person's spiritual link with the
land that confers the rights to use the economic resources of, and
live on, that land.[78]

Not only did the Aborigines lose connections to the land itself, the subsequent alteration of their subsistence patterns meant that important food
ways and taboos were also lost or altered.

The very act of rationing also had a profound effect on Aboriginal life.
Hunting and gathering cultures are centered on the procurement of food.
The process, however, was more than just for subsistence. Through hunting, gathering, and fishing the Aborigines maintained their cultural and
spiritual connection to the land, as well as instilling traditional knowledge
in their children:

As children walked through the country with their parents, they
learnt how to recognize animal tracks and how to hunt. They came
to know the features of the landscape intimately and began learning . . . stories about life and the land. The social and economic
aspects of . . . society were thus integrated with religion in a very
personal way.[79]

Government rations provided an easy source for subsistence, particularly
as access to native goods was cut off. The gathering activities formerly
performed by women, supplying the bulk of the tribe's subsistence, were
made obsolete through European expansion and government rations, and
the position of women within Aboriginal society began to change. Wom-
en lost their position as primary "breadwinners" for their communities.
That position was transferred to men, particularly as they gained employment on pastoral stations. This change in the status of women within the
community was maintained as the Aborigines were forced more and more
to deal with and live in the world of the European colonists.

Aboriginal men, too, faced a change in their cultural and social roles
because of government rationing. While they became the primary breadwinners for their families within the European colonial system, they lost
their traditional social place. As ancient Aboriginal knowledge was lost
due to death, relocation, and European manipulation and intimidation,
the men to whom that knowledge would have passed lost that important
societal role. Government rationing and manipulation also altered the so-

cietal structures, weakening the power and influence of Aboriginal elders.

Despite all its efforts, however, the South Australian government did not completely succeed in its goals of changing Aboriginal culture or inducing the people to abandon their homeland travels. Rather than completely stop their traditional way of life, the Aborigines incorporated rations from the depots and pastoral stations into their established seasonal migration patterns.[80] They moved from ration depot to town as the seasonal availability of rations changed, taking advantage of abundance when it was there and positioning themselves in better locations when it was not.

The openness of the government ration depots in the 1840s and 1850s (not restricting Aborigines from leaving) and the pastoral stations afforded the Aborigines the opportunity to maintain some of their cultural and ceremonial life. Historian Robert Foster explains:

> The system that was put in place to accommodate an Aboriginal presence on pastoral lands, rather than accelerating the breakdown of Aboriginal traditional practices, provided the space in which they could be sustained. There is no question that Aboriginal traditional practices were changed by the presence of Europeans, and that certain practices were modified, or fell into disuse. . . . However, there is equally abundant evidence that Aboriginal people were able to accommodate those aspects of "modernity" that the pastoral industry brought in its train with traditional practices that predated its arrival.[81]

In those areas where the government was able to rely on the pastoral industry and continued native resources to help supplement rationing, the Aborigines were able to maintain some form of their traditional lives, although it placed them at the mercy of a great number of civilians who were generally more interested in their own benefit than in Aboriginal welfare. With the transfer of rationing from Moorundie primarily to pastoral stations, the government lost direct control over "civilization" efforts, and few pastoralists were concerned with the Christianization and education of their laborers or their families. The government, without supervision, merely hoped that the regular employment at the stations would eventually bring "civilization" to the Aborigines. Despite its attempts, however, the South Australian government was never successful in its attempt to assimilate or eradicate Aboriginal culture. Oral histories, music, culture, and some traditions remain. While much was lost under the pressures of European control, much still remains.

The same sort of freedom found at Moorundie and on the pastoral stations, however, was not possible for those tribes who found themselves surrounded by white settlement and who were forced onto restricted reserves and mission stations. Aborigines who found themselves at the missions throughout South Australia faced Europeans who were even more determined to eradicate completely their language, culture, society, and religion. A study of the Port McLeay Mission, especially in terms of rationing, will explore how South Australian policies were applied in this alternate setting.

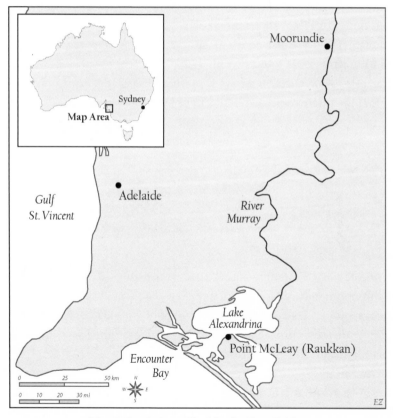

Map 2. South Australia. Map by Ezra Zeitler.

Chapter 7
Point McLeay Mission, 1859–1889

Government depots such as Moorundie were only one of several methods the South Australian government used to distribute rations. Missions, like Point McLeay, also played a crucial role in indigenous relations. While South Australia was founded with a supposedly more humanitarian ideal than other Australian colonies, the passing words and sentiments of those in London rarely translated into actions by colonial leaders or the settlers themselves. Local thoughts on the matter of Aboriginal rights can be seen in an 1838 editorial in the South Australian:

> We wish to see the Aborigines cared for and their rights guarded; but we do not see clearly that each such landed proprietor should be called upon to give so much per cent on the produce of the land as a donation to the natives, much less do we see that the natives can claim such a right.[1]

While there were South Australians who expressed genuine concern about Aboriginal welfare and attempted to aid them in some way, the vast majority of settlers believed Aborigines should be aided only if it did not come at their expense. This type of public opinion helped pave the way for a shift in South Australia's Aboriginal policies.

By the mid-nineteenth century the South Australian government's direct "humanitarian" approach to Aboriginal affairs began to wane. Rather than continuing positions such as the protector of the Aborigines (abolished in 1856), and operating dozens of ration depots throughout the settled districts, the government opted to encourage philanthropic and religious organizations to deal with Aboriginal physical and spiritual well-being. By handing the bulk of Aboriginal concerns over to groups funded largely through private donations, the South Australian government was able to cut drastically the moneys it spent on Aboriginal welfare while ensuring that the people continued on their path toward "civilization" and assimilation.

The government of South Australia was able to place much of the everyday governance of the Aborigines in the hands of private groups in part because of the increasing European population of the colony, particularly in the southern coastal regions. By the 1850s and 1860s many of the Aboriginal nations that had first met the European settlers, such as Kaurnas on the Adelaide Plains, were dead or too reduced in number to present a strong tribal entity. The drastic decrease in the Aboriginal population, through introduced diseases and violence, made it more possible for a few organizations to place the majority of Aborigines living in the heavily Europeanized districts into schools and missions. These institutions often housed Aborigines from a number of different tribes from the surrounding areas. In many ways, this made the assimilationist goals of the institution easier to achieve—it was much more difficult to maintain traditional cultural and social forms, such as food taboos and religious ceremonies, in that type of setting. The Point McLeay Mission, established on the banks of Lake Alexandrina in 1859, however, was unique in that the residents were nearly all members of the Ngarrindjeri. While they were not able to maintain their traditional culture as completely as some Aboriginal nations farther north who had less direct and sustained contact with Europeans, Ngarrindjeris were able to retain their tribal identity while many of their neighbors disappeared.

Ngarrindjeris[2] are one of the peoples of the Riverine region that stretched from New South Wales in the north, through Victoria, to western South Australia.[3] Occupying the coastal areas around the Lower Murray Lakes south past Naracoorte, Ngarrindjeris played a significant role in the early history of South Australia. The earliest European visitors to Australia, whalers and sealers, were frequent visitors to the coastal areas of the Ngarrindjeri that became South Australia looking for water, supplies, and women. Ngarrindjeris were also the focus of early missionary efforts like those of H. E. A. Meyer and Ridgeway Newland.[4] The area quickly attracted explorers and permanent settlers, forever altering Ngarrindjeri life.

Like many Aboriginal language groups, the Ngarrindjeris were composed of a number of individual, but connected, tribes that formed a loose confederation, including Ngangurugu, Ngaralta, Portaulun, Jarildekald, Ramindjeri, and Warki.[5] George Taplin, a missionary-teacher for the Aborigines' Friends' Association, identified eighteen Ngarrindjeri tribes whose names do not necessarily match the later forms found in the National Native Tribunal reports. Taplin's list included Ramindjeri, Tanganarin, Kondarlindjeri, Lungundi, Turarorn, Pankindjeri, Kanmerarorn, Kaikalabindjeri, Mungulindjeri, Rangulindjeri, Karatindjeri, Piltindjeri, Korowalle, Punguratpular, Welindjeri, Luthindjeri, Wunyakulde, and Ngrangatari.[6] Each tribe, or *lakalinyeri*, had its own territory and democratic government. For issues concerning the Ngarrindjeri as a whole, a combined *Tendi*, or government council, was held.[7] Despite the fact that the Tendi was a form of government easily identifiable to the European colonists, even those dealing with the Aboriginal confederation on an official level never recognized it. To do so would have invalidated the ideas underlying British colonization in Australia. Instead, while European officials tried to appease the traditional elders to maintain peaceful relations, they actively worked to undermine traditional Ngarrindjeri power structures by exerting their influence and control over the children of the tribe.

The abundant fish and game of the Lower Murray Lakes region allowed for a fairly dense settlement pattern of semi-permanent villages. These food resources in their waters and on their land are reflected in Ngarrindjeri food ways. Over twenty types of food were taboo for young men and boys, something that could not have been possible in an environment where food was scarcer. Taboo foods were generally easier to obtain, thus ensuring that they remained available for the elderly and those less able to hunt.[8] This same abundance, however, attracted European settlers to Ngarrindjeri lands. Their location at the mouth of the Murray River, and between the European settlements in South Australia and Victoria, also meant that Ngarrindjeri lands were frequently visited by sealers and traversed by explorers and travelers between the colonies.

Even before the influx of permanent European settlers, the Ngarrindjeri population was in decline. As with many Aboriginal nations, introduced diseases had devastating results on the population, often long before any sustained direct contact with Europeans was made. Prior to European settlement, sealers introduced venereal diseases that cut Aboriginal birth-rates. Other epidemic diseases followed Aboriginal trade routes. Smallpox in particular had devastating results. Contracted from explorers and sailors or through Aboriginal contacts and trade routes, smallpox epidemics killed large numbers of Ngarrindjeris in the early nineteenth century.[9] The reduced population numbers, and their cause, was not lost on the leaders of South Australia. George Taplin, who first built the mission at Point McLeay, wrote:

> They have a tradition that some sixty years ago a terrible disease came down the River Murray and carried off the natives by hundreds. This must have been smallpox, as many of the old people now have their faces pitted who suffered from the disease in childhood. The destruction of life was so great as to seriously diminish the tribes. The natives always represent that before this scourge arrived they were much more numerous. They say that so many died that they could not perform the usual funeral rites for the dead, but were compelled to bury them at once out of the way.[10]

According to Taplin's estimates, Ngarrindjeri population numbers began to stabilize to approximately 600 by the 1870s. A population study conducted by Fay Gale placed the Aboriginal population of Point McLeay at 271 people in 1870.[11] Whichever account is more accurate, this represents a significant drop, as much as twenty percent, from an estimated population of 3,000 in the 1840s and likely even larger before colonization.[12]

The massive loss of life caused by smallpox and other introduced diseases had a tremendous effect on all aspects of Ngarrindjeri life. Individuals had specific roles in the cultural, spiritual, and economic life of their communities. With the death of large numbers, as well as the illness of so many others, traditional life among the Ngarrindjeris began to change drastically. The most vulnerable to epic diseases were the very young and the very old. Elders died before they could properly pass on their cultural and religious knowledge. The Ngarrindjeris also lost many of the next generation, leaving fewer to continue the traditional knowledge and customs of their people. The invasion of European settlers continued the degradation of traditional Ngarrindjeri life.

By the time the Point McLeay mission was established in 1859, all the tribes of the Ngarrindjeri Tendi had been affected by the European invasion. The extent of that effect, however, depended greatly upon the territory of the individual tribes. Some, such as the Ramindjeris, had already lost much of their traditional tribal structure due to their proximity to larger European settlements. Other tribes whose territories were less settled by Europeans were able to maintain more independence and retain more of their tribal structures.[13] There were also differences in the condition of each tribe. Those who had adapted more to European ways or still had access to the natural resources of their territories were able to continue traditional lifeways. Those tribes who had been more dispossessed of their lands, such as the remnants of the Tanganarins, lived in destitution. Tribes closest to the mission, and who made up the majority of the core residents, fell in the middle of the spectrum in terms of both their physical well-being and their adaptation to European "civilization," as they were not completely dispossessed of their land. Still, their means of subsistence had been drastically reduced.[14]

By the early 1860s Ngarrindjeri means of subsistence had changed substantially. George Taplin, working with the Ngarrindjeris, wrote journal entries commenting on the *conconbah*, or kangaroo hunts, which became less successful as the growing cattle runs pushed out the larger game.[15] Despite the loss of a few sources of subsistence, even if they were major, the abundance of the Lower Murray region allowed the Ngarrindjeris to continue to survive. Hunger, dependence, and destitution did not become significant problems until European settlers restricted Native access to the land's resources or the people were completely dispossessed of their lands. Taplin observed,

> Their country has been occupied, and the game nearly exterminated. The reeds of which they used to build their houses, and the grass on which they used to sleep, have in many cases been made useless to them. The skins with which they used to make rugs, and the bark with which they made canoes, have been almost destroyed. Their present condition, therefore, is not to be taken as a fair representation of what they were in their natural state; and we must not expect to find amongst their broken and scattered tribes many of those good qualities which they used to possess as savages.[16]

It is the dispossession and European intrusion that created the dependence the Ngarrindjeris experienced by the mid-nineteenth century.

By the late 1850s the situation in which most Aboriginal nations in the settled districts of South Australia found themselves was desperate. Decimated by disease and violence, weakened by starvation, and dispossessed of their land, the Aborigines struggled to survive in the land that was once their home. The South Australian government abandoned the idea of immediate assimilation, most believing it was only a matter of time before the Aborigines died away, and a new policy was developed that focused more on segregation accompanied by gradual assimilation led by philanthropic groups, such as the Aborigines' Friends' Association.

Like many other humanitarian and philanthropic organizations of the time, the Aborigines' Friends' Association (AFA) was firmly rooted in Protestant Christian dogma. Their primary goal was the conversion of the Aborigines to Christianity, with assimilation of other aspects of European culture and concern for their physical well-being following thereafter. No thought or institutional concern was expressed over what the Aborigines themselves wanted, and so the success of the AFA, as well as the other philanthropic groups, in completing its mission depended greatly on the people who worked with the Aborigines on a daily basis rather than the organization as a whole.

Established in Adelaide in 1858, the Aborigines' Friends' Association was primarily concerned with "the moral, spiritual and physical well-being of the natives of this province."[17] To this end they requested that the government make the moneys designated for Aboriginal use directly available to the AFA to establish a school and mission near the town of Goolwa in Ngarrindjeri territory.[18] On March 16, 1859, the AFA appointed George Taplin, a young schoolteacher who had immigrated to Australia at age eighteen, to choose a location and commence building a school and mission for the Ngarrindjeris. He was also considered as a sort of sub-protector of Aborigines, responsible for obtaining and distributing government rations to Ngarrindjeris in his region.[19] In his role as missionary and intermediary between the Aborigines and the Europeans, both in the immediate area and in Adelaide, Taplin was in a position to have a singular influence over Ngarrindjeri adaptation to European civilization for the twenty years of his service, from 1859 to 1879.

George Taplin probably had the most profound influence with Ngarrindjeris of any European in the nineteenth century. While he is generally viewed historically to have been a true friend to the people and to
genuinely have cared about their well-being, there were points of tension
and conflict between the Ngarrindjeris and their missionary. Most of the
tensions arose from traditional customs that Taplin felt interfered with
conversion to Christianity. While he did little to try to change traditional
practices that he believed had nothing to do with religion and spirituality,
he fought vigorously against those that did, and thus he set himself against
the elders of the tribes. Taplin was most concerned with three main cate-
gories of customs: funeral rites, *narumbar* or initiation rites, and sorcery.[20]

The customs surrounding sorcery and superstitions were particularly
vexing to Taplin. Not only did these beliefs encourage the continuation
of practices he wished to abolish, they were the way that the Ngarrindjeri
elders maintained power and control over the nation. Food taboos were
an important element in Ngarrindjeri beliefs and helped guarantee that all
members of the nation had access to subsistence. The taboos also ensured
that sources of food that were easily procured would not be overhunted.
Even within the school dormitories, once they were constructed, Taplin
often found it difficult to sway the children from their beliefs. However, when he was able to convince them to ignore food taboos and prove
that the superstitious consequences would not happen, he was able to chip
away at the foundation of tribal power, as he remarked in his journal on
December 4:

> The schoolboys are glorying in the fact that they have done several
> things in defiance of native custom, and have received no harm.
> They have eaten wallaby, and yet have not turned grey. They have
> eaten tyere, and have no sore legs. They have cooked ngaikunde
> with palye, and yet there are plenty more.[21]

Although he proved the superstitions false, it did not invalidate the underlying reasons for the laws to exist. The taboos remained important in traditional subsistence patterns. However, the increasing European presence,
with rationing, dispossession, and dependence, lessened the importance
of maintaining the taboos. Moreover, in many instances the European
settlers or their livestock decimated the sources of food protected by the
taboos.

Taplin's first order of business in Ngarrindjeri territory was to select a location to build the mission and school. At the suggestion of George Mason, the sub-protector at Wellington (also in Ngarrindjeri territory), Taplin chose a traditional campsite on the banks of Lake Alexandrina called Raukkan.[22]

> I found the land was good, with plenty of limestone and sand, and good water. The landing place is good. In fact I find that this place possesses every requisite for the institution. . . . This is near the boundary of the tribes, is easily accessible, and is much frequented by the natives.[23]

The Lower Murray Lakes location also afforded the mission relatively easy communication with Adelaide. With the site chosen, Taplin proceeded to construct the main buildings: the mission house, chapel, and school.

The school built by Taplin was one of the focal points at Point McLeay. Unlike many of the other Aboriginal schools in South Australia, the school and its dormitories were located within the Raukkan community rather than some distance away. While Taplin shared the belief that the best hope for the assimilation of the Aborigines lay with the children, he reportedly did not condone the forced removal of children from their families. To this end, while students lived in dormitories, they were only admitted, according to Taplin, with approval from their parents. Contradicting this view, Ngarrindjeri oral histories indicate that the idea of parental consent for schooling may not have been as important to Taplin as has been recorded.[24] It was also reported in the *South Australia Register* that the windows of the dormitories were locked with iron bars to prevent parents from removing their children at night.[25]

Since the school was located on mission grounds, families could visit their children on a daily basis if they so desired. It is partially due to Taplin's system that the Point McLeay School was successful. After George Taplin's death in 1879, however, it became more difficult for the missionaries and schoolmasters to maintain attendance levels. In 1889 David Blackwell, who became superintendent at Point McLeay that year, wrote to Protector of Aborigines Edward Lee Hamilton,

> Several natives have removed their children from the school. I would like your opinion as to whether I may refuse them rations

until they return the children; otherwise there is good reason to fear that the school will [be] almost broken up.[26]

Another reason for the school's success was the Ngarrindjeris' perceptions of the value of European education. While the Ngarrindjeris believed that literacy in English was necessary to survive in their increasingly Europeanized world, the closeness of the children meant that many traditional customs could still be observed. The school was also a way for parents to ensure that their children received food on a daily basis, especially during periods of unemployment and low supplies due to financial difficulties.[27]

Although there was little opposition from the Ngarrindjeris to the establishment of the school and mission, this did not mean that they were willing to abandon their own culture for that of the intruders. Interestingly, there was significant opposition to the mission from European settlers in the surrounding area, who saw the mission and congregation of Aborigines in one location as a threat. Many believed that the proximity of an Aboriginal community would negatively impact the value of their lands. There may have also been a fear of the influence that perceived "savages" would have on their families. These Europeans, particularly the mission's immediate neighbors, often expressed their displeasure by refusing to sell meat to Taplin, starting rumors among the Ngarrindjeris, and attacking the AFA, the Point McLeay mission, and George Taplin personally. They had little concern for the larger Aboriginal policies of the state government.

The attacks on the AFA and George Taplin by neighboring pastoralists led the South Australian Parliament to appoint a special committee to investigate the condition of the Aborigines across the colony, especially the Ngarrindjeris, in 1860. The transcripts and report created by the Select Committee of the Legislative Council upon the Aborigines provide an invaluable source for the condition of the Ngarrindjeris at the start of the Point McLeay Mission. Investigators determined that

> contact with Europeans has so changed their habits that they now, in a great measure, depend upon the scanty dole of blankets issued by the Government—which supplies, it appears from evidence, have been most irregular.[28]

It was an established fact that Ngarrindjeri population numbers and birthrates, like those of all Aborigines, had been declining since the founding of the colony. The committee reported that the health of the Aborigines in South Australia had been adversely affected by venereal disease, loss of access to food and medicine, adoption of secondhand European clothing, and, most importantly, the indifference of the colonial government to their suffering.[29]

The findings of the Select Committee seemed to support the popular idea of the time that the Aborigines were a dying race. This belief was used to rationalize the government's lack of attention to Aboriginal welfare in the 1850s and 1860s when, despite widespread hunger and illness, nothing was done to try to fix the problem. This mindset was also shared by many of the philanthropists and missionaries who professed concern for the Native peoples of South Australia, when in fact most cared more about the Aborigines' "spiritual salvation" than their health and physical well-being. Bishop Augustus Short commented,

> I do not think it unadvisable to Christianize them; for I would rather they died as Christians than drag out a miserable existence as heathens. I believe that the race will disappear either way.[30]

Even Taplin, who pointed out that the Ngarrindjeri population on the mission was much more stable than the Aboriginal population in general and who evidenced more concern for their well-being than most Europeans, recorded similar sentiments in his journal when many of his early converts, such as David (son of Pullume), Isaac Waukerri, James Jackson, Allan Jamblyn, and Teenminnie (wife of Pelican) died early deaths.[31]

> It is strange but true that all those natives who have exhibited the most hopeful signs of piety have died. And yet is it not wonderful that in a dying race like this, many should be found who in the general sinking into death, should grasp the cross of Jesus when offered to them.[32]

Despite the desires of the Aborigines' Friends' Association, the Point McLeay Mission was never able to become a self-sustaining enterprise. Financial support for the mission was difficult for Taplin to come by. The government in Adelaide rarely provided an adequate amount of financial support. Other sources of funding, including money from AFA membership dues and public collections, provided little more.[33] In spite of Taplin's frugality in operating Point McLeay, there was often not enough to build and maintain a solid fiscal base for the mission and school. In several instances there was no money to pay laborers to construct or maintain mission buildings, and salaries sometimes could not be paid on time. Supplies such as rations and clothing were also occasionally scarce.

Taplin made several attempts to create a stable financial base not only for the mission, but for Ngarrindjeris as well. The mission barely had enough acreage to make a successful single-family farm, let alone be large enough to support a community of approximately three hundred. While the mission's original 268 acres were rich in natural resources, they were not ideal for European-style agriculture. Even when an additional 250 acres were added in 1865 and 212 acres in 1868, the farm was still unable to support the mission's population. While some Ngarrindjeris were interested in establishing their own small farms, they were reluctant to do so because the AFA only had a twenty-one-year lease on the land at Point McLeay.[34] Few were willing to labor to establish themselves when there was no guarantee they would be able to remain on the land.[35]

Taplin was also unable to transform Ngarrindjeri subsistence fishing into a profitable business. In the time before refrigeration, it was difficult to store and transport the fish that were caught. He found it hard to identify middlemen willing to offer the Ngarrindjeri a fair price for their catch.[36] He was also unable to capitalize on the grazing land, as the AFA did not have the finances to purchase sheep to create a flock for the mission. There were also attempts to create other industries on the mission and to train Ngarrindjeris in different skills such as boot-making, butchering, carpentry, and horticulture, but the financial backing was never enough to make the programs truly successful, leaving the people dependent on far-flung seasonal work and paltry rations.[37]

Finding employment was important to both the Ngarrindjeris and Taplin, but for different reasons. Taplin and other European humanitarians saw the Aborigines entering the workforce as an indication of their assimilation and, in particular, their acceptance of the Protestant work ethic and the tenets of Christianity. The Ngarrindjeris, however, had their own reasons for seeking employment. They recognized that in order to survive in their new European-dominated world and to escape destitution and dependency on government and mission rationing, they needed to enter the colonial economy.[38] Unfortunately, finding employment was always a difficult proposition, even with Taplin's efforts. Seasonal work in farming and pastoral industries was the most available to the Ngarrindjeris, but they presented significant problems as well. Available jobs were often far from the mission settlement, requiring significant travel. In addition, part of the pay for the jobs was usually in rations, and, of course, the work was short-lived.[39]

Unfortunately, even seasonal employment for the Ngarrindjeris was fleeting. As the European population in the colony grew and was more willing to take on seasonal jobs, the Aborigines were increasingly pushed out of their positions. The development of mechanical harvesters and other technological innovations also took jobs from the hands of the Ngarrindjeris, leaving them with fewer options to ensure their subsistence. Unemployment and their increased dependence on rations also had a profound effect on Ngarrindjeri health and physical well-being, despite the efforts of Taplin and his peers.

While the population numbers and health of the Ngarrindjeris, and the Aborigines in general, was declining in the late nineteenth century, the twenty-year administration of George Taplin at Point McLeay broke from this pattern. During this period the mission's population remained fairly stable. However, while mortality rates at Raukkan did not reach those of the Ngarrindjeris living elsewhere, there remained constant and chronic health issues. Despite the introduction of regular vaccinations in 1863, mortality rates remained high, with annual infant mortality rates reaching as high as 75 percent. Yearly epidemics of whooping cough, influenza, and lake fever took their toll, especially on the elderly and in times of extreme deprivation and hunger.[40]

Many whites believed that it was the transition from traditional life to a European lifestyle that caused the greatest health problems for the Aborigines. Poorly built cottages and shacks offered less shelter than traditionally constructed *wurleys*. The adoption of donated and discarded European clothing, without proper washing facilities, was also a health problem.[41] Perhaps the most critical issue, however, was the change in diet. While the Ngarrindjeris' traditional diet was varied and highly nutritious, the European ration diet was far from sound. Consisting largely of bread and meat, with supplemental amounts of flour, rice, sugar, and tea (often of poor quality), the ration diet left the Aborigines in a nutritionally weakened state, making them more susceptible to the problems brought on by poor housing and clothing. While those who completely adopted European culture and those who remained as close to traditional ways as possible had the fewest problems, those who were trapped in the middle of the two worlds had the most difficult time.[42]

In their role as missionaries to the Natives and de facto sub-protectors to the Ngarrindjeris, Taplin and his successors were responsible for the people's physical well-being, including the provision of rations. While there were occasions when all Ngarrindjeris at the Point McLeay Mission received rations, more often they were distributed only to the ill, the elderly, and families with small children who had no other means of subsistence. Children attending the school and living in the dormitories also received daily meals. The effect of the imposed daily meal schedule on those living in the dormitories was significant. Paul Kropinyeri recalled his experience from a later time:

> Then I had the shock of starting to live by time. . . . Before, it was if you're hungry you eat, if you're not you don't, if you're sleepy you sleep, if you feel good you do what you feel like doing. Then all of a sudden you come into a world where you're controlled by the clock. Maybe you're not hungry when you wake up but you've got to eat your breakfast. Then at ten o'clock you're hungry but you can't eat anything until twelve. Then you gobble your lunch because you're starving and by two o'clock you're hungry again, but you can't have anything until six o'clock. You do get used to it, but it affected me, living by time.[43]

The shock of adapting to a life lived by the clock and a set schedule must have been just as drastic for children in the late nineteenth century.

Taplin, and the other missionaries at Point McLeay, used the distribution of rations to encourage certain behaviors from the Ngarrindjeris residing in both the mission village and the surrounding camps.[44] George Taplin treated the rations and supplies for those residing in the two areas very differently. Those in the camps were expected to find much of their subsistence on their own through hunting and fishing. They were also infrequently given bulk rations. Those living in the cottages of the mission village were occasionally given afternoon teas and gifted with prepared meals. Historian Cathy Hayles suggests two possible interpretations of Taplin's intentions with the rationing distinctions: he may have viewed those in the camps as living in a different world from those in the village, or more likely, he could have been using the better rations as an incentive for the Ngarrindjeris to move into the village and adopt a more Europeanized lifestyle.[45]

The acquisition of rations and other supplies proved to be a continual problem for those at the Point McLeay Mission. Often, there was little money available to purchase needed supplies, and the South Australian government was often lax in sending the necessary rations to the mission.[46] Taplin frequently wrote in his journal of the problems he had securing the rations and supplies needed at the mission. In November 1859 he recorded, "I am out of flour. The natives are all very hungary [sic]. I scarcely know what to do with them. The Government are going to send me half a ton."[47] Supplies were still a problem in May 1861:

> No blankets have arrived yet, and they are suffering miserably from cold. No School clothes have arrived yet, and so my school continues miserably thin, and those children which I have are suffering miserably from cold.[48]

Even when supplies were available, their transportation from Adelaide could be problematic. While transportation across the lakes and waterways was easier than going over land, frequent violent storms and poor ships made crossings difficult and often dangerous. Taplin often recorded problems transporting rations because of the unpredictable and hazardous weather on the lakes. In May 1861 a storm prevented the arrival of desperately needed supplies for several days: "The gale still continues and the natives begin to be in distress for food."[49] In addition to preventing the transportation of rations, unexpected storms on Lake Alexandrina occasionally damaged the supplies: "Boat returned last night, almost swamped in a gale on the lake, with the stay broken and the rudder nearly wrenched off. Had a terrible job to get the flour out. It was very wet."[50]

Rationing also created other problems for Taplin. He, like many other humanitarians of his time, believed that the Aborigines were lazy and that the process of rationing was only going to encourage that undesired trait among his charges. While there were no laws or regulations that required work in exchange for rations, much effort was made to avoid what he termed the "pauperization" of the Aborigines. In January 1867 E. B. Scott, the acting South Australia protector of Aborigines, wrote to Taplin,

> [I] regret very much to hear that there are a few Natives in your neighbourhood who refuse to work; but as this is a common occurrence in all parts of this and the other colonies, especially when they can obtain food at the hands of the Government without giving an equivalent in labor I am not at all surprised, of course *you* are aware that there is no *law* to make the Aborigines work against their will . . . but to discourage idleness I should as an Issuer of Stores guard against giving rations to the able bodied.[51]

In order to avoid this "pauperization" of the Ngarrindjeris on the mission, Taplin believed he should only distribute rations to children at the school, the ill, and the elderly, forcing those he deemed physically able to look for employment to survive.[52] Taplin also stopped distributions when he felt the Ngarrindjeris were becoming lazy.

> Today I cannot get a servant altho there are plenty of women who can come but won't because they are so lazy. So I have stopped the Government rations, for I did not think it right to keep them in laziness.[53]

This system left Taplin with the problem of overwhelming unemployment. With the mission farm unable to support the Ngarrindjeri population, and the industries Taplin attempted to start never reaching fruition, it was difficult for all who needed employment to find jobs. Taplin was able to employ some of the mission residents for things such as carpentry, constructing fences, and gardening, for which they were paid in rations and a small amount of money.[54] Despite his efforts, however, rationing and ensuring an adequate food supply were nearly constant problems for the Point McLeay Mission and its residents.

The South Australian government, the AFA, and the Point McLeay missionaries were also concerned about the Ngarrindjeris' perception and expectations of rationing. While a few colonists and humanitarians suggested that European settlers and their government should take responsibility for the subsistence of peoples who had been forcibly dispossessed of their lands, that stance never had wide support, particularly when it would have come at the expense of colonial expansion. Many Aborigines, including the Ngarrindjeris, however, believed that rationing was part of their rights. Based on Aboriginal customs of reciprocity, since white settlers had taken their land and means of subsistence from them, it was considered just for those same settlers to help replace that loss.[55] In March 1860 Taplin recorded the sentiments of the Ngarrindjeris at the mission concerning rationing: "They began to think it their right to be given rations and were often most rude and ungovernable when this right was refused them."[56]

The differences in the perception and understandings of the rationing process between settlers and Ngarrindjeris served to heighten tensions. The Ngarrindjeris viewed rations as their right in exchange for their loss of territory. Taplin and his successors viewed rationing as an encouragement to adopt Christianity and European habits. It was a way to force culture change, weaken the power of tribal elders, and exert control over Aboriginal behavior and migration. The missionaries also viewed rationing as a temporary crutch for the Aborigines as they made a complete transition into the European system, not as a right the Aborigines had gained in response to the loss of their land and subsistence.

Ngarrindjeri dependence on rations at the Point McLeay Mission fluctuated depending on the immediate circumstances, particularly in relation to the seasons. During periods of drought, flood, and bad harvests, their dependence on government rations increased. At times when seasonal employment was abundant, the numbers of Ngarrindjeris collecting rations at the mission decreased. The nature of the work, however, meant that it was difficult for the Ngarrindjeris to remain independent from the rationing system for extended periods of time. The precise composition of the rations and the frequency of their distribution greatly influenced Ngarrindjeri life and health. An examination of the rations in 1883 and 1884, the most complete records extant for the mission, will reveal how actual distributions differed from stated policy and the impact of rationing on the people themselves.

The reported standard government rations distributed to adult Aborigines in the 1880s included seven pounds of flour, fourteen ounces of sugar, three ounces of tea, a half stick of tobacco, a half pound of soap, and occasional small amounts of rice or sago, a starch made from the pith of palm trees.[57] Rations distributed at the mission in 1883 and 1884, however, show a slight difference from the recorded standard government distributions during the superintendency of Frederick Taplin.[58] Taplin distributed daily amounts of bread and meat, as well as weekly amounts of flour, sugar, rice, fruit, and tea. Rations were distributed to family groups (except when the person had no family), and it was left to families to divide the food among themselves.[59]

During the final six months of 1883, with the exception of September, rations were distributed to fourteen or fifteen families, generally consisting of two to three named individuals (adults) and up to three unnamed children. In September only nine family units received rations. Children and adults living and receiving food in the dormitories were not included in the daily ration reports with the others. They received daily meals rather than daily and weekly rations. The total number of adults receiving rations during this period ranged from twenty in September to thirty-six in November. The number of children listed for those families ranged from twelve to twenty. An average of forty-six people, adults and children, received rations each month.[60]

The Ngarrindjeris at Point McLeay in 1883 and 1884 received loaves of bread and portions of meat, either beef or mutton, on a daily basis (see table 7-1). From July through December 1883 between 25.5 and 43 loaves of bread were distributed each month. The supply of bread appears to have been rather steady during this period as the amount distributed corresponded to the number of people receiving rations in any particular month. The amount of meat distributed ranged from fifteen pounds to thirty pounds total per month. Unlike the bread supply, however, the amount of meat distributed did not always increase when the number of people receiving rations grew. In November 1883, when the number of Ngarrindjeris receiving rations was highest, only fifteen pounds of meat were distributed. It was recorded that during George Taplin's time as missionary at Point McLeay neighboring pastoral stations often refused to sell meat to the mission. While the missionaries at Point McLeay following the death of George Taplin kept no journals, it is possible that the problem continued at least sporadically as conflicts flared between pastoralists and the mission.

Table 7-1. Daily Rations, Point McLeay Mission, July–December 1883

Month	Adults	Children	Bread (loaves/diem)	Meat (lb./diem)
July	33	16	37.5	29
August	33	18	38	30
September	20	12	25.5	19
October	29	12	33	22.5
November	36	20	43	15
December	32	18	39	30
Total	183	96	216	175.5

Source: Compiled from Point McLeay Mission Station Daily Ration Book, July 1–December 31, 1883, Mortlock Library of South Australia, State Library of South Australia, Adelaide, SRG 698/2.

Other rations at the Point McLeay Mission were distributed on a weekly, relatively steady basis (see table 7-2). Flour ranged from thirty-eight pounds per week in September to fifty-seven pounds per week in July and August. Sugar ranged from September's fifty-two pounds to August and December's seventy-eight. Ten to twenty-eight pounds of rice and 104 to 156.5 ounces of tea were distributed during the last six months of 1883. The fruit ration for this period was much less. No fruit was included for July or August during the Australian winter. Per week, only five pounds of fruit were distributed in September, seven pounds in October and November, and fourteen pounds in December.

Table 7-2. Weekly Rations, Point McLeay Mission, July–December 1883

Month	Adults	Children	Flour (lb.)	Sugar (lb.)	Rice (lb.)	Fruit (lb.)	Tea (oz.)
July	33	16	57	75	18	0	150
August	33	18	57	78	16	0	156
September	20	12	38	52	10	5	104
October	29	12	47	67	13	7	134
November	36	20	46	74	13	7	125.5
December	32	18	56	78	28	14	156.5
Total	183	96	301	424	98	33	826

Source: Compiled from Point McLeay Mission Station Daily Ration Book, July 1–December 31, 1883, Mortlock Library of South Australia, State Library of South Australia, Adelaide, SRG 698/2.

While each family determined how the rations were divided among themselves, an examination of the average rations that each individual received per day can be informative (see table 7-3). The rations offered at Point McLeay were more extensive than those distributed earlier at Moorundie and at stations further away from the settled districts of the colony. The more extensive rationing was necessary for the Ngarrindjeris to survive surrounded by white pastoralists and nearly completely dispossessed of their land, particularly for those who could not secure seasonal employment. Minimal, if any, hunting and gathering could occur. The average daily bread rations for the final six months of 1883 were approximately three-quarters of a loaf per person. The meat rations averaged half a pound per person per day, with the lowest amount (0.268 pound) distributed in November when the number of Ngarrindjeris receiving rations was at the highest. Despite the drop in the availability of the meat ration, none of the other ration amounts were increased to compensate for the loss of subsistence.

Table 7-3. Average Daily Rations per Person,
Point McLeay Mission, July–December 1883

Month	# of People	Bread (loaves)	Meat (lb.)	Flour (lb.)	Sugar (lb.)	Rice (lb.)	Fruit (lb.)	Tea (oz.)
July	49	0.77	0.59	0.17	0.22	0.05	0	0.44
Aug.	51	0.75	0.59	0.16	0.22	0.05	0	0.44
Sep.	32	0.8	0.59	0.17	0.23	0.05	0.02	0.46
Oct.	41	0.81	0.55	0.16	0.23	0.05	0.02	0.47
Nov.	56	0.78	0.27	0.12	0.19	0.03	0.02	0.32
Dec.	50	0.78	0.6	0.16	0.22	0.08	0.04	0.45
Total	279	0.77	0.52	0.15	0.22	0.05	0.03	0.42
Standard Ration		N/A	N/A	1	0.13	a little	N/A	0.43

Source: Compiled from Point McLeay Mission Station Daily Ration Book, July 1–December 31, 1883, Mortlock Library of South Australia, State Library of South Australia, Adelaide, SRG 698/2.

The average daily personal rations of flour, sugar, rice, and tea for the last half of 1883 remained fairly consistent, with the exception of November when the amounts for all the rations dropped. The daily ration of flour ranged from 0.117 pounds in November to 0.170 pounds in September. The sugar ration averaged 0.217 pounds per-person/per-day. The amount of rice included in the rations was small, averaging only 0.05 pounds per-person/per-day. The small amount of rice included in the rations, when combined with both the amount of bread and flour distributed, indicates that it was considered more a supplement than a staple, though it was apparently better accepted by the Ngarrindjeris at this point than earlier distributions in Adelaide had been. The amount of tea distributed averaged approximately 0.423 ounces per day from July to December 1883. The per-person/per-day fruit ration was extremely low, averaging only 0.026 pounds for the four months that it was included in the distribution.

The demographics of Ngarrindjeris receiving rations at the Point McLeay Mission from January through September 1884 are similar to those from the previous year. An average of twelve family units received rations monthly. An average of twenty-six adults and fourteen children were on the ration sheets for the first nine months of 1884.[61] As with the previous year, September saw the fewest number of Ngarrindjeris receiving rations. This probably indicates the month during which it was easiest for the Aborigines in the Lower Murray Lakes region to obtain seasonal work.

Rations distributed from January through March 1884 continued the patterns established in the previous year (see tables 7-4 and 7-5). Between thirty-two and thirty-eight loaves of bread were distributed daily to forty-one to forty-seven Ngarrindjeris. The daily meat ration ranged from twenty-four pounds to almost thirty pounds. The weekly rations of flour, sugar, rice, and tea were also comparable to those from the previous year. Over the first three months of the year, an average of 51.3 pounds of flour, 67.7 pounds of sugar, 22.5 pounds of rice, and 130.3 ounces of tea were distributed monthly. The fruit ration increased from the previous year, ranging from ten to fourteen pounds per month. Despite the increase, however, fruit remained the smallest component of the rations.

Table 7-4. Daily Rations, Point McLeay Mission, January–March 1884

Month	Adults	Children	Bread	Meat
			(loaves/diem)	(lb./diem)
January	30	17	37.5	29.5
February	29	13	31.5	24.5
March	27	14	32.5	25
Total	86	44	101.5	79

Source: Point McLeay Mission Station Daily Ration Book, January 1–March 31, 1884, Mortlock Library of South Australia, State Library of South Australia, Adelaide, SRG 698/2.

Table 7-5. Weekly Rations, Point McLeay Mission, January–March 1884

Month	Adults	Children	Flour (lb.)	Sugar (lb.)	Rice (lb.)	Fruit (lb.)	Tea (oz.)
January	30	17	56	75	28	14	150
February	29	13	51	63	21.5	10	126
March	27	14	47	65	18	10	115
Total	86	44	154	203	67.5	34	391

Source: Point McLeay Mission Station Daily Ration Book, January 1–March 31, 1884, Mortlock Library of South Australia, State Library of South Australia, Adelaide, SRG 698/2.

The average daily rations per person for January through March of 1884 were similar to those of the previous six months (see table 7-6). Each Ngarrindjeri received an average of 0.781 loaves of bread and 0.608 pounds of meat per day. The daily portions of flour, sugar, rice, and fruit remained small supplements to the bread and meat. The daily tea ration remained fairly steady at a little less than one-half of a ounce per person.

The established distribution pattern continued from April through June 1884, though the total number of Ngarrindjeris receiving the rations declined. Between twenty-eight and thirty-three loaves of bread and twenty-one to twenty-two pounds of meat were distributed daily (see table 7-7). The foodstuffs distributed on a weekly basis also remained fairly steady, as supplements (see table 7-8). An average of 47.7 pounds of flour and 60.3 pounds of sugar was distributed each month. Only an average of 14.7 pounds of rice was distributed during that same period. The fruit ration, again very small, had dipped by two pounds in May.

The average personal daily rations at Point McLeay Mission from April through June 1884 were similar to those from the previous months, though the amounts did decrease slightly (see table 7-9). An average of forty-one people received rations each month. Each received nearly three-quarters of a loaf of bread and slightly more than one-half pound of meat daily. The flour ration averaged 0.166 pounds per person per day. The average daily sugar ration was 0.21 pounds. The average daily fruit ration remained small but steady, despite the onset of winter.

Table 7-6. Average Daily Rations per Person, Point McLeay Mission,
January–March 1884

Month	# of People	Bread (loaves)	Meat (lb.)	Flour (lb.)	Sugar (lb.)	Rice (lb.)	Fruit (lb.)	Tea (oz.)
January	47	0.8	0.63	0.17	0.23	0.09	0.04	0.46
February	42	0.75	0.58	0.17	0.21	0.07	0.03	0.43
March	41	0.79	0.61	0.16	0.23	0.07	0.04	0.43
Total	130	0.78	0.61	0.17	0.22	0.07	0.04	0.43
Standard Ration	N/A	N/A	1	0.13	little	N/A	0.43

Source: Compiled from Point McLeay Mission Station Daily Ration Book,
January 1–March 31, 1884, Mortlock Library of South Australia, State Library of
South Australia, Adelaide, SRG 698/2.

Table 7-7. Daily Rations, Point McLeay Mission, April–June 1884

Month	Adults	Children	Bread (loaves/diem)	Meat (lb./diem)
April	26	13	30.5	22.5
May	23	16	28	21.5
June	27	18	33	22
Total	76	47	91.5	66

Source: Point McLeay Mission Station Daily Ration Book, April 1–June 30, 1884,
Mortlock Library of South Australia, State Library of South Australia, Adelaide,
SRG 698/2.

Table 7-8. Weekly Rations, Point McLeay Mission, April–June 1884

Month	Adults	Children	Flour (lb.)	Sugar (lb.)	Rice (lb.)	Fruit (lb.)	Tea (oz.)
January	30	17	56	75	28	14	150
February	29	13	51	63	21.5	10	126
March	27	14	47	65	18	10	115
Total	86	44	154	203	67.5	34	391

Source: Point McLeay Mission Station Daily Ration Book, April 1–June 30, 1884,
Mortlock Library of South Australia, State Library of South Australia, Adelaide,
SRG 698/2.

Table 7-9. Average Daily Rations per Person, Point McLeay Mission,
April–June 1884

Month	# of People	Bread (loaves)	Meat (lb.)	Flour (lb.)	Sugar (lb.)	Rice (lb.)	Fruit (lb.)	Tea (oz.)
April	39	0.78	0.58	0.18	0.22	0.06	0.04	0.45
May	39	0.72	0.55	0.16	0.21	0.05	0.03	0.41
June	45	0.73	0.49	0.49	0.2	0.04	0.04	0.41
Total	123	0.74	0.54	0.54	0.21	0.05	0.04	0.42
Standard Ration	N/A	N/A	1	0.13	N/A	N/A	0.43

Source: Compiled from Point McLeay Mission Station Daily Ration Book,
April 1–June 30, 1884, Mortlock Library of South Australia, State Library of
South Australia, Adelaide, SRG 698/2.

July, August, and September of 1884 continued the same patterns from
the previous year. As in 1883, the number of Ngarrindjeris receiving rations was lowest in September, indicating that there was more opportunity
for seasonal employment. It is also possible that the availability of rations
was low at the end of the winter and that many Ngarrindjeris sought subsistence away from the mission station. The wool-washing season began in
September and continued for several months.[62] As this was a major source
of seasonal employment for the Ngarrindjeris, it supports the idea that
when employment was available at least some mission residents preferred
traveling rather than remaining at the mission collecting government rations. The amount of food distributed remained comparable to the previous months, with an average of twenty-nine loaves of bread and twenty
pounds of meat distributed daily to the mission's ration-receiving population.[63] The weekly ration distributions also remained comparable to the
previous year. Between July and September 1884 a total of 130 pounds of
flour, 174 pounds of sugar, 42 pounds of rice, 26 pounds of fruit, and 348
ounces of tea were distributed to 113 Ngarrindjeris.[64] The average daily
rations per person from July through September 1884 increased slightly
from the previous three months but remained similar to earlier in the year
(see table 7-10). The people collecting rations during this period received
an average of 0.774 loaves of bread, 0.54 pounds of meat, 0.164 pounds of
flour, 0.22 pounds of sugar, 0.053 pounds of rice, 0.033 pounds of fruit,
and 0.44 ounces of tea daily. This is a decrease in the average daily rations

of most goods that a person received from the same period in 1883. The rations of bread, rice, and fruit increased slightly while rations of meat, flour, sugar, fruit, and tea decreased by a small amount. The difference, however, was small and probably indicated a slight decrease in the available supplies rather than any change in rationing procedures.

Table 7-10. Average Daily Rations per Person, Point McLeay Mission,
July–September 1884

Month	# of People	Bread (loaves)	Meat (lb.)	Flour (lb.)	Sugar (lb.)	Rice (lb.)	Fruit (lb.)	Tea (oz.)
July	40	0.75	0.55	0.17	0.21	0.05	0.04	0.43
Aug.	47	0.79	0.51	0.16	0.23	0.06	0.03	0.45
Sep.	26	0.79	0.58	0.17	0.22	0.06	0.03	0.44
Total	113	0.77	0.54	0.16	0.22	0.05	0.03	0.44
Standard Ration	N/A	N/A	N/A	1	0.13	little	N/A	0.43

Source: Compiled from Point McLeay Mission Station Daily Ration Book, July 1–September 30, 1884, Mortlock Library of South Australia, State Library of South Australia, Adelaide, SRG 698/2.

The death of George Taplin in 1879 marked a profound change in Ngarrindjeri life at the Point McLeay Mission. Few of the men who succeeded him exhibited his concern for the Ngarrindjeris or had as much invested in the mission itself. While conditions at the mission remained fairly static through the end of the 1880s, the Ngarrindjeris continued to adapt and change culturally in response to the "civilization" attempts of their missionaries. By 1890 the effects of rationing on the continuation of bush-knowledge was dramatic. Few of the younger generation of Ngarrindjeris had been taught the skills that would have enabled them to survive through traditional means. There was also a significant loss of traditional cultural knowledge among the younger generations.[65] However, despite the efforts of the government and the Aborigines' Friends' Association, Ngarrindjeri culture was never completely wiped out. Janis Koolmatrie and her family are examples of the continuation of Ngarrindjeri culture and identity.

> It doesn't matter how many qualifications we have in the white man's world, it's still important always to have pride in remembering that we are Ngarinyeri. I'm passing it on to my daughter. I

teach her, my mother teaches her, my brother teaches her. I would like her to grow up in the same way as I grew up, knowing that she is Ngarinyeri.[66]

While the rationing system at Point McLeay did not succeed in completely eliminating Ngarrindjeri identity and culture, it did weaken traditional customs and tribal power structures. George Taplin and the others who followed him used the distribution of rations to elicit desired behaviors and encourage the adoption of European habits and Christianity. The Ngarrindjeris who converted to Christianity and regularly attended services, as well as those who lived in the mission cottages as opposed to the camp wurleys, were often given better or more rations. They were occasionally treated to prepared meals, while those who refused to give up traditional beliefs and customs received bulk rations that were often of questionable quality. Rationing was also used to encourage the Ngarrindjeris to seek work by not providing food to men who were deemed physically able to work and paying those who worked on the mission station primarily in rations.

Rationing was also used as punishment for undesired behaviors and the continuation of traditional customs that were viewed as not conducive to the adoption of "civilization." When Taplin discovered behavior that he believed was wrong, he used his control over the rations as punishment, often affecting the entire Ngarrindjeri mission population, rather than just the offenders. One such incident occurred in September 1864.

> I found today that the bad blacks have been threatening the children if they do not give them bread, so that many of the poor children do not get enough to eat, but are afraid to eat. So I have stopped all giving away whatever, and also stopped the sale of flour.[67]

It is possible that the instances of fewer rations being distributed in 1883–1884 were an example of altering the available food in response to Ngarrindjeri resistance to "civilization" efforts.

When parents refused to send their children to the mission school, the reaction was to withhold rations from those families in hopes of forcing the parents to capitulate. The rationing system was also used to break down Ngarrindjeri tribal identity and their existence as a political entity. Rations and the mission superintendents' control had over their distribution allowed them to challenge traditional food taboos, particularly among the children at the school. When the taboos were broken and the threatened consequences did not happen, the traditional power of the elders over the youth was weakened.

Overall, rationing had a significant effect on the Ngarrindjeris at Point McLeay. While the location of Point McLeay meant that the transportation of ration goods was not as difficult as that to other stations farther away from Adelaide, the frequent storms on Lake Alexandrina were a major concern and often affected the timing and quality of the ration shipments. The mission also faced constant problems with ensuring the necessary quantity of supplies to meet the demands of the Ngarrindjeri population. With the concentration of settlements on the mission station and the encroachment of white settlers, it is unlikely that the Ngarrindjeris would have been able to continue to survive through traditional means. It is also unlikely that there would have been enough seasonal labor available to support the Aboriginal population of the Lower Murray Lakes region. At the same time, however, the rationing system helped create a dependence on the South Australian government and the mission station. The ration diet was nutritionally poor, particularly in comparison to the traditional Ngarrindjeri diet, resulting in malnutrition and poor health, which, in turn, made it more difficult for the Ngarrindjeris to travel and seek the seasonal employment that would allow them to marginally improve their situation.

The last decade of the nineteenth century and first decade of the twentieth century represented a period of significant change for the Ngarrindjeris and the Point McLeay Mission itself. As white settlement continued to expand across South Australia, the number of Ngarrindjeris forced to take refuge on the mission station increased.[68] Despite the addition of more land to the mission, it never had enough acreage to support fully the Aboriginal population that lived there. The situation, combined with a larger white workforce and mechanization in many seasonal industries, created the conditions for increasing Ngarrindjeri dependence on rationing.

The second decade of the twentieth century was a period of dire financial circumstances for Point McLeay and the Aborigines' Friends' Association. Private donations steadily decreased, making it more difficult for the AFA to support Point McLeay and pay the salaries of its workers. By 1913 Point McLeay was the largest mission station in South Australia in terms of population, but this increased population strained the financial reserves of the AFA even more.[69]

On January 1, 1916, the AFA handed over the running of Point Mc-Leay to the South Australian government. After more than fifty years, the state government was once again forced to take a more direct role in Aboriginal affairs and assimilation. The 1911 Aborigines Act made all adult Aborigines in South Australia wards of the state, with little control over their destiny or what happened to their children.[70] However, despite the government's control of Point McLeay and the Aborigines, the AFA continued to influence Ngarrindjeri life by continuing its missionary and medical activities at the station.

After gaining control over the station, the South Australian government did little to improve either the physical buildings or the conditions at Point McLeay. The desperate financial situation of the mission was not alleviated, nor did the government try to increase employment opportunities for those living there. The government also closed the boarding school that had operated at the mission since 1860. Overall, the government takeover of Point McLeay was disastrous to the remaining Ngarrindjeri community. In 1974 the administration of Raukkan was given back to the Ngarrindjeri people.

Chapter 8
Conclusion

The comparison of indigenous policies in the United States and South Australia, with their similar origins in settler colonialism, highlights how even with different circumstances and different cultures, similar methods for handling indigenous populations were developed. The resulting cultural imperialism—the establishment of missions and schools to bring "civilization," restriction of movement within specific areas, and the use of rations to direct cultural change—had a profound effect on both the indigenous peoples and the colonizers. If the ultimate goal was for indigenous peoples to fade away, either to die off peacefully or become acculturated to the point of being culturally indistinct from the lower classes of colonial society, both the United States and South Australia failed.

As with most settler societies, the belief that colonial society would make better use of the land was an overarching idea. As a result, one of the primary goals of the government was the acquisition of land. While not the sole tool, rationing was integral to government policies to achieve this end. Using the manipulation of food, the governments were able to influence and coerce indigenous populations into more closely fitting their perceived version of "civilization." Through the restriction of access to and the planned destruction of traditional sources of food, the selection of distribution sites chosen to encourage or discourage gatherings in particular locations, and the promise of more or the threat of withholding rations for particular behaviors, the United States and South Australia sought a means of dealing with their Native peoples in an increasingly colonized environment.

In the United States rations were distributed to encourage Native nations to gather for treaty negotiations designed to gain land in exchange for a little money and the promise of goods and food for a specified period of time. Restriction to reservations became a key stipulation of these treaties in the mid-nineteenth century. South Australia had similar goals and used rations in a somewhat similar way. While there were no treaties with Aboriginal tribes in South Australia, the government recognized the usefulness of rations in influencing the location and movement of the indigenous peoples. They offered rations at particular locations to try to contain the Aborigines within certain areas. They also offered rations at depots farther from white settlement, such as Moorundie, to try to direct Aboriginal movement away from Adelaide and to compel or coerce the Aborigines into not attacking drovers moving from Victoria into South Australia.

Rationing was also used by the United States and South Australia to coerce cultural and social change—to encourage indigenous populations to adopt "civilization." Agents and governments often adopted a carrot-and-stick system to effect desired changes. George Taplin provided better rations for the Ngarrindjeris who chose to live in the cottages at Point McLeay rather than in wurlies in the more traditional camp settlement. Rations were also used to encourage the Pawnees and the Osages to build European-style houses on farm plots rather than live in traditional communities. When indigenous behavior did not conform to expectations, the people were faced with, at the very least, the threat of withheld rations, if not the withdrawal of the food they had become increasingly dependent on. Native Americans were threatened with the withholding of rations from the entire tribe for actions such as leaving the reservation, individual attacks, and raids. In South Australia rations were withheld from an entire tribe when individuals attacked or stole in an effort to convince the tribe to turn over the perpetrators and pressure others to conform.

Another important goal of the "civilization" efforts made by the United States and South Australia, especially the non-governmental humanitarian organizations that influenced policy, was Christianization. Rationing was used to encourage not only attendance at church services, as Taplin did at Point McLeay, but also the abandonment of traditional beliefs and ceremonies. Rations were withheld from those who participated in ceremonies like the Ghost Dance in the United States and initiation ceremonies in South Australia. Rations were also used to enforce school attendance where children were indoctrinated in Christianity, the English language, and European social norms. When parents resisted sending their children to schools, either local or distant institutions, food was withheld from the family. Extra rations were occasionally offered as inducements to ensure attendance. Some families, especially in times of extreme hunger, saw the schools as the best way to guarantee that their children received regular meals.

Connected to the desired conversion to Christianity was an emphasis on the idea of the individual and nuclear family over the tribe, community, and extended family. Indian agents and protectors and sub-protectors of Aborigines who distributed rations attempted to enforce a preference for the nuclear family through food distributions. In the United States distributions to the tribal chief quickly changed to distributions to heads of families in an attempt to prevent the division of food and goods according to existing cultural standards. Similar efforts were made at Point McLeay and other mission stations in South Australia. At Moorundie flour was distributed to individuals and families, rather than to elders who could then distribute the goods as they saw fit.

The emphasis placed on individuality over community by the governments and humanitarians had several root causes. The governments of both the United States and South Australia both believed that increasing the importance of the individual over the tribe or community weakened the power of the chiefs and elders, which in turn weakened the tribe as a political and military force. Humanitarians saw an increasing emphasis on the nuclear family as an important step towards "civilization" and away from traditional cultural, social, and religious beliefs. In the United States the push for individual family farms, as opposed to communally used land, had the added benefit of opening more territory for settlement.

The imposed ideals of the individual also extended to attempts to enforce the Puritan work ethic on the indigenous population. One of the greatest fears of the governments and humanitarians for the rationing programs was the "pauperization" of the Native peoples receiving the goods. Since most white Americans and South Australians saw rations as charity, they feared that the Native Americans and Aborigines would become lazy and never work for their own support. In order to avoid that possibility, humanitarians lobbied for the end of rationing, despite the lack of alternatives for subsistence for those receiving them.

Agents responsible for distributions on the Pawnee and Osage reservations and at Point McLeay attempted with varying degrees of success to require some amount of work from able-bodied men in exchange for rations. On the isolated reservations in Indian Territory, work was difficult to find. Jobs such as working on the agency farm or fencing certain areas were not adequate to fully employ the reservation population. As a solution, those who accepted farm plots, built their own houses, and farmed their own lands were considered to have met the employment requirements. Similar problems with the availability of jobs existed at Point McLeay. There were a limited number of jobs at the mission but not enough to ensure work for each adult male. Surrounding pastoral stations offered some work, but pastoralists paid in small amounts of rations insufficient to support a family. Moreover, such employment was seasonal and often disappeared when the availability of white labor increased and with the development of new technology. The resulting lack of employment opportunities on both the reservations in the United States and around the mission stations and ration depots in South Australia made it impractical to enforce the idea of no rations without labor.

Ultimately, what the governments of both the United States and South Australia created was a state of dependency. Access to hunting grounds was denied. Native game and vegetation were rapidly diminished. Rations were distributed to supplement the Native diet or to make up for those losses, but the government could not keep up with the increasing need for those provisions. While the Pawnees, Osages, Ngarrindjeris, and Moorundie Aborigines became more dependent on the rations distributed by the governments and the mission, there was no corresponding increase in the amount of food supplied. The consistently low amount and the poor quality of rations ensured that the Native peoples were kept on the edge of subsistence—and frequently on the brink of starvation. This dependency, the governments hoped, would make the indigenous peoples more pliant and open to the change to "civilization."

The governments of the United States and South Australia did not seek to create a constant state of dependency, however. While an initial dependence of indigenous peoples on the government for supplies provided a means to manipulate or coerce behavior and lifeway changes, once that acculturation was underway continued dependence was seen as an impediment to the development of individualism. The desired outcome was to influence the native population to successfully integrate into the lower classes of the larger society as farmers and laborers. Continued dependence was viewed as a failure of indigenous policies and became a problem that vexed both governments into the twentieth century.

Although the underlying goals of the two governments' programs were ultimately similar, the regulations themselves were different. Many of the differences stemmed from the nature of the contact and interaction with the indigenous populations. While Native contact in the United States was primarily with government and military, in South Australia it was primarily through settlers and missionaries. The pace of settlement also progressed more quickly in the American West than across the South Australian outback, especially after the passage in the United States of the Homestead Act in 1862. Because of these differences, the implementation of the rationing policies in the United States was more rigid and regimented than in South Australia.

One of the primary differences between Native policy in the United States and South Australia was the treaties. While the United States negotiated many treaties with individual tribes, South Australian relations were based on a pattern of dispossession without treaties. Treaties, or their lack, had a tremendous effect on the process of rationing in the two locations. Treaties established between the United States and the Pawnees and Osages often stipulated a set amount in annuities to be distributed in exchange for ceded lands. While it was not impossible for the government to change or disregard treaty stipulations, it was more difficult to arbitrarily change or halt those distributions. Treaties have also formed the basis for modern legal arguments for compensation when treaty stipulations were not fully met or broken.

South Australia, on the other hand, never negotiated treaties with the Aboriginal tribes. Therefore, the government's rationing policies were far more fluid than those of the United States. Ration standards, much like Aboriginal policy, could and did vary widely. The South Australian government, with no legal obligation to continue a particular rationing program, was able to alter the distribution of rations to fit current finances and popular sentiment. So while Aborigines near a ration depot or at a mission could expect some type of rations, the consistency of the amount and the frequency of the distributions was unpredictable.

The lack of a legal promise of rations also meant that a wider variety of individuals were responsible for the distribution of rations than in the United States. Instead of relying solely on protectors and sub-protectors, the government of South Australia enlisted police, missionaries, and even private individuals to distribute needed rations in different locations. Whereas the United States government tried to keep firm control over its "civilization" and assimilation efforts, South Australia was content to allow missionaries and others to encourage the adoption of "civilization" as they saw fit. This created varying degrees of assimilation, depending on the personal goals of those distributing the rations. Many pastoralists who distributed rations in order to keep a ready workforce nearby often had little interest in converting the Aborigines as long as they did not steal or kill livestock. The sub-protectors, such as Edward J. Eyre, and police were focused primarily on protecting white settlement and travel lanes from attacks and maintaining the general peace of their areas. Missionaries were the most adamant in their desire to use rationing as a tool in the Christianization and "civilization" of their Aboriginal populations.

Another striking difference between the policies of the United States and South Australia was the use of rations as a tool for confinement. Although both settler societies wanted access to more land, the lower population density and an environment less suited to agriculture in the South Australian outback meant that the approach by each nation was different. The United States restricted the Pawnees and Osages to their reservations, threatening to withhold rations from any who left without permission. This restriction allowed for more land to be opened up to white settlement with a minimum of direct conflict. It was also believed that if they were confined to the reservations, and later forced to accept an allotment of land, the Natives could more easily be persuaded to become self-sufficient farmers (despite the inadequacy of the land itself).

South Australia, however, did not try to restrict the Aborigines onto reservations until later in the nineteenth century, and then only in the more settled regions. Ration depots such as Moorundie were meant to keep peace in the area and to try to keep the Aborigines from traveling to cities like Adelaide rather than to congregate the tribes in one location. While rations could be withheld from those who did journey into the cities, there was no way for the government to prevent the open migration of Aboriginal tribes. Mission stations, like Point McLeay, were established in the more settled districts and therefore were more concerned with the Aborigines maintaining residence on the station. Even in these instances, however, the Aborigines were not prevented from leaving by threats of violence, as in the United States, particularly when it came to travel for seasonal employment.

A more material difference between the rationing programs in the United States and South Australia was the content of the distributions. Rations on the Pawnee and Osage reservations consisted of flour and meat as well as addictive substances like sugar, coffee, and tobacco. It was recognized that the rations were the primary, and often only, source of subsistence, even if quantities did not keep up with that reality. Buffalo hunts were increasingly unsuccessful and eventually ended altogether, while the small game on the reservations was quickly depleted, preventing the possibility of adequately supplementing ration distributions. Despite attempts to instill European-style farming as a primary means of subsistence, the land of the reservations was also unsuitable for extensive and successful farming, trapping the Pawnees and Osages in an ongoing pattern of dependency.

In contrast, the Aborigines in South Australia were expected to continue to hunt, and the composition of the rations reflected this position. Rations there consisted primarily of flour and bread, particularly earlier in the settlement of the colony and in areas more isolated from white settlement. Other goods, such as tea and sugar, were added as pastoralists surrounded mission stations, but meat remained a less fundamental component of the rations, often being distributed only to the elderly and infirm. Rations that served as payment for employment on the cattle runs and pastoral stations were more comprehensive in terms of diversity but were never enough truly to support the worker and his family. Rations in South Australia were never intended to be the sole means of subsistence, even if that occasionally became the case.

The different expectations placed on Native American and Aboriginal ration recipients to find additional sources of subsistence to supplement government distributions influenced the standards set by each government. In the United States, where there was an expectation that the Pawnees and Osages would not continue to hunt buffalo, the ration standards established a fuller, although not complete, diet. The distribution standards included meat as well as flour, corn, and beans. Ration standards in South Australia established considerably smaller distributions. With the expectation that the Aborigines would continue to hunt where possible and find work on settler pastoral runs when necessary, more substantial distributions were deemed unnecessary.

Regardless of the standards established by each government, however, each state faced considerable difficulties in distributing complete rations on a regular basis. Both governments had problems sufficiently and consistently securing adequate funding to supply full rations of acceptable quality. Securing the foodstuffs and goods themselves presented additional challenges. Contractors frequently substituted inferior quality goods in order to increase profits. Distance was yet another issue. Many ration distribution points were initially at some distance from settled areas, making the transportation of large amounts of food difficult and expensive. For governments who ultimately wanted to reduce expenses, there was little concrete effort made to overcome these difficulties. Even today, many Native communities in the United States are located in "food deserts," areas where access to fresh foods is more difficult.[1]

The rationing programs implemented in the United States and South Australia were a mixture of success and disappointment for both the governments and those receiving the goods. Rations, lacking though they were in quality and quantity, were often the only thing preventing mass starvation. However, the nature of the goods themselves created deeper and longer-lasting problems for indigenous communities. When indigenous peoples were restricted to certain areas or removed from their traditional lands altogether and placed on reservations and mission stations, they were not only removed from known sources of food but in most cases their active lifestyle was curtailed as well. As their traditional diets were restricted, and nearly lost altogether, the nutritional health of the Pawnees, Osages, Moorundie Aborigines, and Ngarrindjeris declined.

The traditional diets of hunter-horticulture and hunter-gatherer cultures were marked by their variety and high nutritional content. They were typically high in lean protein, fruits, and vegetables while low in fats and sugars. The ration diet, in both the United States and South Australia, was primarily built on fats and empty calories—foods that could go a long way but were nutritionally poor. Rations could prevent starvation, but they guaranteed malnutrition, especially in a population already susceptible to and weakened by epidemic diseases.

The chronic malnutrition and nutritional deficiencies faced by the indigenous populations had tremendous long-term consequences. Malnutrition affected both the physical and psychological health of Native American and Aboriginal communities.[2] The chronic poor health of the communities often made it more difficult for people to fully take advantage of farming and employment opportunities. The weakness caused by malnutrition made it physically difficult to work, which resulted in few resources for food, which led to more malnutrition. It created a vicious cycle that was almost impossible to break. The continued weakness and deterioration of the community as a result of malnutrition had a profound psychological effect as well. Depression increased as the day-to-day circumstances on the reservations and the mission stations offered little relief or hope for improvement.

The problems stemming from the nutritional shortcomings of the rations diet, and later the overall adopted European diet, continue into the twenty-first century. Many nutrition-based diseases now common among both the Native American and Aboriginal populations, such as Type II diabetes, had no history in those communities prior to colonization and rationing.[3] In 2004–2005, the rate of Type II diabetes for Australian Aborigines was three times higher than for the non-indigenous population. Aboriginal life expectancy between 2005 and 2007 was also an average of 10.5 years lower than the Australian average.[4] Similar consequences are seen in Native American populations, which are more than two times as likely to be diagnosed with Type II diabetes and have a life expectancy six years lower than white Americans.[5]

The problem of poor availability of nutritional foods continues to the present day. The commodity foods offered by the United States, often military and government surplus, are generally highly processed and full of saturated fats, simple sugars, and empty calories.[6] Stores on the reservations also frequently lack significant selections of fresh produce and healthy alternatives, continuing a pattern of poor nutrition and the health problems that result. The Aborigines in South Australia face similar problems, particularly in the more isolated outstation communities. The great distances that goods need to travel to reach these areas make the procurement of fresh produce and meats difficult. Diets still consist primarily of dried and canned vegetables and meats together with goods high in refined sugars and of little nutritional value. The results of these continuing situations are indigenous populations with higher mortality and morbidity rates and shorter life spans than the nonindigenous populations. However, movements to return to more traditional diets in both Native American and Aboriginal communities have begun to create change.

Despite the attention paid to the development and implementation of ration policy, governments and their agents were only one side of the equation. While the governments of the United States and South Australia had specific goals for their rationing programs, the Native American and Aboriginal recipients of those rations did not necessarily view the process in the same ways. The governments viewed rationing as an enticement to adopt, or assistance on the path to, "civilization." However, the recipients accepted rations according to their own cultural understandings. Those distributing rations viewed them as gifts or something that required payment in the form of actions or changing beliefs and ways of living. Those receiving them often viewed them as a right, fitting the process of rationing into their expectations of reciprocity.[7]

Many Native American nations, like the Pawnees and the Osages, saw rations as part of the payment to them for ceding their lands and abandoning their regular buffalo hunts. The goods were a right, not a privilege, in their view. They had ceded their lands, moved onto reservations, and ended their buffalo hunts in exchange for the annuities and rations offered by the government. Based on their cultural understandings of reciprocity, since their means of subsistence had been taken away, it was appropriate for them to receive the goods in exchange. It was the system of reciprocity that ensured support for members of the community who may have otherwise faced hunger. It was a way of viewing relationships that Native Americans expected to continue in their interactions with the United States. Aboriginal peoples, too, had different understandings of the rationing process or refused to conform to government expectations. Rather than use flour to make leavened bread, it was used to make traditional-style dishes. When dining halls were built, the Aborigines continued to eat outside as a community around the fire. Despite government efforts to use food as a means of changing indigenous culture and society, the recipients of rations found ways to resist.

The resistance offered by indigenous communities to the process of rationing took both direct and indirect forms. Direct resistance included actions like the theft of ration goods before they could be distributed. This form of resistance, however, often resulted in the punishment of the entire community in the form of withheld goods. The majority of resistance that the Pawnees, Osages, Moorundie Aborigines, and Ngarrindjeris chose to put up was indirect. Actions such as the redistribution of rations according to traditional cultural values, the continuation of ceremonies banned by the governments and missionaries, and the refusal to build and live in European-style houses allowed indigenous peoples to resist the intentions of the rationing programs without coming into direct conflict with those distributing the rations. Through their direct and especially their indirect resistance to the assimilation and "civilization" attempts of the governments, Native Americans and Australian Aborigines were able to maintain important elements of their cultures in the face of nearly overwhelming colonization.

The disparity in how each side viewed rations and the process of rationing itself ensured that the goals of the United States and South Australia were never fully realized. Despite the agents' best efforts, rations continued to be shared with more than just nuclear families, maintaining the customs that helped guarantee group survival. Even the uses of the goods themselves were also adapted to fit into traditional forms, rather than following European ways. Both the Native Americans and the Aborigines accepted rationing but merged it into their own cultural and social traditions, resisting the efforts of the two governments and humanitarians to assimilate them into the lowest classes of white society.

Ultimately, the rationing programs and policies of the United States and South Australia, as they affected the Pawnees, Osages, Moorundie Aborigines, and Ngarrindjeris, were a mixture of success and failure from both the point of view of the governments and the indigenous peoples receiving the goods. Rationing helped the government agents and missionaries on the reservations and stations influence the behavior and assimilation of their Native residents. Diets and eating habits were altered, and the corresponding traditional cultural knowledge surrounding food practices and taboos began to be forgotten.

The manipulation of rations also encouraged parents to send their children to government and church institutions where they could be indoctrinated in white European ideas and culture while at the same time their Native culture, religion, and language were forced and often beaten out of them. With the education of the children of the communities, the governments and humanitarians hoped to weaken community ties and the power of the elders of the tribes. Knowledge and ceremony were lost as the next generation was removed and isolated for schooling.

Despite the best efforts of the governments to utilize rationing as a tool to enforce "civilization" and acculturation, however, both the Native American and the Aboriginal communities were able to maintain their individual identities. Many important cultural and social ceremonies and traditions were continued. Much traditional knowledge continued to be handed down. People maintained their identity as Pawnee, Osage, or Ngarrindjeri and retained a strong tie to place and community. While many of the customs that surrounded food ways and taboos in both the United States and South Australia were lost as traditional sources of subsistence were lost and replaced by others, some of the social and cultural underpinnings remain. Ultimately, the governments' goals to assimilate the indigenous population into the dominant culture, with the aid of rationing as a tool of influence and coercion, was never completed on the Pawnee and Osage reservations or at Moorundie and Point McLeay. Rations and selective acculturation changed indigenous life. However, even as traditional goods were replaced with new items and non-native foods adopted, cultural and social traditions themselves continued.

In the end, it is the similarities between the United States and South Australia that stand out. Rooted in settler colonialism, both governments sought ways to control indigenous populations while trying to balance the settler desire for land with humanitarian calls for paternalistic compassion. Despite differences in governmental structure and indigenous relations, each adopted the use of rationing as a tool in its arsenal, for strikingly similar reasons. They also faced similar problems, from transportation and quality to Native resistance, for which they found no permanent solutions.

Regardless of the problems, however, the control of food was an effective tool in government attempts to influence tribal movement as well as to encourage the adoption of new societal norms. Rationing did result in a great deal of cultural change and important long-term effects. Neither the United States nor South Australia maintained a consistent approach, vacillating between policies aiming for exclusion and those pushing for assimilation. Often the two competing ideas were applied at the same time, something that actually helped indigenous societies to survive, as Dolores Janiewski argues: "The very effort to isolate and segregate the subordinated racialized cultures from the dominant Euro-American nation ironically aided in the survival of those cultures."[8]

As both nations approached the turn of the twentieth century, their rationing policies began to change. The acquisition of new lands was no longer a driving force, and many Native peoples had been at least partially acculturated into the dominant society. The United States government began phasing out ration distributions at the end of the nineteenth century. The expectation of rations as a temporary necessity during the transition to individual family farming was never abandoned by either the government or humanitarians. Some Native nations, like the Osage in 1879, were able to negotiate annuity distributions in cash. Other Native nations and individuals were granted cash payments when the agent deemed them "civilized enough," usually at the acceptance of allotment. In 1892 Congress approved the transition from annuity payments in goods and rations to cash distributions on a wider scale.

In the more densely settled areas of South Australia, rationing was phased out in the late nineteenth century as well. However, in some of the more isolated regions, periodic ration distributions continued into the 1960s. As indigenous peoples were granted citizenship, in 1924 in the United States and in 1967 in Australia,[9] rationing was replaced with national welfare services and, in the United States, commodity food programs, starting a new phase in the complex relationship between indigenous peoples, governments, and food.

Notes

Plainsword

1. Robert N. Clinton, "Redressing the Legacy of Colonialism: A Vision Quest for a Decolonized Federal Indian Law," 46 Arkansas L. Rev. 77, 86 (1993).
2. Walter R. Echo-Hawk, *In The Light of Justice: The Rise of Human Rights in Native America and the UN Declaration on the Rights of Indigenous Peoples* (Fulcrum Publishing, 2013), 99–132.
3. Walter R. Echo-Hawk, *In the Courts of the Conqueror: The 10 Worst Indian Cases Ever Decided* (Fulcrum Publishing, 2010), 405.
4. Ibid.
5. See in UNDRIP: Article 20 (the right of indigenous peoples to be secure in their own means of traditional subsistence), Article 24 (the right to conservation of vital medicinal plants, animals, and minerals), Article 25 (the right to maintain their distinctive spiritual relationship to traditional lands and resources), and Article 26 (the right of protection for traditional uses of traditional lands and resources).

Chapter 1

1. The area between Mannum on the Murray River north of Murray Bridge and Milang on the western coast of Lake Alexandrina is occupied by Ngarrindjeri clans to the south and members of the Meru language family to the north. David Horton, *Aboriginal Australia* (Canberra: Australian Institute of Aboriginal and Torres Strait Islander Studies, 2000); Graham Jenkin, *Conquest of the Ngarrindjeri: The Story of the Lower Murray Lakes Tribes* (Rigby Ltd, 1979; reprint, Adelaide: Raukkan Publishers, 1985), 23 (page citations are to the reprint edition).
2. State Records of South Australia (hereafter SRSA) GRG 52/1, Aborigines Of-

fice, Correspondence Files of the Aborigines Office and Successor Agencies, file no. 82 of 1872.

3. Ibid., GRG 52/1/1872/91.

4. William Burgess to Barclay White, 15 March 1873, Records of the Superintendency of Iowa 1851–1876, RG 75 (M1166), National Archives; David J. Wishart, "The Dispossession of the Pawnee," *Annals of the Association of American Geographers* 69, no. 3 (1979): 396.

5. Martha Royce Blaine, *Pawnee Passage 1870–1875* (Norman: University of Oklahoma Press, 1990), 184; David J. Wishart, *An Unspeakable Sadness: The Dispossession of the Nebraska Indians* (Lincoln: University of Nebraska Press, 1994), 195–96.

6. Davia Stasiulis and Nira Yuval-Davis, "Introduction: Beyond Dichotomies—Gender, Race, Ethnicity and Class in Settler Societies," in *Unsettling Settler Societies: Articulations of Gender, Race, Ethnicity and Class*, eds. Davia Stasiulis and Nira Yuval-Davis (London: SAGE Publications, 1995), 3.

7. Ibid., 24–25.

8. Ian Tyrrell, "Beyond the View from Euro-America: Environment, Settler Societies, and the Internationalization of American History," in *Rethinking American History in a Global Age*, ed. Thomas Bender (Berkeley: University of California Press, 2002), 169, 183.

9. Stasiulis and Yuval-Davis, "Introduction," 20.

10. Margaret Jacobs, *White Mother to a Dark Race: Settler Colonialism, Maternalism, and the Removal of Indigenous Children in the American West and Australia, 1880–1940* (Lincoln: University of Nebraska Press, 2009), 4–7.

11. Patrick Wolfe, "Settler Colonialism and the Elimination of the Native," *Journal of Genocide Research* 8, no. 4 (December 2006): 390–91.

12. John Wunder, *"Retained by the People": A History of American Indians and the Bill of Rights* (New York: Oxford University Press, 1994), 16–17.

13. Stuart Banner, *Possessing the Pacific: Land, Settlers and Indigenous Peoples from Australia to Alaska* (Cambridge: Harvard University Press, 2007); Jacobs, *White Mother*; Robert Foster, "Feasts of the Full Moon: The Distribution of Rations to Aborigines in South Australia: 1836–1861," *Aboriginal History* 13, no. 1 (1989): 63–78; Tim Rowse, *White Flour, White Power: From Rations to Citizenship in Central Australia* (Cambridge: Cambridge University Press, 1998).

14. Carole M. Counihan, "The Social and Cultural Uses of Food," in *The Cambridge World History of Food*, eds. Kenneth F. Kiple and Kriemhild Coneè Ornelas (Cambridge: Cambridge University Press, 2000), 1513.

15. Peter Scholliers, "Meals, Food Narratives, and Sentiments of Belonging in

Past and Present," in Peter Scholliers, ed., *Food, Drink and Identity: Cooking, Eating and Drinking in Europe since the Middle Ages* (Oxford: Berg, 2001), 4.

16. Ibid.

17. David L. Howell, "Ainu Ethnicity and the Boundaries of the Early Modern Japanese State," *Past and Present* 142, no. 1 (February 1994): 69–79; Takakura Shinichiro, *The Ainu of Northern Japan: A Study in Conquest and Acculturation*, trans. John A. Harrison (Philadelphia: American Philosophical Society, 1960), 51–52.

18. *Instructions to Officials in Charge of the Management of Ezo* (1799); quoted in Shinichiro, 55.

19. Alice C. Fletcher and Francis LaFlesche, *The Omaha Tribe* (Lincoln: University of Nebraska Press, 1992), 493–500.

20. Peter Farb and George J. Armelagos, *Consuming Passions* (Boston: Houghton Mifflin, 1980), 14.

21. Richard Baker, *Land is Life: From Bush to Town, The Story of the Yanyuwa People* (St. Leonards, NSW: Allen & Unwin, 1999), 48–50.

22. Carol A. Bryant et al., *The Cultural Feast: An Introduction to Food and Society*, 2nd ed. (Belmont, CA: Thomson Wadsworth, 2003), 203–4.

23. Peter K. Latz, *Bushfires and Bushtucker* (Alice Springs, NT: Institute for Aboriginal Development Press, 1995), 27; Dolores Janiewski, "Gendering, Racializing and Classifying: Settler Colonization in the United States, 1590–1990," in *Unsettling Settler Societies*, 135.

24. Lorna Marshall, *The !Kung of Nyae Nyae* (Cambridge, MA: Harvard University Press, 1976), 295.

25. Edward John Eyre, "Manners and Customs of the Aborigines," in *Journals of the Expedition of Discovery into Central Australia and Overland from Adelaide to King George's Sound in the Years 1840–1*, vol. 2 (London: T. and W. Boone, 1845; reprint, Adelaide: Libraries Board of South Australia, 1964), 484.

26. Scholliers, *Food, Drink and Identity*, 5.

27. Ibid., 3.

28. Ibid., 8.

29. Patricia Albers, "Labor and Exchange in American Indian History," in *A Companion to American Indian History*, eds. Philip J. Deloria and Neal Salisbury (Malden, MA: Blackwell Publishers, 2002), 281.

30. Blaine, *Pawnee Passage*, 33.

31. Fletcher and LaFlesche, *Omaha Tribe*, 537–38.

32. Carl Waldman, *Encyclopedia of Native American Tribes* (New York: Facts On File, 1999), 87–88.

33. Claude Grignon, "Commensality and Social Morphology: An Essay of Typology," in *Food, Drink and Identity*, ed. Peter Scholliers (New York: Berg, 2001), 23.

34. Clayton Roberts and David Roberts, *A History of England*, vol. 2, *1688 to the Present*, 3rd ed. (Englewood Cliffs, NJ: Prentice Hall, 1991), 672.

35. Rowse, *White Flour*, 3.

36. Ibid., 4–5.

37. SRSA GRG 52/1/1872/91.

38. Foster, "Feasts of the Full Moon," 75.

39. Bryant et al., *Cultural Feast*, 222.

40. United Kingdom, Hansard Parliamentary Debates, Commons, 3d ser., vol. 29 (14 July 1835), cols. 549–553.

41. Mark Nathan Cohen, "History, Diet, and Hunter-Gatherers," in *The Cambridge World History of Food*, eds. Kenneth F. Kiple and Kriemhild Coneè Ornelas (Cambridge: Cambridge University Press, 2000), 68.

42. Anne O'Brien, "Kitchen Fragments and Garden Stuff," *Australian Historical Studies* 39, no. 2 (June 2008): 150, 152; Andrew Porter, "Introduction: Britain and the Empire in the Nineteenth Century," in *Oxford History of the British Empire*, vol. 3, *The Nineteenth Century*, ed. Andrew Porter and Alaine Low (Oxford: Oxford University Press, 1999), 22.

43. Gary Smithers, "The 'Pursuits of Civilized Man': Race and the Meaning of Civilization in the United States and Australia, 1790s–1850s," *Journal of World History* 20, no. 2 (June 2009): 245–72.

44. Alan Lester, "British Settler Discourse and the Circuits of Empire," *History Workshop Journal* 54 (2002): 26, 30.

45. Andrew Porter, "Trusteeship, Anti-Slavery, and Humanitarianism," in *Oxford History of the British Empire*, vol. 3, *The Nineteenth Century*, ed. Andrew Porter and Alaine Low (Oxford: Oxford University Press, 1999), 199, 205.

46. Julie Evans, "Re-reading Edward Eyre: Race, Resistance and Repression in Australia and the Caribbean," *Australian Historical Studies* 118 (2002): 188.

47. For a more thorough discussion of the conflict between humanitarians and settlers, see Alan Lester, "British Settler Discourse" and Lester, "Colonial Networks, Australian Humanitarianism and the History Wars," *Geographical Research* 44, no. 3 (September 2006): 229–41.

48. O'Brien, "Kitchen Fragments," 165.

49. Eyre, *Journals*, vol. 1, 171.

50. Lester, "British Settler Discourse," 27.

51. Richard White, *Roots of Dependency: Subsistence, Environment, and Social Change among the Choctaws, Pawnees, and Navajos* (Lincoln: University of Nebraska Press, 1983), xvi.

52. Ibid., xvii.
53. Baker, *Land Is Life*, 24.
54. White, *Roots of Dependency*, 320-21.
55. Edward Eyre, the first distributor of rations at Moorundie, did not specify which tribes were coming in to receive food. Most other government residents followed in the same suit. However, in his reports Eyre indicated that the most numerous Aborigines were coming from north of the station. Based on his statements and a map of language group areas, the most likely tribe was Meru. They are members of a larger language group and were probably subdivided into different clans or dialects. See Horton, *Aboriginal Australia*.
56. SRSA 52/1/1872/134.
57. Burgess to White, 4 July 1873, RG 75 (M1166); Blaine, *Pawnee Passage*, 184–85.

Chapter 2

1. A comprehensive discussion of colonial-Native relations, including Russian, British, French, Spanish, and Dutch, can be found in Alan Taylor, *American Colonies: The Settling of North America* (New York: Penguin Books, 2001). For examples of Spanish-Native relations, see Lee Miller, ed., *From the Heart: Voices of the American Indian* (New York: Vintage Books, 1995), 289–91. For examples of British and French-Native relations, see Daniel K. Richter, *Facing East from Indian Country: A Native History of Early America* (Cambridge, MA: Harvard University Press, 2001), and Michael N. McConnell, *A Country Between: The Upper Ohio Valley and Its Peoples, 1724–1774* (Lincoln: University of Nebraska Press, 1992). For a discussion of Dutch-Native relations, see Russell Shorto, *The Island at the Center of the World: The Epic Story of Dutch Manhattan and the Forgotten Colony That Shaped America* (New York: Doubleday, 2004). For a discussion of Russian-Alaska Native relations, see Lydia T. Black, *Russians in Alaska, 1732–1867* (Fairbanks: University of Alaska Press, 2004).
2. "Treaty of Holston," 2 July 1791, Article iv, United States Statutes at Large 7, sec. 39.
3. Francis Paul Prucha, *American Indian Treaties: The History of a Political Anomaly* (Berkeley: University of California Press, 1994), 138–39; Prucha, *The Great Father: The United States Government and the American Indians*, vol. 1 (Lincoln: University of Nebraska Press, 1986), 170–71; Wishart, *Unspeakable Sadness*, 24, 68.
4. Annuity goods ranged from clothing and blankets to bedsteads, axle grease, and wheelbarrows. Rations and food goods included basic items such as beef

and flour and unfamiliar goods like allspice, ground ginger, and maraschino cherries. For a sample list of annuity goods, see United States Bureau of Indian Affairs, "Abstract of Annuity Goods, fiscal year 1885–1886," RG75 (864), National Archives, Washington, DC.

5. "Treaty with the Osage," 2 June 1825, Article iv, United States Statutes at Large 7, sec. 240.

6. Lewis Cass, "A Memorandum of Lewis Cass: Concerning a System for the Regulation of Indian Affairs," eds. Francis Paul Prucha and Donald F. Carmony, *Wisconsin Magazine of History* 52, no. 1 (Autumn 1968): 35–50. Provides a transcript of a memorandum sent by Cass to the Secretary of War in 1816.

7. Prucha, *Great Father,* vol. 1, 170.

8. "Act to Amend an Act entitled 'An Act to Provide for the better Organization of the Department of Indian Affairs,'" 1847, United States Statutes at Large 66, sec. 10.

9. Prucha, *Great Father,* vol. 1, 332.

10. In the 1831 Supreme Court decision *Cherokee Nation v. Georgia,* Chief Justice John Marshall ruled that native tribes were "domestic dependent nations" and that the political position of the United States was one of guardian. *Cherokee Nation v. Georgia,* 30 US 1 (1831). For a discussion of the Cherokee legal cases, see Jill Norgren, *The Cherokee Cases: The Confrontation of Law and Politics* (New York: McGraw-Hill, 1996).

11. United States Office of Indian Affairs, Annual Report of the Commissioner of Indian Affairs to the Secretary of the Interior for the Year 1848 (Washington, DC: Government Printing Office, 1848), 386.

12. United States Office of Indian Affairs, Annual Report of the Commissioner of Indian Affairs to the Secretary of the Interior for the Year 1872 (Washington, DC: Government Printing Office, 1872), 10–11.

13. United States Office of Indian Affairs, Annual Report of the Commissioner of Indian Affairs to the Secretary of the Interior for the Year 1875 (Washington, DC: Government Printing Office, 1875), 265.

14. For a sample of weekly ration distributions for several tribes in 1877, see United States Bureau of Indian Affairs, Records of the Central Superintendency of Indian Affairs, 1813–1878, File M856, RG75, 1877, National Archives, Washington, DC.

15. Cyrus Beede, Osage agent, to William Nicholson, superintendent, 3 January 1877, in ibid.

16. William Burgess, Pawnee agent, to Barclay White, superintendent, 2 February 1874; 20 March 1874, United States Bureau of Indian Affairs, Records

of the Northern Superintendency of Indian Affairs, 1851–1876, File M1070, RG75, National Archives, Washington, DC.

17. Elizabeth Mulligan, "Accounts of the 'Cherokee Trail of Tears' with reference to 'Princess Otahki,'" *St. Louis* [MO] *Post-Dispatch*, January 18, 1970.

18. Richard N. Ellis, "General Pope and the Old 'Hand-to-Mouth Way'" in *The Western American Indian: Case Studies in Tribal History*, ed. Richard N. Ellis, 63–75.

19. Wah-ti-anka, "Minutes of Council held in Osage Council House," United States Bureau of Indian Affairs, Reports of Inspections of the Field Jurisdictions of the Office of Indian Affairs, 1873–1900, File M1070, RG75, 18 January 1878, National Archives, Washington, DC.

20. Lewis Meriam, *The Problem of Indian Administration* (Baltimore: Johns Hopkins Press, 1928), 221.

21. United States Office of Indian Affairs, Annual Report of the Commissioner of Indian Affairs to the Secretary of the Interior for the Year 1877 (Washington, DC: Government Printing Office, 1877), 4–5.

22. United States Office of Indian Affairs, Report of the Commissioner of Indian Affairs (1892), quoted in *The American Indian and the United States: A Documentary History*, ed. Wilcomb E. Washburn (New York: Random House, 1973), 618.

23. The same fears of "pauperization" can be seen in humanitarian arguments concerning Aboriginal rations in Australia, where on many stations rations were not distributed to the able-bodied without work.

24. Most Native American nations were receiving rations and goods as part of treaty obligations on the part of the federal government. While many humanitarians, government officials, and United States citizens viewed rations as free handouts, most tribes viewed them as payments for land ceded.

25. Cited in Merrill E. Gates, "Land and Law as Agents in Educating Indians," in *Americanizing the American Indian: Writings by the "Friends of the Indian," 1880–1900*, ed. Francis Paul Prucha (Lincoln: University of Nebraska Press, 1978), 47.

26. United States Office of Indian Affairs, Annual Report of the Commissioner of Indian Affairs to the Secretary of the Interior for the Year 1867 (Washington, DC: Government Printing Office, 1868), 190.

27. Robert M. Utley and Wilcomb E. Washburn, *Indian Wars* (Boston: Houghton Mifflin, 1977), 201–2.

28. United States Bureau of Indian Affairs, Procedural Issuances: Orders and Circulars, File M1121, RG75, 17 July 1874, National Archives, Washington, DC.

29. Felix Cohen, *Felix Cohen's Handbook of Federal Indian Law* (Albuquerque: University of New Mexico Press, 1971), 244.
30. United States Department of the Interior, Office of Indian Affairs, Circular #112, 31 May 1883. Of course, many reservations did not have resident physicians, and the likelihood of finding two disinterested whites, especially near the more remote reservations, would have been low. It is also worth noting that this federal law quickly followed the Resolution of 1871, prohibiting the making of any more Indian treaties.
31. Despite these orders, however, the people found ways of maintaining important cultural patterns, as will be discussed in a later chapter.
32. United States Bureau of Indian Affairs, Procedural Issuances, Circular #93, Accounts 1882.
33. Francis Paul Prucha, *American Indian Policy in Crisis: Christian Reformers and the Indian, 1865–1900* (Norman: University of Oklahoma Press, 1976), 211.
34. United States Congress, House of Representatives, Instructions to Agents in Regard to Manner of Issuing Beef, 51st Cong., 2nd sess., 1890, H. Doc. 1, part 5, vol. 2, Serial 2841.
35. United States Statutes at Large, "Act Making Appropriations for the Current and Contingent Expenses of the Indian Department," 1892, *Statutes at Large* 27, sec. 8.

Chapter 3

1. Anne Pattel-Gray, *The Great White Flood: Racism in Australia* (Atlanta: Scholars Press, 1998), 16.
2. Andrew Fitzmaurice defines natural law as a mentality that informed both formal legal systems and European thinking about the world. See Andrew Fitzmaurice, "The Genealogy of Terra Nullius," *Australian Historical Studies* 38, no. 129 (April 2007): 2.
3. C. D. Rowley, *The Destruction of Aboriginal Society* (Ringwood: Penguin, 1972), 13.
4. A. D. Douglas, "How the Blacks Might Be Civilized," in *Queenslander* [Brisbane], 7 March 1891.
5. United Kingdom, Hansard Parliamentary Debates, Commons, 3d ser., vol. 24 (1 July 1834), cols. 1061–1063; and ibid., 3d ser., vol. 29 (14 July 1835), cols. 549–53.
6. United Kingdom, First Annual Report of the Colonization Commissioners of South Australia (28 July 1836), 8.
7. United Kingdom, South Australia Colonization Act (15 August 1834), 1.

8. This pattern of dispossession came to be called *terra nullius*. Recent scholarship has challenged the assertion that terra nullius was used as the legal basis of Australian colonization. For a discussion of the evolution of the term and practice of terra nullius, see Fitzmaurice, "The Genealogy of Terra Nullius," 1–15.

9. Stuart Macintyre, *A Concise History of Australia* (Cambridge: Cambridge University Press, 1999), 34.

10. Governor George Grey to Lord John Russell, State Records of South Australia GRG 2/5 Governor's Dispatches, file no. 52 of 1841.

11. Alan Lester, "Obtaining the 'Due Observance of Justice': The Geographies of Colonial Humanitarianism," *Environment and Planning D: Society and Space* 20 (2002): 278–83.

12. Cass argued that the most effective way to maintain peace between settlers and American Indians was to give gifts and supplement Native subsistence efforts. Far from having Natives' best interests at heart, Cass was motivated by a desire to ease and quicken the pace of settler expansion in the United States. See Prucha, *Great Father*, 1:170.

13. In the 1990s the Australian Institute of Health and Welfare found that life expectancy for the Aborigines was as much as twenty years less than the national average. There are also higher rates of chronic disease, such as diabetes, as well as problems like depression. For a discussion of present Aboriginal health issues as well as their historical bases, see Justin Healey, "Aboriginal Health and Welfare," in *Issues in Society*, ed. Justin Healey (Balmain, NSW: Spinney Press, 2000), 129: 2–15; Basil S. Hetzel, "Historical Perspectives on Indigenous Health in Australia," *Asia Pacific Journal of Clinical Nutrition* 9, no. 3 (2000): 157–63; and H. J. Frith and Basil S. Hetzel, eds., *The Changing Nutrition of Aborigines in the Ecosystem* (Melbourne: CSIRO, 1978).

14. John Harris, *One Blood: 200 Years of Aboriginal Encounter with Christianity: A Story of Hope* (Sutherland, NSW: Albatross Books Pty, 1990), 309.

15. John Hindmarsh, "Proclamation by His Excellency John Hondmarsh, Knight of the Royal Hanovarian Guelphic Order Governor and Commander-in-Chief of His Majesty's Province of South Australia," in *Seed of the Coolibah: A History of the Yandruwandha and Yawarrawarrka People*, by H.M. Tolcher (Adelaide, SA: Openbook Print, 2003), epigraph.

16. South Australian Colonization Commission, Letters Sent to Officers in South Australia, State Records of South Australia, GRG 48/1, file no. 16 of 1836.

17. The colonial government in South Australia proclaimed that lands under cultivation, fixed residences, and land used as cemeteries were protected. This, of course, did not fit into Aboriginal cultural and social practices and in reality left very little protected. Harris, *One Blood*, 310–11.

18. *South Australian Government Gazette* [Adelaide], 11 July 1839, 1.

19. Ann McGrath, *Contested Ground: Australian Aborigines under the British Crown* (St. Leonards, NSW: Allen & Unwin, 1995), 58.

20. Fay Gale, "The History of Contact in South Australia," in *The Aborigines of South Australia: Their Present Condition and Future Development* (Adelaide: University of Adelaide, Department of Adult Education, 1969), 29, 31.

21. Christobel Mattingley and Ken Hampton, eds., *Survival in Our Own Land: "Aboriginal Experiences in South Australia" since 1836, Told by Nungas and Others* (Adelaide: Wakefield Press, 1988), 20.

22. South Australia, Colonial (Later Chief) Secretary's Office, Letters and other Communications Received by the Colonial Secretary, Governor and Other Government Officials, State Records of South Australia, Adelaide, SA, GRG 24/1, file no. 169 of 1837.

23. Rowse, *White Flour*, 17.

24. "Protector's Report," *The Register*, 25 May 1839; quoted in Foster, "Feasts of the Full Moon," 67.

25. Mattingley and Hampton, *Survival*, 20.

26. Edward John Eyre, "Manners and Customs of the Aborigines of Australia," in *Journals*, 2: 483–84.

27. South Australia, Colonial (later, Chief) Secretary's Office, Letters Received by the Colonial (later, Chief) Secretary's Office, State Records of South Australia, GRG 24/6, file no. 286 of 1847.

28. There were 283 Kaurnas at the celebration in 1840. By 1843 450 Aborigines, both Kaurna and other groups from the Adelaide area, attended the celebration. Tom Gara, "Life and Times of Mullawirraburka ('King John') of the Adelaide Tribe," in *History in Portraits: Biographies of Nineteenth Century South Australian Aboriginal People*, ed. Jane Simpson and Luise Hercus (Sydney: Southwood Press, 1998), 119.

29. William Anderson Cawthorne, "Diaries," 21 October 1843, State Library of New South Wales, Sydney; quoted in Gara, "Life and Times," 120.

30. Mattingley and Hampton, *Survival*, 21; South Australia, Colonial (later, Chief) Secretary's Office, Letters Sent by the Colonial (later, Chief) Secretary's Office, GRG 24/4, file no. 151 of 1844, State Records of South Australia.

31. Matthew Moorhouse, "Protector's Report 9 October 1839," British Parliamentary Papers (1842), 321; quoted in Foster, "Feasts of the Full Moon," 65.

32. Foster, "Feasts of the Full Moon," 65.

33. Ibid., 63.

34. Neville Wanklyn, "Confrontation at Port Lincoln," *Origin* 3, no. 2 (1970): 7.

35. Aborigines' Protection Society, Report of the Sub-Committee on Australia (London: Aborigines' Protection Society, 1838), 19–20.

36. McGrath, *Contested Ground*, 222.
37. An example can be seen in an 1866 letter from Phillip Levi to the Protector of Aborigines concerning the withdrawal of the police who had been distributing rations in his area. He requests that he be permitted to distribute the rations from his station so that the area's Aboriginal workforce will not leave. South Australia, Aborigines Office, Correspondence Files of the Aborigines Office and Successor Agencies, GRG 52/1, file no. 63 of 1866, State Records of South Australia.
38. Foster, "Feasts of the Full Moon," 73.
39. South Australia. Aborigines Office, Correspondence Files, file no. 305 of 1867.
40. "Ration Day," *Illustrated Australian News*, 26 December 1884.
41. Baker, *Land is Life*, 128–29.
42. Rowley, *Destruction of Aboriginal Society*, 77.
43. Barry Morris, *Domesticating Resistance: The Dhan-gadi Aborigines and the Australian State* (Oxford: Berg Publishers, 1989), 85–88.

Chapter 4

1. Jane F. Smith and Robert M. Kvasnicka, eds., *Indian-White Relations: A Persistent Paradox* (Washington, DC: Howard University Press, 1981), 161.
2. Ralph H. Vigil, Frances W. Kaye, and John R. Wunder, eds., *Spain and the Plains: Myths and Realities of Spanish Exploration and Settlement on the Great Plains* (Niwot: University Press of Colorado, 1994), 15, 95–97.
3. Wishart, *Unspeakable Sadness*, 9.
4. Clifton Wharton, "Journal," 26, 52, Nebraska State Historical Society, Lincoln, NE.
5. Wishart, *Unspeakable Sadness*, 94.
6. White, *Roots of Dependency*, 151–56; David Wishart, "The Pawnee Claims Case, 1947–64," in *Irredeemable America: The Indians' Estate and Land Claims*, ed. Imre Sutton and Ralph Leon Beals (Albuquerque: University of New Mexico Press, 1985), 163.
7. Although the lands south of the Platte River were ceded to the United States government, the Pawnee maintained the right to hunt in those lands. See United States Statutes at Large, "Treaty with the Pawnee," 9 October 1833, Articles i–ii, 7 (1834): 448.
8. Ibid., Articles iii–viii.
9. Wishart, *Unspeakable Sadness*, 66.
10. United States Statutes at Large, "Treaty with the Pawnee," 24 September 1857, Article i–ii, 11 (1858): 729.

11. United States Bureau of Indian Affairs, "Pawnee, Abstracts of Estimates of Goods Needed for Fiscal Year 1879–1880," Records of the Bureau of Indian Affairs Finance Division, RG75 (862), National Archives, Washington, DC.

12. United States Statutes at Large, "Treaty with the Pawnee," Article xiii (1858).

13. Blaine, *Pawnee Passage*, 13.

14. John Dunbar, "John Dunbar Manuscript," in John Dunbar Papers, p. 6, Nebraska State Historical Society, Lincoln, NE.

15. Jacob Troth, Pawnee agent, to Barclay White, superintendent, 31 January 1872–1 April 1872, in United States Bureau of Indian Affairs, Records of the Northern Superintendency of Iowa, 1851–76, File M1166, RG75 1872, National Archives, Washington, DC.

16. Ibid., 9 July 1872.

17. Barclay White, "Barclay White Journals, 1871–1876," p. 296, Nebraska State Historical Society, Lincoln.

18. William Burgess, agent, to Barclay White, superintendent, 4 July 1873 in United States Bureau of Indian Affairs, Records of the Northern Superintendency of Iowa, 1851–76, File M1166, RG75.

19. Ruby E. Wilson, *Frank J. North: Pawnee Scout Commander and Pioneer* (Athens, OH: Swallow Press, 1984), 195.

20. William Burgess, Pawnee agent, to Barclay White, superintendent, 2 February 1874, in United States Bureau of Indian Affairs, Records of the Northern Superintendency of Iowa, 1851–76, File M1166, RG75.

21. William Burgess, Pawnee agent, to Barclay White, superintendent, 31 August 1874, in ibid.

22. Burgess to White, 15 March 1873, in ibid.; Clyde A. Milner, *With Good Intentions: Quaker Work among the Pawnees, Otos, and Omahas in the 1870s* (Lincoln: University of Nebraska Press, 1982), 62–63.

23. White, *Roots of Dependency*, 205.

24. Edmond Dounias et al., "No Longer Nomadic: Changing Punan Tubu Lifestyle Requires New Health Strategies," *Cultural Survival Quarterly* 28, no. 2 (2004): 16.

25. White, *Roots of Dependency*, 211.

26. Wishart, *Unspeakable Sadness*, 193.

27. Wishart, "Dispossession of the Pawnee," 399.

28. Barclay White, "Barclay White Journals Vol. 1, 1873," p. 390, Nebraska State Historical Society, Lincoln.

29. There has been some debate over the true desire of Pawnees in the move to Indian Territory. Some historians believe the desire to move was genuine, while others argue that the United States government, traders, or local white settlers were behind the change in Pawnee sentiment. See Wishart, "Dispossession of the Pawnee," 401; and Blaine, *Pawnee Passage*, 214–33.

30. "An Act to Authorize the Sale of the Pawnee Reservation," 10 April 1876, 19 Stat. 28, Sec. 2, in *Indian Affairs: Laws and Treaties*, vol. 1, *Laws*, ed. Charles J. Kappler (Washington, DC: Government Printing Office, 1903), 160, http://digital.library.okstate.edu/kappler/.

31. Ibid., sec. 3.

32. Each sack of flour contains approximately 100 pounds. See William Burgess, agent to Barclay White, superintendent, 16 March 1875, United States Bureau of Indian Affairs, Records of the Northern Superintendency, 1851–1876, File M1166, RG75.

33. Milner, *With Good Intentions*, 85; and Blaine, *Pawnee Passage*, 247.

34. Elliott West, *The Way to the West: Essays on the Central Plains* (Albuquerque: University of New Mexico Press, 1995), 31–32, 37–40; Elliott West, *The Contested Plains: Indians, Goldseekers, and the Rush to Colorado* (Lawrence: University Press of Kansas, 1998), 89–90.

35. Blaine, *Pawnee Passage*, 245.

36. Ibid., 239–40.

37. Ibid., 269; and Milner, *With Good Intentions*, 86.

38. E. P. Smith to the Secretary of the Interior, 44th Cong., First Sess., Ex. Doc. No. 80, 6 March 1875, p. 4.

39. Smith to Secretary of the Interior, 1 November 1875, in United States Office of Indian Affairs, Annual Report for the Year 1875, 78.

40. Martha Royce Blaine, *Some Things Are Not Forgotten: A Pawnee Family Remembers* (Lincoln: University of Nebraska Press, 1997), 18.

41. John Williamson, "John Williamson Manuscripts: The Story of the Pawnee's Removal South," film MS2710, p. 42, Nebraska State Historical Society, Lincoln.

42. Smith to Secretary of the Interior, 30 October 1876, in United States Congress, House of Representatives, Report of the Secretary of the Interior, 44th Cong., 2nd sess., 1876, H. Ex. Doc. 1, Part 5, Serial 1749, III-XXV, 5, 20.

43. William Burgess, agent, to William Nicholson, superintendent, 26 June 1876 and 4 July 1876, United States Bureau of Indian Affairs, Records of the Central Superintendency.

44. Ruby Wilson, *Frank J. North*, 203.

45. Barclay White, "Barclay White Journals, Vol. 3, 1876," p. 272, Nebraska State Historical Society, Lincoln.

46. Milner, *With Good Intentions*, 91–93.

47. Blaine, *Some Things*, 22.

48. Ibid.

49. G. Nicholson, acting superintendent, to Burgess, 2 December 1876, United States Bureau of Indian Affairs, Records of the Central Superintendency.

50. Burgess to Nicholson, 7 February 1877, in ibid.

51. Ibid., 13 February 1877.

52. Pawnee Agency, Weekly Ration Reports, 1877, United States Bureau of Indian Affairs, Records of the Central Superintendency.

53. Weekly Ration Reports, Pawnee Agency, 17 March 1877 and 31 March 1877, in ibid.

54. Ibid., 7 April–28 April 1877.

55. Burgess to Nicholson, 24 March 1877, in ibid.

56. Nicholson to Burgess, 2 February 1877, in ibid.

57. Charles H. Searing, Pawnee Agent, to Nicholson, 30 May 1877, in ibid.

58. Nicholson to Burgess, 7 April 1877, in ibid.; and Pawnee Agency, Weekly Ration Reports, 21 April 1877, in ibid.

59. Ibid., 26 May 1877.

60. Searing to Nicholson, 1 June 1877, in ibid.

61. Nicholson to Searing, 18 September 1877, in ibid.

62. Pawnee Agency, Weekly Ration Reports, 27 October 1877, in ibid.

63. E. Hayt, commissioner, to Searing, 12 November 1877, in ibid.

64. Burgess to Nicholson, 13 February 1877, in ibid.

65. Searing to Nicholson, 26 July 1877, in ibid.

66. Ibid., 3 October 1877.

67. Blaine, *Pawnee Passage*, 292.

68. Blaine, *Some Things*, 17.

69. Garland J. and Martha R. Blaine Collection, "Unpublished Notes and Pawnee Music," quoted in Blaine, *Pawnee Passage*, 290.

70. Joseph Hertford to Nicholson, 7 November 1877, Bureau of Indian Affairs, Letters Received, 1824–1881, File M234, RG75, National Archives, Washington, DC.

71. Ibid., 6 November 1877; and Hertford to Barclay White, 15 June 1878, in ibid.

72. Pawnee Petition, 29 August 1891, United States Bureau of Indian Affairs, Reports of Inspections of the Field Jurisdictions of the Office of Indian Affairs, 1873–1900, File M1070, RG75, National Archives, Washington, DC.

73. "An act making appropriations for current and contingent expenses, and fulfilling treaty stipulations with Indian tribes, for fiscal year ending June thirtieth, eighteen hundred and ninety-four," 27 Stat. 612, Sec. 12, Art. III, in Kappler, *Indian Affairs*, 1: 498.

Chapter 5

1. Willard Hughes Rollings, *Unaffected by the Gospel: Osage Resistance to the*

Christian Invasion (1673–1906): A Cultural Victory (Albuquerque: University of New Mexico Press, 2004), 3–4.

2. Osage territory at the turn of the nineteenth century included portions of Missouri, Arkansas, Kansas, and Oklahoma.

3. In contrast to the Pawnees, however, the Osages relied more on the hunt and abundance of wild foods than cultivation, particularly in the eighteenth and nineteenth centuries. This difference made the United States "civilization" program a poor fit with the Osage Nation.

4. Willard H. Rollings, *The Osage: An Ethnohistorical Study of Hegemony on the Prairie-Plains* (Columbia: University of Missouri Press, 1992), 64.

5. Spanish authorities also developed relations with other Native peoples to act as a barrier between their settlements and the Osages. Colin G. Calloway, *One Vast Winter Count: The Native American West before Lewis and Clark* (Lincoln: University of Nebraska Press, 2003), 364–65, 380–81.

6. Rollings, *Osage*, 154.

7. The Osages signed treaties in 1808, 1818, 1825, 1839, and 1865, all of which ceded large portions of their lands to the US government.

8. The Osages moved westward in the face of American encroachment, giving up much of their woodland territory and depending more and more on the buffalo hunt for their subsistence.

9. Many settlers who viewed the Osages as savages were not averse to the idea of wiping them out militarily. As more white settlers moved west, they saw little need, and had little desire, to negotiate the purchase of Osage lands and thus aided the government in its coercive policy of removal.

10. Louis F. Burns, *A History of the Osage People* (Fallbrook, CA: printed by author, 1989), 133.

11. Ibid., 135.

12. United States Statutes at Large, "Treaty with the Osage," 10 November 1808, Article ii–v, 7 (1808): 107.

13. Ibid., Article viii.

14. Burns, *Osage People*, 154. Other native nations that were moved to Osage territory included the Sac-Fox, Kickapoos, Shawnees, and Delawares, among others.

15. United States Statutes at Large, "Treaty with the Osage," 25 September 1818, Article i, 7 (1818): 183.

16. United States Statutes at Large, "Treaty with the Osage," 2 June 1825, Article i, 7 (1825): 240.

17. Ibid., Article iii.

18. Ibid., Article iv.

19. Rollings, *Osage*, 45, 61.
20. United States Statutes at Large, "Treaty with the Osage," 1825, Article iv, 7 (1825): 240.
21. Paul Liguest Chouteau to Lewis Cass, 6 April 1832, in United States Bureau of Indian Affairs, Letters Received.
22. Burns, *Osage People*, 166.
23. United States Statutes at Large, "Treaty with the Osage," 11 January 1839, 7 (1839): 576.
24. The policy of issuing treaty goods to heads of families rather than through chiefs, designed to hasten the breakdown of the tribe as a political and social entity, did not begin until 1847.
25. United States Statutes at Large, "Treaty with the Osage," 1839, Article ii, 7 (1839): 576.
26. Burns, *Osage People*, 165.
27. Joseph Paw ne no pa she, Osage governor to Enoch Hoag, superintendent, 12 August 1875, United States Bureau of Indian Affairs, Records of the Central Superintendency.
28. For a detailed discussion of religious missions to the Osages see Rollings, *Unaffected by the Gospel.*
29. John R. Chenault to Office of Indian Affairs, 27 September 1849, United States Bureau of Indian Affairs, Letters Received.
30. United States Statutes at Large, "Treaty with the Osage," 29 September 1865, 14 (1865): 687.
31. The excess funds diverted into the "civilization fund" were in excess of $776,900. The Osages received less than $200 from this fund. See Burns, *Osage People*, 282.
32. United States Statutes at Large, "Treaty with the Osage," 1865, Article I, 14 (1865): 687.
33. Ibid., Article v.
34. Burns, *Osage People*, 314. The old view of the removal as a simple move with little loss of life is disputed by Burns. He offers four sources to support his assertions: grave markers on the Caney River watershed, Osage annuity rolls, eyewitness accounts, and the Osage Mission register.
35. Ibid., 317.
36. Vouchers for Osage Annuity Goods, 8 November 1858, United States Bureau of Indian Affairs, Records of the Central Superintendency.
37. United States Statutes at Large, "Act of 15 July 1870," 16 (1870): 362.
38. The gifts that were traditionally given at the conclusion of negotiations, the expenses of the government officials, and the survey of the ninety-sixth me-

ridian were all paid for from the $50,000 removal fund. Burns, *Osage People*, 323.

39. Article xvi of the 1865 Osage Treaty granted the Osages complete ownership of their new lands in Indian Territory. Theoretically, this should have better protected Osage lands from encroaching American settlement.

40. Burns, *Osage People*, 321.

41. United States Statutes at Large, "Act to Confirm to the Great and Little Osage Indians a Reservation in the Indian Territory," 5 June 1872, 17 (1872): 228.

42. Despite efforts to gain possession of their title, it continues to be held by the United States government in trust for the Osage Nation.

43. The Osage reservation was divided by the "Osage Allotment Act of 1906," United States Statutes at Large 34, sec. 539.

44. Garrick Alan Bailey, "Changes in Osage Social Organization, 1673–1906," Anthropological Papers, Department of Anthropology, University of Oregon, no. 5 (1973): 80; Terry P. Wilson, *The Underground Reservation: Osage Oil* (Lincoln: University of Nebraska Press, 1985), 25; Murray R. Wickett, *Contested Territory: Whites, Native Americans, and African Americans in Oklahoma, 1865–1907* (Baton Rouge: Louisiana State University Press, 2000), 206.

45. Cyrus Beede, agent to William Nicholson, superintendent, 15 October 1876, United States Bureau of Indian Affairs, Records of the Central Superintendency.

46. Isaac Gibson, agent to Edward P. Smith, commissioner, 1 October 1874, in ibid.

47. United States Statutes at Large, "Act Making Appropriations for Current and Contingent Expenses, and Fulfilling Treaty Stipulations with Indian Tribes," 27 (1983): 612. This regulation was carried out from the 1860s through the turn of the twentieth century.

48. The Drum Creek Treaty, which attempted to remove the Osages from Kansas, was the last treaty negotiated with the Osage nation, but it was rejected by Congress. The removal of the Osage nation was completed by an act of Congress passed in 1870.

49. G. C. Snow, 24 July 1869, United States Office of Indian Affairs, Annual Report of the Commissioner of Indian Affairs for the Year 1869 (Washington, DC: Government Printing Office, 1870), 380–81; Rollings, *Osage*, 166.

50. Isaac Gibson, agent, to Enoch Hoag, superintendent, 11 February 1871, United States Bureau of Indian Affairs, Records of the Central Superintendency.

51. Gibson to Hoag, 28 March 1871, in ibid.

52. Ibid.

53. In 1875 Chetopah, acting governor of the Osages, wrote to the Commission-

er of Indian Affairs asking that their annuity be paid in cash so the people could decide what goods to buy. Chetopah to Commissioner of Indian Affairs, 30 August 1875, United States Bureau of Indian Affairs, Letters Received.

54. Gibson to Hoag, 11 February 1871, United States Bureau of Indian Affairs, Records of the Central Superintendency.

55. Gibson to Hoag, 2 April 1872, in ibid.

56. Gibson to Hoag, 1 January 1873, in ibid.

57. Gibson to Hoag, 3 September 1874, in ibid.; Gibson, Annual Report, 1 September 1874, in ibid.

58. Isaac Gibson, Annual Report, 1 September 1874, in ibid.; Gibson, agent, to Enoch Hoag, superintendent, 3 September 1874, in ibid.

59. United States Office of Indian Affairs, Annual Report of the Commissioner of Indian Affairs for the Year 1873 (Washington, DC: Government Printing Office, 1874), 218.

60. Gibson to Hoag, 3 September 1874, United States Bureau of Indian Affairs, Records of the Central Superintendency.

61. Isaac Gibson, agent, to Edward P. Smith, commissioner, 1 October 1874, in ibid.

62. Gibson to Smith, Monthly Report, 1 December 1874, United States Bureau of Indian Affairs, Letters Received.

63. Gibson to Smith, 15 November 1875, United States Bureau of Indian Affairs, Records of the Central Superintendency.

64. Gibson to Smith, Monthly Report, 1 November 1874, in ibid.

65. Gibson to Smith, Monthly Report, 28 February 1875, in ibid.

66. Gibson to Hoag, 20 March 1875, in ibid.

67. Gibson to Smith, 24 October 1875, in ibid.

68. Gibson to Hoag, 6 November 1875, in ibid.

69. Gibson to Smith, Monthly Report, 31 January 1876, in ibid.

70. Cyrus Beede, agent, to William Nicholson, superintendent, 29 March 1876, in ibid.

71. Beede to Nicholson, 17 July 1876, 24 July 1876, 18 August 1876, in ibid.

72. Beede to Nicholson, 18 August 1876, in ibid.

73. Beede to Nicholson, 5 June 1876, in ibid.

74. Nicholson to Beede, 31 July 1876, in ibid.

75. Beede to Nicholson, superintendent, 9 October 1876, 15 October 1876, in ibid.

76. Beede to Nicholson, 7 August 1876, in ibid.

77. Nicholson to Beede, 2 February 1877, in ibid.; Beede to Nicholson, 19 November 1877, in ibid.

78. Beede to Nicholson, 9 March 1877, in ibid.

79. Beede to Nicholson, 15 June 1877, in ibid.

80. Beede to Nicholson, 17 July 1877, in ibid.

81. Beede to Nicholson, 27 July 1877, in ibid.

82. Nicholson to Beede, 23 October 1877, in ibid.

83. Dennis McAuliffe, Jr., *Bloodland: A Family Story of Oil, Greed and Murder on the Osage Reservation* (San Francisco, CA: Council Oak Books, 1999), 44.

84. Burns, *Osage People*, 177.

85. Minutes of Council held in Osage Council House, 18 January 1878, United States Bureau of Indian Affairs, Inspections of the Field Jurisdictions.

86. E. C. Watkins to E. A. Hayt, commissioner, 29 January 1878, in ibid.

87. Resolution of Osage Council, 5 August 1878, in ibid.

88. Ibid.

89. McAuliffe, *Bloodland*, 160.

90. United States Statutes at Large, "Act Making Appropriations," 13 July 1892, 27 (1893): sec. 8.

Chapter 6

1. A more comprehensive list of Aboriginal nations in South Australia can be found in Mattingly and Hampton, *Survival*, 3.

2. Ibid., 4.

3. The title of sub-protector was given to the deputies of the protector of Aborigines. Sub-protectors were responsible for maintaining peace with the Aborigines in a specified region as well as distributing rations and handling colonist-Aboriginal disputes.

4. Eyre, "Manners and Customs of the Aborigines of Australia," in *Journals*, 2: 158.

5. Ibid., 478.

6. Ibid., 479, 480.

7. Foster, "Feasts of the Full-Moon, 77.

8. Nathanial Hales, "Account of a Visit to Port Lincoln," quoted in Mattingly and Hampton, *Survival*, 20.

9. Harry Palada Kulamburut, "Strange Food," transcriber Michael Walsh, in *This is What Happened: Historical Narratives by Aborigines*, ed. Luise Hercus and Peter Sutton (Canberra: Australian Institute of Aboriginal Studies, 1986), 57–58.

10. Robert Foster, De Rose Hill Native Title Claim History Report (Native Title Unit, ALRM, 2000), 61.

11. *South Australian Government Gazette* [Adelaide], 4 July 1839, 4.

12. Eyre, "Manners and Customs," in *Journals*, 2: 160–61.
13. Specific goals of the rationing policies of South Australia are discussed in the next section.
14. For an in-depth study of a situation such as this, see Rowse, *White Flour*.
15. Laws, Statutes, etc., Imperial Crown Land Sale Act, 1846, 5 & 6 Vic., c. 36. Also referred to as the Sale of Waste Lands Act 1842 and the Australian Colonies Waste Lands Act 1842. The South Australian government did not recognize legal Aboriginal ownership of the land, nor did the proceeds from sales of the lands go solely to the traditional inhabitants of that area. However, South Australian law, in conjunction with the act, dictated that proceeds from land sales be used to offset the costs of maintaining the Aboriginal population.
16. Eyre, "Manners and Customs," in *Journals*, 2: 165.
17. Advocate-General Charles Mann, Statement in Court Hearing, 2 May 1839, quoted in *South Australian Register* (Adelaide), 4 May 1839.
18. Resident magistrates were civil officers who had limited judicial powers in a specific area. In the case of government-run ration depots in South Australia, the resident magistrate was in charge of distributing rations as well as maintaining peace, particularly between Aborigines and settlers. Not all ration depots were managed by resident magistrates, especially as the number of depots grew and distributions were taken over by police, station managers, and missionaries.
19. Government Resident Magistrate, Guichen Bay to Colonial Secretary, 29 May 1847, South Australia, Colonial (later, Chief) Secretary's Office, Letters Received by the Colonial (later, Chief) Secretary's Office, GRG 24/6, file no. 640 of 1847, State Records of South Australia, Adelaide.
20. J.A.H., "Letter to the Editor," *Adelaide Observer* (South Australia), 10 April 1869, 3G.
21. Stuart Rintoul, *The Wailing: A National Black Oral History* (Port Melbourne: William Heinemann Australia, 1993), 6.
22. Protector of Aborigines to Colonial Secretary, 23 June 1847, SRSA GRG 24/6/1847/ 697.
23. George Grey, Governor, to Lord John Russell, Secretary of State, 30 October 1841, reprinted in Edward J. Eyre, Report and Letters to Governor Grey from E. J. Eyre at Moorunde (Adelaide: Sullivan's Cove, 1985), 11.
24. Sustainable Recreation Steering Committee, *A Sustainable Recreation Strategy for the River Murray and Lower Lakes in South Australia* (Adelaide, SA: QED Pty, 2002), 6. The spelling of the name of the ration depot varies: Moorundie, Moorunde, Moorundee. The first two spellings occur most frequently.

25. Moorunidie was selected as a case study to represent the depot-type of ration stations because the first sub-protector of Aborigines, John Eyre, helped develop much of South Australia's policies and is representative of the prevailing humanitarian views in South Australia at the time.

26. Horton, *Aboriginal Australia*. The group names presented in this map may include smaller groups such as clans, dialects, or individual languages, and so is not exact.

27. National Native Title Tribunal, "First Peoples of the River Murray and Mallee Region," (Commonwealth of Australia, 2004); Sustainable Recreation Steering Committee, *Sustainable Recreation Strategy*, 2.

28. Colonial Secretary to Commissioner of Police, 20 April 1847, SRSA, GRG 24/6/1848/1486.

29. Eyre, "Manners and Customs," in *Journal*, 2: 434.

30. A. M. Mundy to Eyre, 11 April 1844, SRSA, GRG 24/4/1844/151I.

31. Mattingly and Hampton, *Survival*, 22.

32. Edward J. Eyre to J. A. Jackson, Colonial Secretary, 10 January 1842, reprinted in Eyre, Report and Letters, 20.

33. Jackson to Eyre, 16 December 1842, South Australia, Colonial (later, Chief) Secretary's Office, Letters Received by the Colonial (later, Chief) Secretary's Office, SRSA, GRG 24/6, file no. 262F of 1842.

34. Eyre to Colonial Secretary, 7 December 1842, SRSA, GRG 24/6/1842/1000.

35. Eyre to Governor Grey, 24 January 1842, reprinted in Eyre, Report and Letters, 22.

36. Resident Magistrate's Report for 1843, 20 January 1844, SRSA, GRG 24/6/1844/111.

37. Colonial Secretary to Commissioner of Police, 20 April 1847, SRSA, GRG 24/6/1848/1486.

38. Eyre to Colonial Secretary, 28 February 1844, SRSA, GRG 24/6/1844/228; A.M. Mundy to Eyre, 12 March 1844, South Australia, Colonial (later, Chief) Secretary's Office, Letters Sent by the Colonial (later, Chief) Secretary's Office, GRG 24/4, file no. 112I of 1844.

39. Similar situations can be found in the United States rationing program on the Pawnee and Osage reservations.

40. Eyre to Colonial Secretary, 16 March 1844, SRSA, GRG 24/6/1844/284.

41. Eyre to Colonial Secretary, 7 February 1843, SRSA, GRG 24/6/1843/193.

42. Moorhouse to Colonial Secretary, 18 May 1849, SRSA, GRG 24/6/1849/929.

43. Resident Magistrate's Report for 1843, 20 January 1844, SRSA 24/6/1844/111.

44. Instructions to W. Nation as Resident Magistrate, 14 October 1844, SRSA, GRG 24/4/1844/345H.

45. Resident Magistrate's Report (W. Nation acting), 30 June 1845, SRSA, GRG 24/6/1845/752.

46. Eyre, "Manners and Customs," in *Journal*, 2: 430.

47. In the nineteenth century South Australia did not intend to educate all Aboriginal children in schools. Therefore, the need to ensure attendance was a far less pressing problem than in the United States.

48. Richard Broome, *Aboriginal Australians: Black Responses to White Dominance, 1788–1994*, 2nd ed. (St. Leonards, NSW: Allen & Unwin, 1994), 61.

49. Macintyre, *Concise History of Australia*, 14.

50. Broome, *Aboriginal Australians*, 61.

51. Eyre, "Manners and Customs," in *Journal*, 2: 371.

52. Protector of the Aborigines Moorhouse, Quarterly Report, 22 February 1848, SRSA GRG 24/6/1848/225.

53. Eyre, *Journals*, 1: 192.

54. The distribution of blankets depended greatly on supply, not weather. The blankets were valuable commodities and were therefore sought after regardless of the weather conditions or season.

55. Protector of the Aborigines to Colonial Secretary, 28 January 1848, SRSA, GRG 24/6/1848/112; and Protector of the Aborigines to Colonial Secretary, 19 May 1849, SRSA, GRG 24/6/1849/943.

56. B. Finniss to Protector of the Aborigines, 8 June 1852, SRSA, GRG 24/4/1852/543T.

57. Protector of the Aborigines to Colonial Secretary, 3 June 1852, SRSA, GRG 24/6/1852/1652.

58. *South Australian Government Gazette* [Adelaide], 14 October 1847, 320.

59. Eyre, "Manners and Customs," in *Journal*, 2: 218.

60. Baker, *Land is Life*.

61. James Potter, "Chittleborough's Adelaide," *History SA: The Newsletter of the Historical Society of South Australia* (July 2003): 16.

62. Fay Gale, *A Study of Assimilation: Part-Aborigines in South Australia* (Adelaide: Libraries Board of South Australia, 1964), 76.

63. A. W. Sturt to Sub-Protector of the Aborigines at Moorunde, 3 June 1851, SRSA, GRG 24/4/1851/320S.

64. "Protector of Aborigines' Report," *Adelaide Observer* [South Australia], 3 July 1852, 6BCD.

65. "Protector of Aborigines' Report," *Adelaide Observer*, 3 June 1854, 10E.

66. "Protector of the Aborigines' Report," *South Australian Government Gazette*, 28 July 1853, 499.

67. South Australian Parliamentary Papers (1856), Paper No. 12; "Report on the

Aborigines of the Murray and Lakes Districts," *Adelaide Observer* (26 March 1859), 7H.

68. The position was re-created after the Select Committee investigation.

69. Robert Foster, "Rations, Co-Existence, and the Colonization of Aboriginal Labour in South Australian Pastoral Industry, 1860–1911," *Aboriginal History* 24, no. 1 (2000): 1.

70. A. Whitefellow, "The Aborigines," *Adelaide Observer*, 1 August 1857, Supp. 3G.

71. Protector of the Aborigines, General Report on Aborigines, 9 April 1863, Department of Lands, Crown Lands and Immigration/Crown Lands Office, Letters Received, GRG 35/1, file no. 791 of 1863, State Records of South Australia, Adelaide.

72. Ibid., 35/1/1863/791.

73. South Australian Parliamentary Debates (30 April 1861), 11.

74. Protector of Aborigines, General Report on Aborigines, April 9, 1863, Correspondence Files, Crown Lands and Immigration Office, GRG 35/1/14/1863/791, State Records of South Australia, Adelaide.

75. Ibid.

76. Foster, "Rations, Coexistence," 1.

77. Broome, *Aboriginal Australians*, 147, 174; L. R. Smith, *The Aboriginal Population of Australia* (Canberra: Australian National University Press, 1980), 143.

78. Petronelle Vaarzon-Morel, ed., *Warlpiri Karnta Karnta-Kurlangu Yimi (Warlpiri Women's Voices: Our Lives Our History)* (Alice Springs: IAD Press, 1995), 6.

79. Ibid., 7.

80. Foster, "Feasts of the Full-Moon," 76.

81. Foster, De Rose Hill, 66.

Chapter 7

1. *South Australian* (Adelaide), 15 September 1838.

2. Also spelled Narrinyeri, particularly in older writings.

3. Horton, *Aboriginal Australia*, map.

4. Warren Bury, "The Foundation of the Point McLeay Aboriginal Mission," BA Honor's thesis, University of Adelaide, 1964, 75.

5. National Native Title Tribunal, *Research Report Bibliography: Ngarrindjeri* (Commonwealth of Australia, January 2003, No. 1/2003), 2.

6. Graham Jenkin, *Conquest of the Ngarrindjeri*, 23.

7. The combined Tendi still existed as late as the 1870s. Ibid., 13; George Taplin, "Journal of George Taplin," 20 March 1875, 3: 495, Mortlock Library of South

Australia, State Library of South Australia, Adelaide. [Page numbers refer to typescript by Edith Beaumont.]

8. Jenkin, *Conquest of the Ngarrindjeri*, 13–14.

9. Ibid., 28–30.

10. George Taplin, *The Narrinyeri Tribe*, 2nd ed. (Adelaide: E. S. Wigg & Son, 1878), 44.

11. Fay Gale, "A Changing Aboriginal Population," in *Settlement and Encounter: Geographical Studies Presented to Sir Grenfell Price*, ed. Fay Gale and Graham H. Lawton (Melbourne: Oxford University Press, 1969), 69.

12. Ibid., 9; Jenkin, 11.

13. Bury, "Point McLeay Aboriginal Mission," 16–17.

14. Jenkin, *Conquest of the Ngarrindjeri*, 82–83. The tribes closest to Raukkan included Karatindjeris and probably Rangulindjeris.

15. Ibid., 82.

16. Taplin, *Narrinyeri Tribe*, 16.

17. *Observer* [Adelaide], 4 September 1858.

18. Jenkin, *Conquest of the Ngarrindjeri*, 77–78.

19. Bury, "Point McLeay Aboriginal Mission," 4.

20. Jenkin, *Conquest of the Ngarrindjeri*, 100–102.

21. Taplin, *Narrinyeri Tribe*, 98. Tyere and ngaikunde are both types of fish.

22. Taplin, *Journal*, 14 Apr 1859, 1: 5; Gale, "Changing Aboriginal Population," 65.

23. Taplin, *Journal*, 18 April 1859, 1: 5.

24. Diane Bell, *Ngarrindjeri Wurruwarrin: A World That Is, Was and Will Be* (North Melbourne, Victoria: Spinifex Press Pty, 1998), 106.

25. *South Australia Register* [Adelaide], 20 March 1879.

26. David Blackwell, Point McLeay to Edward Lee Hamilton, Protector of Aborigines, 16 August 1889, Aborigines Office, Correspondence Files of the Aborigines Office and Successor Agencies, GRG 52/1, file no. 283 of 1889, State Records of South Australia, Adelaide.

27. Cathy Hayles, "George Taplin's Reconstruction of Landscape on the Point McLeay Aboriginal Mission," *Journal of the Anthropological Society of South Australia* 30–31(1993): 101.

28. South Australia, Parliament, Report of the Select Committee of the Legislative Council upon the Aborigines (Adelaide: W. C. Cox, Government Printer, 1860), 3.

29. Ibid.

30. Ibid., Minutes of Evidence, question 98.

31. Mattingley and Hampton, *Survival*, 186.

32. Taplin, *Journal*, 1 August 1865, 2: 245.

33. Jenkin, *Conquest of the Ngarrindjeri*, 113–14.

34. C. E. Bartlett, *A Brief History of the Point McLeay Reserve and District* (Adelaide: Aborigines' Friends' Association in connection with the Point McLeay Centenary, 1959), 10–11; Mattingley and Hampton, *Survival*, 183; Broome, *Aboriginal Australians*, 75.

35. Broome, *Aboriginal Australians*, 79.

36. Jenkin, *Conquest of the Ngarrindjeri*, 97–98.

37. Hayles, "Reconstruction of Landscape," 106.

38. Jenkin, *Conquest of the Ngarrindjeri*, 106.

39. George Taplin to Scott, Acting Protector of Aborigines, 17 May 1867, GRG 52/1/1867/197; Bury, "Point McLeay Aboriginal Mission," 92–93; Jenkin, *Conquest of the Ngarrindjeri*, 109–10.

40. Jenkin, *Conquest of the Ngarrindjeri*, 123–25.

41. Ibid., 125.

42. Ibid.

43. Paul Kropinyeri, in *Survival*, ed. Mattingley and Hampton, 138.

44. Taplin, *Journal*, 22 November 1864, 1: 217. For example, Taplin refused to distribute rations to women who came in without cleaning their faces.

45. Hayles, "Reconstruction of Landscape," 95.

46. Bury, "Point McLeay Aboriginal Mission," 16–17; Jenkin, *Conquest of the Ngarrindjeri*, 180.

47. Taplin, *Journal*, 1 November 1859, 1: 28.

48. Ibid., 1 May 1861, 1: 99.

49. Ibid., 2 May 1861.

50. Ibid., 25 June 1862, 1: 156.

51. E. B. Scott, acting protector of Aborigines, to George Taplin, 28 January 1867, GRG 52/1/1867/33.

52. Bury, "Point McLeay Aboriginal Mission," 92; Taplin, *Journal*, vol. 3.

53. Taplin, *Journal*, 29 November 1864, 1: 218.

54. Ibid., 20 September 1862, 1: 160, and 21 July 1873, 3: 451; Bury, "Point McLeay Aboriginal Mission," 92–93.

55. Broome, *Aboriginal Australians*, 53.

56. Taplin, *Journal*, 2: 21 March 1860, p.66.

57. Jenkin, *Conquest of the Ngarrindjeri*, 180.

58. Frederick Taplin, son of George Taplin, succeeded his father as superintendent at Point McLeay. He ran the mission from 1879 until his death in 1889.

59. July–December 1883, Point McLeay Mission Station Daily Ration Book, 1 July 1883 to 30 September 1884, Mortlock Library of South Australia, State Library of South Australia, Adelaide, SRG 698/2.

60. Point McLeay Mission Station Daily Ration Book, July 1–December 31, 1883, Mortlock Library of South Australia, State Library of South Australia, Adelaide, SRG 698/2.

61. Point McLeay Mission Station Daily Ration Book, January 1–September 30, 1884, The Mortlock Library of South Australia, State Library of South Australia, Adelaide, SRG 698/2.

62. Jenkin, *Conquest of the Ngarrindjeri*, 109.

63. Point McLeay Mission Station Daily Ration Book, July 1–September 30, 1884, Mortlock Library of South Australia, State Library of South Australia, Adelaide, SRG 698/2.

64. Ibid.

65. Jenkin, *Conquest of the Ngarrindjeri*, 172.

66. Janis Koolmatrie, in Mattingley and Hampton, *Survival*, 188.

67. Taplin, *Journal*, 26 September 1864, 1: 209.

68. Jenkin, *Conquest of the Ngarrindjeri*, 215.

69. South Australia, Parliament, Progress Report of the Royal Commission on the Aborigines (Adelaide, 1913), iv.

70. Jenkin, *Conquest of the Ngarrindjeri*, 246.

Chapter 8

1. Gretchen Goetz, "Nutrition a Pressing Concern for American Indians," *Food Safety News*, March 5, 2012, http://www.foodsafetynews.com/ 2012/03/nutrition-a-pressing-concern-for-american-indians/#.UhTt4H_OAuc.

2. M. Yvonne Jackson, "Diet, Culture, and Diabetes," in *Diabetes as a Disease of Civilization: The Impact of Culture Change on Indigenous Peoples*, ed. Jennie Joe and Robert S. Young (Berlin: Mouton de Grouter, 1994), 381.

3. Joe and Young, "Introduction," in ibid., 7; Goetz, "Nutrition."

4. Australian Institute of Health and Welfare, "Populations of Interest," http://www.aihw.gov.au/diabetes/populations-of-interest/; "The Health and Welfare of Australia's Aboriginal and Torres Strait Islander Peoples, Oct 2010," Australian Bureau of Statistics, http://www.abs.gov.au/AUSSTATS/abs@.nsf/lookup/4704.0Chapter218Oct+2010.

5. United States Department of Health and Human Services, Office of Minority Health, "Diabetes and American Indians/Alaska Natives," http://minorityhealth.hhs.gov/templates/content. aspx?lvl=2&lvlID=52&ID=3024; American Psychiatric Association, Office of Minority and National Affairs, "Mental Health Disparities: American Indians and Alaska Natives," fact sheet, http://www.psych.org.

6. Cynthia J. Smith, Elaine M. Manhattan, and Sally G. Palo, "Food Habit and

Cultural Changes among the Pima Indians," in *Diabetes as a Disease of Civilization: The Impact of Culture Change on Indigenous Peoples*, ed. Jennie Rose Joe and Robert S. Young (Berlin: Mouton de Gruyter, 1994), 415.

7. Carrol Counihan, *The Anthropology of Food and Body: Gender, Meaning, and Power* (New York: Routledge, 1999), 14.

8. Janiewski, "Gendering, Racializing," 133–34.

9. Individuals could apply for and, if they met certain criteria, receive citizenship prior to those dates.

Bibliography

Primary: United States

Allis, Samuel. "Samuel Allis Manuscript, (1876?)." Nebraska State Historical Society Archives, Lincoln, NE.

Cass, Lewis. "A Memorandum of Lewis Cass: Concerning a System for the Regulation of Indian Affairs." Edited by Francis Paul Prucha and Donald F. Carmony. *Wisconsin Magazine of History* 52, no. 1 (Autumn 1968): 35–50. http://www.jstor.org/stable/4634379.

Dunbar, John. "John Dunbar Papers." Nebraska State Historical Society Archives, Lincoln, NE.

Martin, Viahnett Sprague. *Years with the Osages, 1877–1886*. Houston, TX: Edgemoor Publishing, 1889.

United States Bureau of Indian Affairs. "Abstract of Annuity Goods, fiscal year 1885–1886." File 864. RG 75. National Archives, Washington, DC.

———. "Letters Received, 1824–1881." File M234. RG 75. National Archives, Washington, DC.

———. "Pawnee, Abstracts of Estimates of Goods Needed for Fiscal Year 1879–1880." Records of the Bureau of Indian Affairs Finance Division, RG75 (862), National Archives, Washington, DC.

———. "Procedural Issuances: Orders and Circulars." File M1121. RG 75. National Archives, Washington, DC.

———. "Records of the Bureau of Indian Affairs Finance Division." File 862. RG 75. National Archives, Washington, DC.

———. "Records of the Central Superintendency of Indian Affairs, 1813–1878." File M856. RG 75. National Archives, Washington, DC.

———. "Records of the Northern Superintendency of Indian Affairs, 1851–1876."

File M1166. RG 75. National Archives, Washington, DC.

———. "Records of the Northern Superintendency of Iowa, 1851–76., "File M1166. RG75, 1872. National Archives, Washington, DC.

———. "Reports of Inspections of the Field Jurisdictions of the Office of Indian Affairs, 1873–1900." File M1070. RG 75. National Archives, Washington, DC.

———. "Special Files of the Office of Indian Affairs, 1807–1904." RG 75. National Archives, Washington, DC.

United States Congress. House of Representatives. Instructions to Agents in Regard to Manner of Issuing Beef. 51st Cong., 2nd sess., 1890. H. Doc. 1. Serial 2841.

———. Report of the Secretary of the Interior. 44th Cong., 2nd sess., 1876. H. Ex. Doc. 1. Serial 1749.

United States Department of Health and Human Services, Office of Minority Health, "Diabetes and American Indians/Alaska Natives," http://minority-health.hhs.gov/templates/content. aspx?lvl=2&lvlID=52&ID=3024.

United States Department of the Interior, Office of Indian Affairs, Circular #112, 31 May 1883.

United States Department of State. "Treaty of Holston," 2 July 1791.

United States Office of Indian Affairs. Annual Report of the Commissioner of Indian Affairs to the Secretary of the Interior for the Year 1848. Washington, DC: Government Printing Office, 1848.

———. Annual Report of the Commissioner of Indian Affairs for the Year 1869. Washington, DC: Government Printing Office, 1867.

———. Annual Report of the Commissioner of Indian Affairs for the Year 1869. Washington, DC: Government Printing Office, 1870.

———. Annual Report of the Commissioner of Indian Affairs to the Secretary of the Interior for the Year 1872. Washington, DC: Government Printing Office, 1872.

———. Annual Report of the Commissioner of Indian Affairs to the Secretary of the Interior for the Year 1873. Washington, DC: Government Printing Office, 1874.

———. Annual Report of the Commissioner of Indian Affairs to the Secretary of the Interior for the Year 1875. Washington, DC: Government Printing Office, 1875.

———. Annual Report of the Commissioner of Indian Affairs to the Secretary of the Interior for the Year 1877. Washington, DC: Government Printing Office, 1877.

United States Statutes at Large. "Act to Amend an Act entitled 'An Act to Provide for the better Organization of the Department of Indian Affairs.'" 9 (1847): 203.

——. "Act to Confirm to the Great and Little Osage Indians a Reservation in the Indian Territory." 17 (1872): 228.

——. "Act of 15 July 1870." 16 (1870): 362.

——. "Act Making Appropriations for Current and Contingent Expenses, and Fulfilling Treaty Stipulations with Indian Tribes." 27 (1893): 612.

——. "Act Making Appropriations for the Current and Contingent Expenses of the Indian Department," 27 (1892).

——. "Treaty with the Osage," 7 (1808): 107.

——. "Treaty with the Osage," 7 (1818): 183.

——. "Treaty with the Osage," 7 (1825): 240.

——. "Treaty with the Osage," 7 (1839): 576.

——. "Treaty with the Osage," 14 (1865): 687.

——. "Treaty with the Pawnee," 7 (1834): 448.

——. "Treaty with the Pawnee," 11 (1858): 729.

Wharton, Clifton. "Clifton Wharton Journal, 1844." Nebraska State Historical Society Archives, Lincoln, NE.

White, Barclay. "Barclay White Journals, 1871–1876." Nebraska State Historical Society Archives, Lincoln, NE.

Williamson, John. "John Williamson Manuscripts." Nebraska State Historical Society Archives, Lincoln, NE.

Primary: Australia

Aborigines' Protection Society. Report of the Sub-Committee on Australia. London: Aborigines' Protection Society, 1838.

Eyre, Edward J. *Report and Letters to Governor Grey from E. J. Eyre at Moorunde.* Adelaide: Sullivan's Cove, 1985.

Point McLeay Mission Station Daily Ration Book, 2 July 1885 to 30 September 1884. The Mortlock Library of South Australia, State Library of South Australia, Adelaide, SA.

South Australia. Aborigines Office. Correspondence Files of the Aborigines Office and Successor Agencies. GRG 52/1. State Records of South Australia, Adelaide, SA.

South Australia. Colonial (Later Chief) Secretary's Office. Letters Received by the Colonial (Later Chief) Secretary's Office. GRG 24/6. State Records of South Australia, Adelaide, SA.

——. Letters Sent by the Colonial (Later Chief) Secretary's Office. GRG 24/4. State Records of South Australia, Adelaide, SA.

——. Letters and Other Communications Received by the Colonial Secretary, Governor and Other Government Officials. GRG 24/1. State Records of South Australia, Adelaide, SA.

South Australia. Department of Lands. Crown Lands and Immigration/Crown Lands Office. GRG 35/1. State Records of South Australia, Adelaide, SA.

South Australia. Parliamentary Debates. 30 April 1861.

South Australia. Parliament. Progress Report of the Royal Commission on the Aborigines. Adelaide: South Australia Parliament, 1913.

———. Report of the Select Committee of the Legislative Council upon the Aborigines. Adelaide: W. C. Cox, Government Printer, 1860.

South Australian Colonization Commission. Letters Sent to Officers in South Australia. GRG 48/1. State Records of South Australia, Adelaide, SA.

South Australian Government Gazette [Adelaide].

Taplin, George. "Journal of George Taplin." 3 vols. Mortlock Library of South Australia, State Library of South Australia, Adelaide, SA.

United Kingdom. First Annual Report of the Colonization Commissioners of South Australia. 28 July 1836.

———. Hansard Parliamentary Debates. 3d ser., vol. 24 (1834), cols. 1061–1063.

———. Hansard Parliamentary Debates. 3d ser., vol. 29 (1835), cols. 549–553.

———. South Australian Colonization Act. 15 August 1834.

Secondary

Albers, Patricia. "Labor and Exchange in American Indian History." In *A Companion to American Indian History*, edited by Philip J. Deloria and Neal Salisbury. Malden, MA: Blackwell Publishers, 2002.

American Psychiatric Association. Office of Minority and National Affairs. "Mental Health Disparities: American Indians and Alaska Natives." Fact Sheet. http://www.psych.org.

Andrist, Ralph K. *The Long Death: The Last Days of the Plains Indians*. New York: MacMillan, 1964.

Australian Institute of Health and Welfare. "Populations of Interest." http://www.aihw.gov.au/ diabetes/populations-of-interest/.

Bailey, Garrick Alan. "Changes in Osage Social Organization, 1673–1906." Anthropological Papers, Department of Anthropology, University of Oregon, no. 5, 1973.

Baker, Richard. *Land Is Life: From Bush to Town, the Story of the Yanyuwa People*. St. Leonards, NSW: Allen & Unwin, 1999.

Banner, Stuart. *Possessing the Pacific: Land, Settlers and Indigenous Peoples from Australia to Alaska*. Cambridge, MA: Harvard University Press, 2007.

Barsh, Russell. "Ecocide, Nutrition and the 'Vanishing Indian.'" In *State Violence and Ethnicity*, edited by P. L. van den Berghe, 221–52. Niwot, CO: University of Colorado Press, 1990.

Bartlett, C. E. *A Brief History of the Point McLeay Reserve and District.* Adelaide: Aborigines' Friends' Association in connection with the Point McLeay Centenary, 1959.

Bell, Diane. *Ngarrindjeri Wurruwarrin: A World That Is, Was and Will Be.* North Melbourne, Victoria: Spinifex Press, 1998.

Berkhofer, Robert F. *The White Man's Indian: Images of the American Indian, from Columbus to the Present.* New York: Vintage Books, 1979.

Berman, Tressa. *Circle of Goods: Women, Work, and Welfare in a Reservation Community.* Albany: State University of New York Press, 2003.

Black, Lydia T. *Russians in Alaska, 1732–1867.* Fairbanks: University of Alaska Press, 2004.

Blaine, Martha Royce. *Pawnee Passage, 1870–1875.* Norman: University of Oklahoma Press, 1990.

———. *The Pawnees: A Critical Bibliography.* Bloomington: Indiana University Press, 1980.

———. *Some Things Are Not Forgotten: A Pawnee Family Remembers.* Lincoln: University of Nebraska Press, 1997.

Boughter, Judith A. *Betraying the Omaha Nation, 1790–1916.* Norman: University of Oklahoma Press, 1998.

Broom, Leonard, and F. Lancaster Jones. *A Blanket a Year.* Canberra: Australian National University Press, 1973.

Broome, Richard. *Aboriginal Australians: Black Responses to White Dominance, 1788–1994.* 2nd ed. St. Leonards, NSW: Allen & Unwin, 1994.

Bryant, Carol A., Kathleen M. DeWalt, Anita Courtney, and Jeffery Schwartz. *The Cultural Feast: An Introduction to Food and Society.* 2nd ed. Belmont, CA: Thomson Wadsworth, 2003.

Burns, Louis F. *A History of the Osage People.* Fallbrook, CA: printed by author, 1989.

Bury, Warren R. "The Foundation of the Point McLeay Aboriginal Mission." BA Honors thesis, University of Adelaide, 1964.

Butlin, N. G. *Our Original Aggression: Aboriginal Populations of Southeastern Australia, 1788–1850.* Sydney: G. Allen & Unwin, 1983.

Calloway, Colin G. *One Vast Winter Count: The Native American West before Lewis and Clark.* Lincoln: University of Nebraska Press, 2003.

Calloway, D. H., R. D. Giauque, and F. M. Costa. "The Superior Mineral Content of Some American Indian Foods in Comparison to Federally Donated Counterpart Commodities." *Ecology of Food and Nutrition* 3 (1974): 203–11.

Chapman, Carl H. *The Origin of the Osage Indian Tribe.* New York: Garland Publishing, 1974.

Cohen, Felix. *Felix Cohen's Handbook of Federal Indian Law*. Albuquerque: University of New Mexico Press, 1971.

Cohen, Mark Nathan. "History, Diet, and Hunter-Gatherers." In *The Cambridge World History of Food*, edited by Kenneth F. Kiple and Kriemhild Coneè Ornelas. Cambridge: Cambridge University Press, 2000.

Counihan, Carole. *The Anthropology of Food and Body: Gender, Meaning, and Power*. New York: Routledge, 1999.

———. "The Social and Cultural Uses of Food." In *The Cambridge World History of Food*, edited by Kenneth F. Kiple and Kriemhild Coneè Ornelas, 1513–20. Cambridge: Cambridge University Press, 2000.

Cutter, T. "Nutrition and Food Habits of the Central Australian Aboriginal." In *The Changing Nutrition of Aborigines in the Ecosystem of Central Australia*, edited by Basil S. Hetzel and H. J. Frith, 63–70. Melbourne: CSIRO, 1978.

Daunton, Martin, and Rick Halpern, eds. *Empire and Others: British Encounters with Indigenous Peoples, 1600–1850*. Philadelphia: University of Pennsylvania Press, 1999.

Deloria, Philip J., and Neal Salisbury, eds. *A Companion to American Indian History, Blackwell Companions to American History*. Malden, MA: Blackwell Publishers, 2002.

Dippie, Brian W. *The Vanishing American: White Attitudes and US Indian Policy*. Middletown, CT: Wesleyan University Press, 1982.

Dounias, Edmond, Misa Kishi, Audrey Selzner, Iwan Kunlawan, and Patrice Levang. "No Longer Nomadic: Changing Punan Tubu Lifestyle Requires New Health Strategies." *Cultural Survival Quarterly* 28, no. 2 (2004): 15–19.

Elkin, A. P. "Reaction and Interaction: A Food Gathering People and European Settlement in Australia." *American Anthropologist* 53, no. 2 (1951): 164–86.

Ellis, Richard N. "General Pope and the Old 'Hand-to-Mouth Way.'" In *The Western American Indian: Case Studies in Tribal History*, edited by Richard N. Ellis, 63–75. Lincoln: University of Nebraska Press, 1972.

Evans, Julie. "Re-reading Edward Eyre: Race, Resistance and Repression in Australia and the Caribbean." *Australian Historical Studies* 118 (2002): 175–98.

Eyre, Edward John. *Journals of the Expedition of Discovery into Central Australia and Overland from Adelaide to King George's Sound in the Years 1840–1*. 2 vols. London: T. and W. Boone, 1845; reprint Adelaide, SA: Libraries Board of South Australia, 1964.

Farb, Peter, and George J. Armelagos. *Consuming Passions*. Boston: Houghton Mifflin, 1980.

Finney, Frank F. "The Osages and Their Agency During the Term of Isaac T. Gibson, Quaker Agent." *Chronicles of Oklahoma* 36, no. 4 (1958–1959): 416–28.

Fitzmaurice, Andrew. "The Genealogy of Terra Nullius." *Australian Historical Studies* 38, no. 129 (April 2007): 1–15.

Fletcher, Alice C., and Francis La Flesche. *The Omaha Tribe*. Reprint, Lincoln: University of Nebraska Press, 1992.

———. "The Osage or Wazha'zhe Tribe." In Smithsonian Institution Bureau of American Ethnology 27th Annual Report. Washington, DC: Government Printing Office, 1911.

Foster, Robert. De Rose Hill Native Title Claim History Report. Native Title Unit, ALRM, 2000.

———. "Feasts of the Full Moon: The Distribution of Rations to Aborigines in South Australia, 1836–1861." *Aboriginal History* 13, no. 1 (1989): 63–78.

———. "Rations, Coexistence, and the Colonisation of Aboriginal Labour in the South Australian Pastoral Industry, 1860–1911." *Aboriginal History* 24, no. 1 (2000): 1–26.

Frith, H. J., and Basil S. Hetzel, eds. *The Changing Nutrition of Aborigines in the Ecosystem*. Melbourne: CSIRO, 1978.

Gale, Fay. "A Changing Aboriginal Population." In *Settlement and Encounter: Geographical Studies Presented to Sir Grenfell Price*, edited by Fay Gale and Graham H. Lawton, 65–88. Melbourne: Oxford University Press, 1969.

———. "The History of Contact in South Australia." In *The Aborigines of South Australia: Their Present Condition and Future Development*, 27–35. Adelaide: University of Adelaide, Department of Adult Education, 1969.

———. "Roles Revisited: The Women of Southern South Australia." In *Women Rites and Sites: Aboriginal Women's Cultural Knowledge*, edited by Peggy Brock, 120–35. Sydney: Allen & Unwin, 1989.

———. *A Study of Assimilation: Part-Aborigines in South Australia*. Adelaide: Libraries Board of South Australia, 1964.

Gara, Tom. "The Aborigines of the Great Victoria Desert: The Ethnographic Observations of the Explorer Richard Maurice." *Journal of the Anthropological Society of South Australia* 27, no. 6 (1989): 15–47.

———. "Life and Times of Mullawirraburka ('King John') of the Adelaide Tribe." In *History in Portraits: Biographies of Nineteenth Century South Australian Aboriginal People*, edited by Jane Simpson and Luise Hercus. Sydney: Southwood Press, 1998.

Gilmore, Melvin R. *Uses of Plants by the Indians of the Missouri River Region*. Enlarged ed. Reprint, Lincoln: University of Nebraska Press, 1991.

Goetz, Gretchen. "Nutrition a Pressing Concern for American Indians." *Food Safety News*, March 5, 2012. http://www.foodsafetynews.com/ 2012/03/ nutrition-a-pressing-concern-for-american-indians/#.UhTt4H_OAuc.

Gray, Sharon A. *Health of Native People of North America: A Bibliography and*

Guide to Resources, Native American Bibliography Series, No. 20. Lanham, MD: Scarecrow Press, 1996.

Gringnon, Claude. "Commensality and Social Morphology: An Essay of Typology." In *Food, Drink and Identity*, edited by Peter Scholliers. New York: Berg, 2001.

Haebich, Anna. *Broken Circles: Fragmenting Indigenous Families 1800–2000*. Fremantle, WA: Fremantle Arts Centre Press, 2000.

Harris, John. *One Blood: 200 Years of Aboriginal Encounter with Christianity: A Story of Hope*. Sutherland, NSW: Albatross Books Pty, 1990.

Harrison, Brian. "Philanthropy and the Victorians." *Victorian Studies* 9, no. 4 (June 1966): 353–74.

Hassell, Kathleen. *The Relations between the Settlers and Aborigines in South Australia, 1836–1860*. Adelaide: Libraries Board of South Australia, 1966.

Hayles, Cathy. "George Taplin's Reconstruction of Landscape on the Point McLeay Aboriginal Mission." *Journal of the Anthropological Society of South Australia* 30–31 (1993): 89–109.

Hays, Robert G. *A Race at Bay:* New York Times *Editorials on "The Indian Problem," 1860–1900*. Carbondale: Southern Illinois University Press, 1997.

Healey, Justin, ed. *Issues in Society*. Balmain, NSW: Spinney Press, 2000.

"The Health and Welfare of Australia's Aboriginal and Torres Strait Islander Peoples, Oct 2010." Australian Bureau of Statistics. http://www.abs.gov.au/ AUSSTATS/abs@.nsf/ lookup/4704.0Chapter218Oct+2010.

Hemming, Steve, ed. *Troddin Thru Raukkan, Our Home: Raukkan Re-Union, 1994*. Adelaide: Raukkan Council South Australian Museum, 1994.

Hercus, Luise, and Peter Sutton, eds. *This Is What Happened: Historical Narratives by Aborigines*. Canberra: Australian Institute of Aboriginal Studies, 1986.

Hetzel, Basil S. "Historical Perspectives on Indigenous Health in Australia." *Asia Pacific Journal of Clinical Nutrition* 9, no. 3 (2000): 157–63.

Hill, Edward E. *The Office of Indian Affairs, 1824–1880: Historical Sketches*. The Library of American Indian Affairs. New York: Clearwater, 1974.

Holder, Preston. *The Hoe and the Horse on the Plains: A Study of Cultural Development among North American Indians*. Lincoln: University of Nebraska Press, 1974.

Horton, David. *Aboriginal Australia*. Canberra: Australian Institute of Aboriginal and Torres Strait Islander Studies, 2000.

Howell, David L. "Ainu Ethnicity and the Boundaries of the Early Modern Japanese State." *Past and Present* 142, no. 1 (February 1994): 69–93.

Jacobs, Margaret. *White Mother to a Dark Race: Settler Colonialism, Maternalism,*

*and the Removal of Indigenous Children in the American West and Australia,
1880–1940.* Lincoln: University of Nebraska Press, 2009.

Janiewski, Dolores. "Gendering, Racializing and Classifying: Settler Colonization
in the United States, 1590–1990," in *Unsettling Settler Societies: Articulations
of Gender, Race, Ethnicity and Class,* edited by Davia Stasiulis and Nira Yuval-Davis, 132–61. London: SAGE Publications, 1995.

Jenkin, Graham. *Conquest of the Ngarrindjeri: The Story of the Lower Murray
Lakes Tribes.* Rigby Ltd, 1979. Reprint, Adelaide: Raukkan Publishers, 1985.

Joe, Jennie, and Robert S. Young. *Diabetes as a Disease of Civilization: The Impact
of Culture Change on Indigenous Peoples.* Berlin: Mouton de Gruter, 1994.

Johnson, Steven L. *Guide to American Indian Documents in the Congressional
Serial Set, 1817–1899: A Project of the Institute for the Development of Indian
Law.* New York: Clearwater, 1977.

Kappler, Charles J., ed. *Indian Affairs, Laws and Treaties.* Washington, DC: Government Printing Office, 1903. http://digital.library.okstate.edu/kappler/.

Kenen, Regina H. "Health Status: Australian Aborigines and Native Americans—A Comparison." *Australian Aboriginal Studies* No. 1 (1987): 34–45.

Kiple, Kenneth F., and Kriemhild Coneè Ornelas. *The Cambridge World History
of Food.* New York: Cambridge University Press, 2000.

Kouris-Blazos, Antigone, and Mark Wahlqvist. "Indigenous Australian Food
Culture on Cattle Stations Prior to the 1960s and Food Intake of Older
Aborigines in a Community Studied in 1988." *Asia Pacific Journal of Clinical
Nutrition* 9, no. 3 (2000): 224–31.

Kvasnicka, Robert M., and Herman J. Viola. *The Commissioners of Indian Affairs,
1824–1977.* Lincoln: University of Nebraska Press, 1979.

Latz, Peter K. *Bushfires and Bushtucker.* Alice Springs, NT: Institute for Aboriginal Development Press, 1995.

La Vere, David. *Contrary Neighbors: Southern Plains and Removed Indians in
Indian Territory.* Norman: University of Oklahoma Press, 2000.

Lester, Alan. "British Settler Discourse and the Circuits of Empire." *History
Workshop Journal* 54 (2002): 25–48.

———. "Colonial Networks, Australian Humanitarianism and the History Wars."
Geographical Research 44, no. 3 (September 2006): 229–41.

———. "Obtaining the 'Due Observance of Justice': The Geographies of Colonial Humanitarianism." *Environment and Planning D: Society and Space* 20
(2002): 277–93.

Lupton, Deborah. *Food, the Body and the Self.* London: SAGE Publications, 1996.

Macintyre, Stuart. *A Concise History of Australia.* Cambridge: Cambridge University Press, 1999.

Maddock, K. *The Australian Aborigines: A Portrait of Their Society.* Ringwood, Victoria: Penguin, 1974.

Maggiore, Pat. "Analysis of Australian Aboriginal Bush Foods." *Australian Aboriginal Studies* No. 1 (1993): 55–58.

Marshall, Lorna. *The !Kung of Nyae Nyae.* Cambridge, MA: Harvard University Press, 1976.

Mattingley, Christobel, and Ken Hampton, eds. *Survival in Our Own Land: "Aboriginal Experiences in South Australia" since 1836, Told by Nungas and Others.* Adelaide: Wakefield Press, 1988.

McAuliffe, Denis, Jr. *Bloodland: A Family Story of Oil, Greed and Murder on the Osage Reservation.* San Francisco, CA: Council Oak Books, 1999.

McConnell, Michael N. *A Country Between: The Upper Ohio Valley and Its Peoples, 1724–1774.* Lincoln: University of Nebraska Press, 1992.

McGrath, Ann. *Contested Ground: Australian Aborigines under the British Crown.* St. Leonards, NSW: Allen & Unwin, 1995.

Meriam, Lewis. *The Problem of Indian Administration.* Baltimore: Johns Hopkins Press, 1928.

Miller, Lee, ed. *From the Heart: Voices of the American Indian.* New York: Vintage Books, 1995.

Milner, Clyde A. *With Good Intentions: Quaker Work among the Pawnees, Otos, and Omahas in the 1870s.* Lincoln: University of Nebraska Press, 1982.

Morris, Barry. *Domesticating Resistance: The Dhan-gadi Aborigines and the Australian State.* Oxford: Berg Publishers, 1989.

Morrison, T. F. "The Osage Treaty of 1825." *Kansas State Historical Society Collections* 17 (1928): 692–708.

Murphy, D., R. Joyce, and C. Hughed, eds. *Labor in Power.* St. Lucia: University of Queensland Press, 1980.

National Native Title Tribunal. *First Peoples of the River Murray and Mallee Region.* Commonwealth of Australia, 2004.

———. *Research Report Bibliography: Ngarrindjeri.* Commonwealth of Australia, January 2003, No. 1/2003.

Norgen, Jill. *The Cherokee Cases: The Confrontation of Law and Politics.* New York: McGraw-Hill, 1996.

O'Brien, Anne. "Kitchen Fragments and Garden Stuff." *Australian Historical Studies* 39, no. 2 (June 2008): 150–66.

Pattel-Gray, Anne. *The Great White Flood: Racism in Australia.* Atlanta: Scholars Press, 1998.

———. *Through Aboriginal Eyes: The Cry from the Wilderness.* Geneva: WCC Publications, 1991.

Pope, Alan. "From Feast to Famine: The Food Factor in European-Aboriginal Relations, South Australia 1836–45." *Forum* 10, no. 1 (1988): 47–54.

———. *Resistance and Retaliation: Aboriginal-European Relations in Early Colonial South Australia.* Bridgewater, SA: Heritage Action, 1989.

Pope, Polly. "Trade in the Plains: Affluence and Its Effects." *Kroeber Anthropological Society Papers* 34 (1966): 53–61.

Porter, Andrew, and Alaine Low, ed. *Oxford History of the British Empire.* Vol. 3, *The Nineteenth Century.* Oxford: Oxford University Press, 1999.

Potter, James. "Chittleborough's Adelaide." *History SA: The Newsletter of the Historical Society of South Australia* (July 2003): 10–16.

Priest, Loring Benson. *Uncle Sam's Stepchildren: The Reformation of United States Indian Policy, 1865–1887.* Lincoln: University of Nebraska Press, 1975.

Prucha, Francis Paul. *American Indian Policy in Crisis: Christian Reformers and the Indian, 1865–1900.* Norman: University of Oklahoma Press, 1976.

———. *American Indian Treaties: The History of a Political Anomaly.* Berkeley: University of California Press, 1994.

———. ed. *Americanizing the American Indian: Writings by the "Friends of the Indian," 1880–1900.* Lincoln: University of Nebraska Press, 1978.

———. ed. *Documents of United States Indian Policy.* Lincoln: University of Nebraska Press, 2000.

———. *The Great Father: The United States Government and the American Indians.* 2 vols. Lincoln: University of Nebraska Press, 1986.

Richter, Daniel K. *Facing East from Indian Country: A Native History of Early America.* Cambridge, MA: Harvard University Press, 2001.

Rintoul, Stuart. *The Wailing: A National Black Oral History.* Port Melbourne: William Heinemann Australia, 1993.

Roberts, Clayton, and David Roberts. *A History of England.* Vol. 2, *1688 to the Present.* 3rd ed. Englewood Cliffs, NJ: Prentice Hall, 1991.

Rollings, Willard H. *The Osage: An Ethnohistorical Study of Hegemony on the Prairie-Plains.* Columbia: University of Missouri Press, 1992.

———. *Unaffected by the Gospel: Osage Resistance to the Christian Invasion (1673–1906): A Cultural Victory.* Albuquerque: University of New Mexico Press, 2004.

Rowley, C. D. *Aboriginal Policy and Practice.* Canberra: Australian National University Press, 1970.

———. *The Destruction of Aboriginal Society.* Ringwood: Penguin, 1972.

Rowse, Tim. *White Flour, White Power: From Rations to Citizenship in Central Australia.* Cambridge: Cambridge University Press, 1998.

Russell, Lynette, ed. *Colonial Frontiers: Indigenous-European Encounters in Settler Societies.* Manchester, UK: Manchester University Press, 2001.

Scholliers, Peter, ed. *Food, Drink and Identity: Cooking, Eating and Drinking in Europe since the Middle Ages*. New York: Berg, 2001.

Scrimshaw, Nevin S. "The Value of Contemporary Food and Nutrition Studies for Historians." In *Hunger and History: The Impact of Changing Food Production and Consumption Patterns on Society*, edited by Robert I. Rotberg and Theodore K. Rabb, 331–36. Cambridge: Cambridge University Press, 1983.

Shaw, Bruce. *Our Heart Is in the Land: Aboriginal Reminiscences from the Western Lake Eyre Basin*. Canberra: Aboriginal Studies Press, 1995.

Shinichiro, Takakura. *The Ainu of Northern Japan: A Study in Conquest and Acculturation*. Translated by John A. Harrison. Philadelphia: American Philosophical Society, 1960.

Shorto, Russell. *The Island at the Center of the World: The Epic Story of Dutch Manhattan and the Forgotten Colony That Shaped America*. New York: Doubleday, 2004.

Simpson, Jane, and Luise Hercus, eds. *History in Portraits: Biographies of Nineteenth Century South Australian Aboriginal People*. Sydney: Southwood Press, 1998.

Smith, Cynthia J., Elaine M. Manhattan, and Sally G. Palo. "Food Habit and Cultural Changes among the Pima Indians." In *Diabetes as a Disease of Civilization: The Impact of Culture Change on Indigenous Peoples*, edited by Jennie Rose Joe and Robert S. Young, 381–434. Berlin: Mouton de Gruyter, 1994.

Smith, Jane F., and Robert M. Kvasnicka, eds. *Indian-White Relations: A Persistent Paradox*. Washington, DC: Howard University Press, 1981.

Smith, L. R. *The Aboriginal Population of Australia*. Canberra: Australian National University Press, 1980.

Smith, Pamela A., and Richard M. Smith. "Diets in Transition: Hunter-Gatherer to Station Diet and Station Diet to the Self-Select Store Diet." *Human Ecology* 27, no. 1 (1999): 115–33.

Smithers, Gary. "The 'Pursuits of Civilized Man': Race and the Meaning of Civilization in the United States and Australia, 1790s–1850s." *Journal of World History* 20, no. 2 (June 2009): 245–72.

South Australia State Records. *Aboriginal Resource Kit: An Introduction to Primary Sources Held by State Records Relating to Aboriginal People*. Adelaide: State Records of South Australia, 1993.

———. *Guide to Records Relating to Aboriginal People*. 5 vols. Adelaide: State Records of South Australia, 1988.

Stanner, W. E. H. "Native Food Rations: A Thorough Investigation Necessary." *The Aborigines' Protector* 1, no. 1 (1935): 16.

Stasiulis, Davia, and Nira Yuval-Davis, eds. *Unsettling Settler Societies: Articulations of Gender, Race, Ethnicity and Class*. London: SAGE Publications, 1995.

Stone, Sharman N., ed. *Aborigines in White Australia: A Documentary History of the Attitudes Affecting Official Policy and the Australian Aborigine, 1697–1973*. South Yarra, Victoria: Heinemann Educational Australia Pty, 1974.

Sunder, John E. *Joshua Pilcher, Fur Trader and Indian Agent*. Norman: University of Oklahoma Press, 1968.

Sustainable Recreation Steering Committee. *A Sustainable Recreation Strategy for the River Murray and Lower Lakes in South Australia*. Adelaide, SA: QED Pty, 2002.

Sutton, Imre, and Ralph Leon Beals, eds. *Irredeemable America: The Indians' Estate and Land Claims*. Albuquerque: University of New Mexico Press, 1985.

Taplin, George, ed. *The Folklore, Manners, Customs and Languages of the South Australian Aborigines*. Adelaide: Johnson Reprint, 1879.

———. *The Narrinyeri Tribe*. 2nd ed. Adelaide: E. S. Wigg & Son, 1878.

Taylor, Alan. *American Colonies: The Settling of North America*. New York: Penguin Books, 2001.

Tolcher, H. M. *Seed of the Coolibah: A History of the Yandruwandha and Yawarrawarrka People*. Adelaide, SA: Openbook Print, 2003.

Trennert, Robert A. *Alternative to Extinction: Federal Indian Policy and the Beginnings of the Reservation System, 1846–51*. Philadelphia, PA: Temple University Press, 1975.

———. *White Man's Medicine: Government Doctors and the Navajo, 1863–1955*. Albuquerque: University of New Mexico Press, 1998.

Tyrrell, Ian. "Beyond the View from Euro-America: Environment, Settler Societies, and the Internationalization of American History." In *Rethinking American History in a Global Age*, edited by Thomas Bender, 168–91. Berkeley: University of California Press, 2002.

United States Department of Health and Human Services. Office of Minority Health. "Diabetes and American Indians/Alaska Natives." http://minorityhealth.hhs.gov/templates/content.aspx? lvl=2&lvlID=52&ID=3024.

Utley, Robert M., and Wilcomb E. Washburn. *Indian Wars*. Boston: Houghton Mifflin, 1977.

Vaarzon-Morel, Petronella, ed. *Warlpiri Karnta Karnta-Kurlangu Yimi (Warlpiri Women's Voices: Our Lives Our History)*. Alice Springs: IAD Press, 1995.

Vigil, Ralph H., Frances W. Kaye, and John R. Wunder, eds. *Spain and the Plains: Myths and Realities of Spanish Exploration and Settlement on the Great Plains*. Niwot: University Press of Colorado, 1994.

Waldman, Carl. *Encyclopedia of Native American Tribes*. New York: Facts on File, 1999.

Wanklyn, Neville. "Confrontation at Port Lincoln." *Origin* 3, no. 2 (1970): 7.

Washburn, Wilcomb E. *The American Indian and the United States: A Documentary History*. New York: Random House, 1973.

West, Elliott. *The Contested Plains: Indians, Goldseekers, and the Rush to Colorado*. Lawrence: University Press of Kansas, 1998.

———. *The Way to the West: Essays on the Central Plains*. Albuquerque: University of New Mexico Press, 1995.

White, Richard. *Roots of Dependency: Subsistence, Environment, and Social Change among the Choctaws, Pawnees, and Navajos*. Lincoln: University of Nebraska Press, 1983.

Wickett, Murray R. *Contested Territory: Whites, Native Americans, and African Americans in Oklahoma, 1865–1907*. Baton Rouge: Louisiana State University Press, 2000.

Will, George F., and George E. Hyde. *Corn among the Indians of the Upper Missouri*. Lincoln: University of Nebraska Press, 1964.

Wilson, Ruby E. *Frank J. North: Pawnee Scout Commander and Pioneer*. Athens, OH: Swallow Press, 1984.

Wilson, Terry P. *Bibliography of the Osages*. Metuchen, NJ: Scarecrow Press, 1985.

———. *The Underground Reservation: Osage Oil*. Lincoln: University of Nebraska Press, 1985.

Wishart, David J. "The Dispossession of the Pawnee." *Annals of the Association of American Geographers* 69, no. 3 (1979): 382–401.

———. "The Pawnee Claims Case, 1947–64." In *Irredeemable America: The Indians' Estate and Land Claims*, edited by Imre Sutton and Ralph Leon Beals. Albuquerque: University of New Mexico Press, 1985.

———. *An Unspeakable Sadness: The Dispossession of the Nebraska Indians*. Lincoln: University of Nebraska Press, 1994.

Wolfe, Patrick. "Settler Colonialism and the Elimination of the Native." *Journal of Genocide Research* 8, no. 4 (December 2006): 387–409. http://dx.doi.org/10.1080/14623520601056240.

Worcester, Donald Emmet. *Forked Tongues and Broken Treaties*. Caldwell, ID: Caxton Printers, 1975.

Wunder, John. *"Retained by the People": A History of American Indians and the Bill of Rights*. New York: Oxford University Press, 1994.

Index